The Rugby League Challenge Cup

The Rugby League Challenge Cup

AN ILLUSTRATED HISTORY

by Les Hoole

Breedon Books
Publishing Company
Derby

First published in Great Britain by
The Breedon Books Publishing Company Limited
Breedon House, 44 Friar Gate, Derby, DE1 1DA.
1998

ISBN 1 85983 094 3

Printed and bound by Butler & Tanner Ltd., Selwood Printing Works, Caxton
Road, Frome, Somerset.

Colour separations by Freelance Repro, Leicester.

Jackets printed by Lawrence-Allen, Avon.

Contents

Introduction
7

Challenge Cup Results
8

The Lance Todd Trophy
202

The Cup Comes Home
204

Statistics
206

Bibliography
208

Acknowledgements

I would like to thank the following people who have helped in providing information, encouragement and for granting permission for the reproduction of photographs held in their collections: Steve Brady, editor of *Rugby Leaguer,* Dave Makin, Robert Gate, Mike Gardner, Sam Coulter, Tim Auty, Curtis Johnson and Dianne, Verity and Ben Hoole.

Introduction

THE Rugby Football League can trace its history back to 29 August 1895 when a group of northern-based Rugby Union clubs voted to break away from the English Union and form their own, independent, Northern Union.

The new Union flourished and within months of its first full season its committee decided to introduce a knockout competition open to all member clubs.

The decision was hardly a surprising one. Yorkshire clubs, who had dominated the Yorkshire Rugby Union Cup, knew how popular a sudden-death competition was with the growing number of fee-paying spectators. The third round Yorkshire Cup game between Leeds and Halifax in 1892-93 had attracted a crowd of 27,654, more than 2,000 above the estimated attendance at the 1892 FA Cup Final.

On 5 March 1896, at a meeting of the Northern Union, the Challenge Cup was officially established and the committee set about the task of providing a cup and medals to play for. The Bradford-based company of Fattorini & Son was chosen to supply the trophy. When delivered the silver cup weighed 189 ounces, stood 36 inches high and cost the Union the sum of £60. Two sets of medals were also supplied, winners' at a cost of three guineas and losers' at 30 shillings.

The draw for the first round of the inaugural Northern Union Challenge Cup was made on 3 September 1896, well in advance of the first matches which were to be played in March and April 1897.

There is little doubt those committee men of March 1896 made the right decision, for the Challenge Cup was an instant success and has become the code's premier competition. The brave decision to take the Final to Wembley in 1929 also proved to be a masterstroke of forward planning.

The game's annual showcase in London is one of the most popular events in the British sporting calendar and the television coverage is beamed around the globe. Here, then, is the story of each of those 101 Finals and the statistics behind how the two teams got there.

'*A BIG success, financially, socially and from a football point of view,*' is how the first-ever Challenge Cup Final was described by the *Leeds Mercury*.

On the social side the Northern Union held a committee meeting at the Mitre Hotel and then hosted a lunch for various guests at Brayshays Restaurant on Bond Street. The party then made their way to Headingley in a fleet of horse-drawn carriages, calling at the Mitre Hotel to collect the Batley team who had arrived in Leeds at around 2pm. Despite a dull and cold day, the city of Leeds was invaded by supporters of St Helens and Batley all anxious to catch an early glimpse of the Challenge Cup as it was paraded through the streets on its journey to Headingley.

St Helens won the toss and took advantage of the wind blowing across the ground from the Kirkstall end. Batley attacked from the kick-off and after about five minutes play Goodhall dropped a goal directly from a scrum in front of the St Helens posts.

The goal against them spurred St Helens on and they had a good but brief spell on attack with Little coming close on one occasion but then spoiling a good attack with a wild pass which Fitzgerald intercepted well.

Batley rallied and their forwards swept into the Saints half with a long dribbling rush. St Helens held out the attacks with some sturdy tackling but were beaten when Davies kicked across field for J.Goodhall to collect the ball and score a clever, well-worked try at the side of the posts. The usually sound goal-kicker, Wharton 'Wattie' Davies, missed the simple conversion attempt.

In the second half Batley resumed their onslaught of the St Helens defence and came close several times before St Helens finally gave their fans something to cheer about. An eyewitness account describes the action: '*Then came a sudden and startling transformation, effected by the finest incident in the whole match. Close to his own line Doherty took the ball from a kick and dashed straight down the field on the uncovered stand side, handing off beautifully until he had reached the centre line, where he passed to Traynor, and the latter, though closely pursued, managed to cross the line and score in a good position.*'

Jacques failed with the conversion attempt.

Batley adopted a safety-first strategy for the remainder of the game and kept the ball with the forwards. Following several very near-misses and some clever defensive work, Batley finally scored their second try when Munns touched down after the ball had been driven over the line in a loose maul. It was the final score of the match, Davies once again missing the conversion attempt and Batley's Gallant Youths thus beating St Helens 10-3 to become the first holders of the trophy.

Batley's 1897 Challenge Cup Final squad photographed at their Mount Pleasant base. Back row (left to right): Gath, Munns, Lowrie, Wilby, J.B.Goodhall, Stubley, H.Goodhall, Barraclough, Fisher. Middle row: Shackleton, Oakland, Naylor, Littlewood. Front row: Wilson (trainer), Shaw, Garner, Spurr, Main, Bennett (trainer).

Northern Union Cup Results

First Round

Bradford	7	Oldham	3
Bramley	8	Morecambe	8
Broughton R	0	Warrington	0
Castleford	43	Allerton	3
Eastmoor	26	Oldham Juniors	8
Halifax	55	Stockport Rangers	5
Holbeck	38	Latchford Rangers	3
Hull	9	Walkden	0
Hunslet	75	Broughton Recreation	5
Leeds	11	Rochdale St Clements	0
Leeds Parish Church	42	Runcorn Recreation	0
Leigh	0	Wakefield T	0
Manningham	31	Dukinfield	3
Rochdale H	63	Waterhead Hornets	3
Runcorn	65	Warrington Locos	0
St Helens	58	Lees	0
Salford	28	Warrington St Mary's	0
Swinton	12	Huddersfield	4
Widnes	55	Atherton Hornets	0
Wigan	3	Radcliffe	0

Byes: Batley, Bradford Church Hill, Brighouse R, Crompton, Heckmondwike, Liversedge, St Helens Rec, Stockport, Swinton Church, Thornton Rangers, Tyldesley and Werneth.
Morecambe, Runcorn Rec, Stockport R and Warrington St Mary's gave up ground advantage.

First Round Replays

Bramley	6	Morecambe	4
Wakefield T	13	Leigh	4
Warrington	3	Broughton R	0

Second Round

Bradford	68	Swinton Church	3
Bramley	0	Batley	11
Brighouse R	11	Wakefield T	4
Crompton	26	Bradford Church Hill	0
Eastmoor	3	Stockport	3
Leeds Parish Church	0	Halifax	11
Liversedge	9	Heckmondwike	4
Rochdale H	8	St Helens Rec	0
Runcorn	52	Thornton Rangers	4
St Helens	17	Castleford	3
Salford	30	Werneth	0
Swinton	15	Hunslet	0
Tyldesley	9	Leeds	3
Warrington	24	Holbeck	0
Widnes	11	Hull	0
Wigan	7	Manningham	0

St Helens Recreation, Swinton Church, Thornton Rangers and Werneth gave up ground advantage.

Second Round Replay

Stockport	28	Eastmoor	8

Third Round

Batley	6	Brighouse R	3
Bradford	4	Tyldesley	8
Halifax	50	Crompton	0
Rochdale H	3	Swinton	3
St Helens	11	Wigan	0
Stockport	8	Salford	0
Warrington	6	Liversedge	0
Widnes	14	Runcorn	6

Third Round Replay

Swinton	10	Rochdale H	0

Fourth Round

Batley	10	Widnes	0
St Helens	12	Tyldesley	0
Swinton	3	Stockport	0
Warrington	10	Halifax	8

Semi-finals

Batley	6	Warrington	0

At Fartown, Huddersfield.
Attendance: 5,500

St Helens	7	Swinton	0

At Wheater's Field, Broughton
Attendance: 20,000

Final

Saturday, 24 April at Headingley, Leeds.

	T	G	P		T	G	P
Batley	**2**	**1**	**10**	**St Helens**	**1**	**0**	**3**
A.Garner				T.Foulkes			
W.P.Davies				R.Doherty			
D.Fitzgerald				D.Traynor	T		
J.B.Goodall	T			J.Barnes			
I.Shaw				W.Jaques			
J.Oakland		G		R.O'Hara			
H.Goodall				F.Little			
M.Shackleton				T.Winstanley			
J.Gath				W.Briers			
G.Maine				W.Winstanley			
R.Spurr				T.Reynolds			
F.Fisher				J.Thompson			
C.Stubley				T.Dale			
J.Littlewood				S.Rimmer			
J.T.Munns	T			W.Whiteley			

Referee: J.H.Smith (Widnes) *Half-time: 7-0*
Attendance: 13,492 *Receipts: £624*

Cup presented by Mrs Waller, wife of the President of the Union.

1898 Batley 7 Bradford 0

BATLEY held possession of the Challenge Cup thanks to a brilliant display by their forwards who were at their very best controlling almost all aspects of the game. The *Leeds Mercury* wrote of the Batley eight: *'Their greatest merit is their irresistible dash and cleverness with both feet and hands in the open. In a scrimmage they shove like cart horses; but at its break up can dribble, or pick up, handle, and pass like threequarters.'*

Bradford's forwards played a good game but where beaten by a far better pack. Their backs, however, let the side down badly, one newspaper commenting: *'Bradford's weak spot was in the backs, whose fielding, fairly good at the start, grew perceptibly worse as the game progressed and became wretchedly poor towards the finish. Not the slightest excuse can be offered for the miserably incompetent and helplessly incapable way in which they stood and looked at each other and the ball, and allowed it to go beyond them without making an attempt to take it.'*

Bradford started the game well and were soon pressing into the Batley '25' with a series of dangerous rushes, one of which was stopped by Jack Goodhall when he was *'bowled over'* whilst saving a rush by the Bradford forwards. A series of stubborn scrums near the Batley line was finally halted when Bradford were awarded the first penalty of the match, but Cooper missed the relatively easy shot at goal. Bradford continued to attack and had a try disallowed when Kelsey grounded the ball over the line but play was brought back for a scrummage. Gradually Batley began to take control and following a rare but brief passing bout 'Wattie' Davies dropped a goal to give the Gallant Youths the lead.

Jack Toothill, Bradford's loose forward, one of the stars of the 1898 Final.

Bradford rallied well after the score against them and their forwards swept all before them and dashed well into the Batley half. With only Garner to beat it seemed nothing would prevent a try, but the full-back plucked the ball from the boot of a Bradford forward and managed to evade several attempted tackles to clear with a brilliant kick. The failure to score took the heart out of the Bradford side and for the last ten minutes of the game they were a hopelessly beaten and despondent side.

A strong rush by the Batley forwards brought the ball almost to the line and Jack Goodhall picked up and, although tackled by Cooper, managed to ground the ball for the only try of the game. Davies squandered the conversion attempt with a poor kick but Jack Goodhall made amends minutes later by taking a short pass from his brother Harry and dropping a goal to give Batley a 7-0 lead and the Cup for the second time.

Northern Union Cup Results

First Round

Altrincham	8	Salford St Bartholomew's	0
Barrow	13	Dalton	3
Barton	16	Rochdale Rangers	3
Batley	12	St Helens	7
Birkenhead Wanderers	17	Runcorn Recreation	0
Bradford	7	Swinton	2
Castleford	18	Wigan	2
Eastmoor	22	Smallbridge	3
Fleetwood	6	Warrington St Mary's	3
Halifax	17	St Helens Recreation	0
Hull	8	Morecambe	0
Hull KR	46	Hull Marlborough	0
Hunslet	8	Lancaster	3
Leeds PC	7	Bramley	10
Leigh	7	Heckmondwike	0
Manningham	5	Huddersfield	11
Mossley	0	Lees	9
Oldham	8	Leeds	3
Rochdale H	10	Holbeck	6
Salford	9	Millom	2
Stockport	5	Brighouse R	6
Tyldesley	2	Broughton R	3
Ulverston	2	Runcorn	19
Wakefield T	5	Warrington	3
Walkden	22	Swinton Church	0
Werneth	14	Oldham Juniors	0
Whitworth	2	Rochdale Athletic	2
Widnes	26	Liversedge	0

Walkover: Abbey Hills, Lostock Gralam, Morley and Radcliffe
Millom gave up ground advantage.

First Round Replay

Rochdale Athletic	0	Whitworth	4

Second Round

Altrincham	11	Eastmoor	2
Barton	16	Werneth	4
Batley	8	Walkden	0
Birkenhead Wanderers	0	Bradford	5
Brighouse R	3	Runcorn	3
Broughton R	3	Wakefield T	0
Castleford	14	Whitworth	7
Halifax	3	Oldham	8
Huddersfield	14	Barrow	6
Hull	18	Radcliffe	0
Hull KR	11	Morley	0
Leigh	59	Abbey Hills	0
Lostock Gralam	0	Fleetwood	10
Rochdale H	3	Bramley	4
Salford	65	Lees	2
Widnes	8	Hunslet	7

Abbey Hills, Lees, Radcliffe and Walkden gave up ground advantage.

Second Round Replay

Runcorn	11	Brighouse R	0

Third Round

Altrincham	0	Salford	16
Barton	3	Bramley	9
Castleford	4	Batley	10
Fleetwood	0	Hull KR	31
Huddersfield	0	Broughton R	6
Hull	2	Bradford	6
Leigh	3	Widnes	3
Oldham	11	Runcorn	0

Third Round Replay

Widnes	22	Leigh	3

Fourth Round

Batley	3	Oldham	0
Bradford	7	Broughton R	5
Hull KR	0	Widnes	0
Salford	12	Bramley	2

Fourth Round Replay

Widnes	6	Hull KR	5

Semi-finals

Batley	5	Salford	0

At Watersheddings, Oldham
Attendance: 15,000

Bradford	13	Widnes	0

At Hanson Lane, Halifax
Attendance: 14,000

Final

Saturday, 23 April at Headingley, Leeds

	T	G	P		T	G	P
Batley	1	2	7	**Bradford**	0	0	0
A.Garner				B.Patrick			
P.Davies		G		T.H.Dobson			
J.B.Goodall	T	G		F.W.Cooper			
D.Fitzgerald				W.Murgatroyd			
E.Fozzard				F.Murgatroyd			
J.Oakland				R.Wood			
H.Goodall				H.Prole			
M.Shackleton				T.Broadley			
J.Gath				J.Fearnley			
G.Maine				R.J.Robertson			
R.Spurr				H.Holden			
F.Fisher				E.Kelsey			
C.Stubley				B.Holt			
J.T.Munns				J.McLoughlin			
J.Rogers				J.Toothill			

Referee: J.H.Smith (Widnes)   *Half-time: 0-0*
Attendance: 27,941   *Receipts: £1,586*

Cup presented by Mrs Warren, wife of the President of the Union.

1899 Oldham 19 Hunslet 9

Oldham's 1899 Cup-winning squad. Back row (left to right): Edwards, Moffatt, Bonsor, Ellis, A.Lees, Broome, J.Lees, Frater. Middle row: Fletcher, Sellars, Thomas, S.Lees, Davies. Front row: Martin, Williams, Lawton, Barnes.

OLDHAM were generally regarded to be the finest combination in Lancashire and their performances in the rounds leading to the Final made them favourites for the game. Hunslet had one of the finest packs in the Northern Union and were five pounds a man heavier than Oldham; Lawton, the lightest of the Roughyeds' eight was 17 pounds behind the smallest of his opponents. The *Manchester Guardian* commented: '*Lightness in the scale, however, has its compensating advantage, almost always in fleetness of foot, and often in staying power.*'

Hunslet won the toss and playing with the wind behind them started in a determined mood, their forwards soon driving the ball down the field. After only two minutes play, Albert Goldthorpe scored the first points of the game with a penalty-goal. Within three minutes a dangerous forward rush swept past Hunslet full-back Mitchell and J.Lees scored a try for Oldham which he converted himself. Hunslet's determination continued and their forwards charged towards Oldham, twice forcing full-back Thomas to touch down behind his own line. On a rare Oldham attack, centre Fletcher flung out a wild pass which Albert Goldthorpe snapped up with a fine interception. He quickly made ground and, as the Oldham cover came across, whipped a pass to his brother Walter who raced clear and scored a fine try. Albert converted and then moments later lived up to his reputation as one of the

game's deadliest kickers when he dropped a goal from around the half-way line to give Hunslet a 9-5 half-time lead.

With the wind facing them in the second half the powerful Hunslet forwards soon began to feel the pace of the game, and with their weight advantage now working against them began to visibly wilt. The followers of Oldham took great delight in this and many of them took to shouting, "Yorkshire puddings," at the floundering forwards.

Oldham took full advantage and from a scrum in the Hunslet '25', the ball was whipped through four pairs of hands for Williams to score in the corner. Moments later Oldham centre Fletcher kicked ahead, regained possession almost on the Hunslet line and threw the ball to Moffatt, whose superb backing up earned him an easy try and gave Oldham a two-point lead. The conversion attempt was missed but moments later, J.Lees gathered the ball in a loose scrummage near the Hunslet line and darted over for a try, which was again unconverted.

Oldham were now a very confident side and their threequarters opened the game out whenever they had the opportunity. A fine passing movement started by Fletcher and Sam Lees ended with Williams crossing the line for his second try of the afternoon. Full-back Thomas landed the conversion attempt and Oldham were 19-9 winners and the first Lancashire side to collect the Cup.

Northern Union Cup Results

First Round

Batley	38	Rochdale Athletic	0
Bowling	12	Warrington St Mary's	0
Bradford	8	Wakefield T	0
Brighouse R	10	Stockport	0
Broughton R	59	Rothwell	8
Castleford	8	Halifax	0
Dewsbury	2	Tyldesley	0
Elland	13	Workington	5
Holbeck	9	Birkenhead Wanderers	3
Huddersfield	43	Saddleworth Rangers	2
Hull	21	Featherstone	0
Hull KR	11	Manningham	2
Hunslet	11	Maryport	2
Leeds	20	Rochdale Rangers	0
Leeds PC	11	Idle	0
Leigh	14	Bramley	0
Liversedge	0	York	4
Millom	24	Ulverston	2
Morecambe	30	Latchford Rangers	0
Oldham	63	Goole	0
Outwood Church	8	Altrincham	3
Radcliffe	0	Normanton	5
Rochdale H	28	Dalton	0
Runcorn	77	Runcorn Recreation	0
St Helens	12	Whitworth	3
Salford	63	Luddendenfoot	3
Swinton	40	Fletcher, Russell & Co	5
Warrington	12	Barrow	2
Werneth	4	Salford St Bartholomew's	2
Widnes	48	Fleetwood	3
Wigan	28	Groves United	3

Walkover: Heckmondwike

Goole, Groves United, Rochdale Rangers, Runcorn Recreation, Saddleworth and Salford St Bartholomew's gave up ground advantage.

Second Round

Batley	29	York	5
Bradford	19	Rochdale H	5
Broughton R	10	Hull KR	5
Castleford	10	Brighouse R	2
Elland	10	Bowling	3
Huddersfield	17	Heckmondwike	0
Hull	21	Millom	0
Leeds	3	Wigan	0
Leigh	4	Runcorn	2
Normanton	7	Holbeck	2
Oldham	14	Warrington	0
Outwood Church	0	Leeds PC	6
St Helens	0	Morecambe	0
Salford	31	Werneth	0
Swinton	0	Hunslet	2
Widnes	28	Dewsbury	0

Second Round Replay

Morecambe	5	St Helens	5

Second Round Second Replay

St Helens	17	Morecambe	5

Third Round

Bradford	3	Oldham	23
Broughton R	6	Leeds PC	7
Huddersfield	23	Normanton	2
Hull	86	Elland	0
Hunslet	16	Castleford	0
Leigh	16	Batley	6
Salford	16	St Helens	0
Widnes	11	Leeds	8

Fourth Round

Hunslet	9	Hull	0
Leeds PC	5	Leigh	10
Oldham	20	Widnes	0
Salford	8	Huddersfield	0

Semi-finals

Hunslet	15	Salford	8

At Park Avenue, Bradford
Attendance: 7,000

Oldham	16	Leigh	2

At Wheater's Field, Broughton
Attendance: 20,000   *Receipts: £534*

Final

Saturday, 29 April at Fallowfield, Manchester

	T	G	P		T	G	P
Oldham	5	2	19	**Hunslet**	1	3	9
R.L.Thomas		G		J.Mitchell			
S.Williams	2T			W.Hannah			
S.Lees	T	G		A.E.Goldthorpe		3G	
T.Fletcher				W.Goldthorpe	T		
T.Davies				J.W.Wright			
A.Lees				H.Robinson			
J.R.Lawton				E.Fletcher			
E.W.Telfer				T.Leach			
W.Barnes				T.C.Young			
G.Frater				H.Wilson			
H.Ellis				R.Rubrey			
E.Bonser				O.Walsh			
J.Moffatt	T			T.Walsh			
J.Lees	T			J.Ramage			
H.Broome				J.Harrison			

Referee: T.H.Marshall (Bradford)   *Half-time: 5-9*
Attendance: 15,762   *Receipts: £946*

Cup presented by Mrs Burnley, wife of the President of the Union.

1900 Swinton 16 Salford 8

THE Final between the great Manchester rivals generated such interest that the Northern Union Cup committee again decided to stage the game at Fallowfield, the home of the Manchester Athletic Club, although the game had originally been earmarked to return to Yorkshire. Despite the official attendance being recorded as 17,864 it was thought that around 25,000 people actually witnessed the match, many of whom gained free admission.

The game began in fine style with Swinton pressing the Salford line almost straight from the kick-off and, following a stylish bout of passing from the backs, Evans crossed the line but was called back for a knock-on. Salford's forwards dribbled and hacked the ball the length of the field and from a scrum Griffiths passed to Williams who slipped through the Lions defence to score a good try. Griffiths converted to give the Reds a 5-0 lead. Within two minutes Swinton had equalised. An eye witness account describes the try: *'Davies, Morgan and R.Valentine got away with a neat passing bout at midfield, and the last named handing the ball to Messer. This clever threequarter put on top speed, and dodging and outpacing his opponents in really wonderful style, ran nearly half the length of the field and scored.'*

Jim Valentine converted the goal to bring the scores level at 5-5, Salford's forwards were now beginning to control the game, the *Manchester Guardian* commenting: *'The Salford forwards did splendidly. If it had been simply a case of forwards versus forwards Salford would have no doubt won.'*

Their play, however, was at times a little too robust and Brown was sent off for an unfair tackle on Lewis, the Swinton wingman. Shortly after the incident Swinton's veteran captain, Jim Valentine, dislocated his collar bone, but after receiving treatment off the field returned to play in the threequarters.

Shortly before half-time Hampson and Chorley missed a loose ball allowing a trio of Salford forwards to dribble the ball over the Swinton line where Pearson dropped on it to score.

Swinton hit back immediately when Lewis scored a try following an excellent passing movement from a scrum on the Salford '25'.

In the second half Swinton's backs took control of the game and, although helped at times by Salford mistakes, they played a superb game. One newspaper observed: *'The Swinton halves played with excellent judgement throughout and the threequarters gave one of the best displays that have been seen this season.'*

The Lions added a try when Pearson, Salford's wingman, carelessly passed the ball to a Salford forward, who quickly transferred to R.Valentine who scored a try. After scoring he walked back and gave the ball to his brother Jim, who despite having the injury to his collar bone struck a superb conversion to give Swinton a five-point lead. Davies, Swinton's stand-off, added the final try to give the Lions a 16-8 victory.

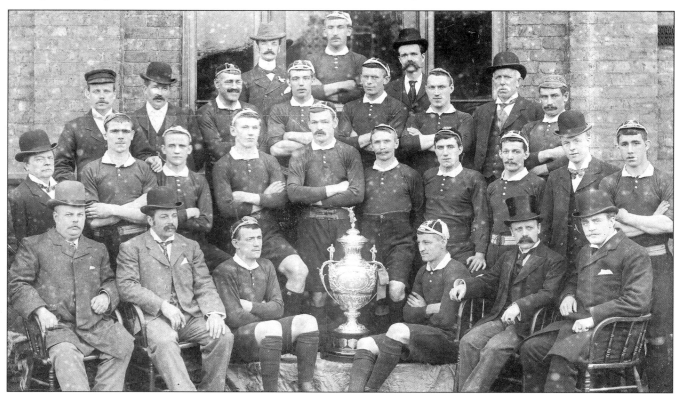

Swinton's 1900 Cup-winning squad. Players only: Back row (left to right): G.Jones. Third row: Jack Evans, Preston, Vigors, Pollitt, B.Murphy. Second row: Tickle, Hampson, R.Valentine, J.Valentine, Messer, Lewis, Chorley, Harris. Front row: Morgan, Dai Davies.

Northern Union Cup Results

First Round

Alverthorpe	2	Workington	8
Altrincham	24	Pontefract	0
Barrow	2	Bradford	3
Birkenhead Wanderers	4	Werneth	6
Brighouse R	16	Todmorden	5
Broughton R	22	Lancaster	7
Castleford	0	Batley	0
Dewsbury	3	Wigan	0
Goole	8	Heckmondwike	6
Halifax	19	Featherstone	2
Huddersfield	22	Idle	0
Hull	52	Wath Brow	0
Hull KR	3	Millom	0
Kendal Hornets	0	Maryport	9
Leeds PC	5	Seaton	0
Liversedge	8	Leigh	12
Manningham	3	Oldham	3
Morecambe	19	Whitehaven Recreation	0
Normanton	5	Leeds	0
Ossett	5	Elland	0
Outwood Church	5	Widnes	24
Radcliffe	13	Whitworth	0
Runcorn	42	Birstall	0
St Helens	0	Warrington	6
Salford	9	York	0
Stockport	2	Hunslet	0
Swinton	53	Eastmoor	0
Tyldesley	12	Brookland Rovers	0
Wakefield T	15	Hebden Bridge	0
Windhill	0	Rochdale H	11

Walkover: Bramley and Holbeck
Featherstone and Hebden Bridge gave up ground advantage.

First Round Replays

Batley	5	Castleford	0
Oldham	18	Manningham	3

Second Round

Bramley	8	Hull	5
Bradford	12	Ossett	0
Brighouse R	0	Wakefield T	4
Dewsbury	0	Widnes	2
Halifax	5	Oldham	10
Holbeck	8	Swinton	17
Huddersfield	13	Workington	0
Leeds PC	15	Altrincham	3
Leigh	2	Salford	9
Morecambe	0	Broughton R	7
Normanton	0	Batley	3
Radcliffe	2	Werneth	0
Rochdale H	13	Hull KR	5
Runcorn	12	Maryport	0
Stockport	5	Tyldesley	2
Warrington	44	Goole	0

Altrincham gave up ground advantage.

Third Round

Bradford	0	Runcorn	0
Bramley	3	Widnes	3
Broughton R	5	Wakefield T	3
Leeds PC	7	Batley	2
Rochdale H	3	Warrington	0
Salford	6	Huddersfield	5
Stockport	24	Radcliffe	3
Swinton	14	Oldham	2

Third Round Replays

Widnes	8	Bramley	0
Runcorn	3	Bradford	3

Third Round Second Replay

At Wheater's Field, Broughton

Runcorn	6	Bradford	2

Fourth Round

Leeds PC	5	Runcorn	5
Salford	11	Rochdale H	3
Stockport	0	Widnes	3
Swinton	9	Broughton R	0

Fourth Round Replay

Runcorn	6	Leeds PC	8

Semi-finals

Salford	11	Widnes	0

At Fartown, Huddersfield
Attendance: 15,500   *Receipts: £420*

Swinton	8	Leeds PC	0

At Watersheddings, Oldham
Attendance: 14,000   *Receipts: £313*

Final

Saturday, 28 April at Fallowfield, Manchester

	T	G	P		T	G	P
Swinton	4	2	16	**Salford**	2	1	8
A.Chorley				D.Smith			
J.T.Lewis	T			A.Pearson	T		
R.J.Messer	T			T.Williams	T		
R.Valentine	T			E.Harter			
V.R.Hampson				H.Hadwen			
D.Davies	T			B.Griffiths		G	
F.J.Morgan				I.Grey			
E.Vigors				H.Shore			
G.Harris				R.Shaw			
J.Preston				P.Tunney			
G.R.Jones				M.Gledhill			
J.Valentine		2G		W.Brown			
C.Pollitt				G.Fisher			
J.Evans				J.Williams			
B.Murphy				J.Rhapps			

Referee: F.Renton (Hunslet)   *Half-time: 8-8*
Attendance: 17,864   *Receipts: £1,110*

Cup presented by Mrs Smith, wife of the President of the Union.

1901 Batley 6 Warrington 0

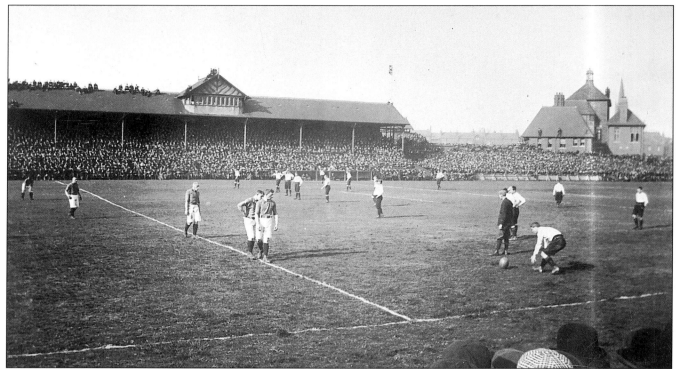

A rare action photograph of the 1901 Final at Headingley shows a Batley player, believed to be Wattie Davies, preparing to take a shot at the Warrington goal.

A RECORD crowd of 29,569 assembled at Headingley for the game that was billed as a Yorkshire v Lancashire affair, proving that the Northern Union game was as popular as ever and did not need the very best clubs to create interest.

Batley were generally expected to win their third trophy, the *Bradford Observer* commenting: '*Batley can seize an opportunity or cover a mistake equally well, although it is in defence that we think the present team excel. Davies, Goodhall and Oakland are past masters in their knowledge of tactics whilst the forwards possess energy and staying power in a marked degree.*'

Warrington's backs had paved the way for their Headingley appearance, although it was thought that some of their opponents in the rounds were hardly determined opposition. The *Bradford Observer* said: '*The impression we gather of Warrington is of a very fast but rather uneven body of men. Brilliant in attack behind the scrummage on their day, but not tacticians enough for hard Cup-tie work against determined foes.*'

The game was a poor one and hardly deserved the huge attendance to witness it. One newspaper observed: '*In the main the play was of a scrambling, rough and tumble character, unrelieved by no more than half a dozen bits of really smart work.*'

The opening minutes of the game were taken up by a rather pointless kicking duel between the half-backs but soon settled down when Warrington pressed into the Batley half. From the very first scrum of the game Garner, the

Batley full-back, misfielded the ball. Wattie Davies made an attempt to collect it but he slipped and Warrington's Harris seized his chance well and ran over the line to touch down. Referee Kidd disallowed the claim and ordered another scrum.

The *Manchester Guardian* commented: '*It seemed rather hard lines for Warrington, who, granted this early success, might have played with more confidence than they did and have been less subject to what has aptly been termed stage fright of a Cup-tie match.*'

After 15 minutes Warrington attempted a passing movement but Dickenson, the Wire centre, tumbled badly and allowed Goodall to collect the ball. The Batley threequarter seized his chance and sped towards the Warrington line and, when faced with Hallam, passed to Wattie Davies who ran unopposed to the line for a try. Davies missed the conversion attempt.

Two minutes later a clever piece of passing between Oakland, Goodall and Fitzgerald gave Wilf Auty the room to score another try.

In the second half the game developed into a series of monotonous scrummages and meaningless kicking. The play was also a great deal keener and eventually Batley forward George Maine was sent-off for an unfair tackle.

The only highlights for the vast crowd were brilliant runs from Batley's Wattie Davies and Warrington's Jack Fish.

With no further scoring, Batley were 6-0 winners and collected their third trophy.

Northern Union Cup Results

First Round

Aspatria	4	Altrincham	3
Barrow	11	Brighouse R	0
Birkenhead W	2	Millom	0
Bradford	7	Swinton	2
Broughton R	24	Tyldesley	3
Dewsbury	9	Featherstone	5
Goole	2	St Helens	12
Hebden Bridge	6	Whitworth	0
Heckmondwike	8	Seaton	0
Huddersfield	6	Hull	3
Hull KR	4	Salford	0
Hunslet	8	Wath Brow	0
Keighley	13	Kinsley	0
Lancaster	3	Maryport	3
Leeds	0	Warrington	19
Leeds PC	11	Radcliffe	0
Leigh	38	Alverthorpe	0
Liversedge	3	Normanton	2
Manningham	0	Castleford	0
Morecambe	11	Pontefract	0
Oldham	19	Otley	0
Outwood Church	2	Holbeck	5
Rochdale H	3	Bramley	7
Runcorn	18	Wigan	0
Stockport	13	Shipley	2
Todmorden	2	Sowerby Bridge	11
Wakefield T	28	Eastmoor	6
Whitehaven Rec	0	Widnes	3
Windhill	3	Ossett	5
York	10	Halifax	2

Walkover: Batley and Workington.
Otley gave up ground advantage.

First Round Replays

Barrow	0	Brighouse B	2
Castleford	21	Manningham	2
Maryport	3	Lancaster	0

Second Round

Batley	6	Huddersfield	2
Bramley	7	Oldham	10
Castleford	3	Workington	2
Dewsbury	8	Morecambe	0
Hebden Bridge	3	Broughton R	33
Holbeck	3	Bradford	6
Hull KR	11	Maryport	0
Keighley	5	York	5
Liversedge	0	Leeds PC	5
Ossett	5	Birkenhead W	5
Runcorn	16	Leigh	4
St Helens	0	Stockport	0
Sowerby Bridge	3	Brighouse R	6
Wakefield T	21	Aspatria	2
Warrington	19	Heckmondwike	2
Widnes	8	Hunslet	0

Aspatria and Maryport gave up ground advantage.

Second Round Replays

Birkenhead W	20	Ossett	2
Stockport	5	St Helens	11
York	12	Keighley	0

Third Round

Birkenhead W	2	Widnes	10
Brighouse R	0	Hull KR	7
Broughton R	4	Oldham	11
Dewsbury	3	Castleford	5
Runcorn	21	York	0
St Helens	5	Batley	7
Wakefield T	4	Bradford	5
Warrington	11	Leeds PC	0

Fourth Round

Batley	5	Runcorn	2
Hull KR	5	Castleford	5
Warrington	10	Bradford	8
Widnes	0	Oldham	8

Fourth Round Replay

Castleford	7	Hull KR	2

Semi-finals

Batley	9	Oldham	2

At Fartown, Huddersfield
Attendance: 16,000

Warrington	21	Castleford	5

At Wheater's Field, Broughton
Attendance: 9,000

Final

Saturday, 27 April at Headingley, Leeds

	T	G	P		T	G	P
Batley	2	0	6	**Warrington**	0	0	0
A.Garner				E.Hallam			
W.P.Davies	T			J.Fish			
D.Fitzgerald				D.Isherwood			
J.B.Goodall				J.Dickenson			
F.W.H.Auty	T			E.Harris			
J.Oakley				P.Bate			
J.Midgley				J.Duckworth			
F.Fisher				G.Boardman			
P.Judge				J.Fell			
J.Rodgers				W.Edmondson			
C.Stubley				J.Scholtze			
R.Spurr				J.Eden			
G.Maine				J.Cunningham			
F.Fozzard				J.Morrison			
F.Hollingworth				E.Swift			

Referee: J.Kidd (Millom)   *Half-time: 6-0*
Attendance: 29,569   *Receipts: £1,644*

Cup presented by Mrs Hutchinson, wife of the President of the Union.

1902 Broughton Rangers 25 Salford 0

Broughton Rangers pose with the Challenge Cup in 1902. Seated directly behind the trophy is Bob Wilson, the first man to score a hat-trick of tries in the Final.

IN A match that was described as *'the most wonderful final on record'*, Bob Wilson, the Rangers captain, played one of the finest games of his career with Broughton. Wilson was a sensation from the very kick-off, a contemporary newspaper report wrote of him: *'To him more than any other man on the side the great triumph of the south Manchester team was due. The Broughton skipper is not merely a sprinter. In tackling, marking, and defensive play generally he is equally at home. Really in the first half it was a case of Salford v Wilson.'*

Salford arrived late at Rochdale and the kick-off was delayed for an hour. When the game did get under way it was Salford who attacked the Rangers line for the first ten minutes of play, their forwards controlling the scrummages well.

From a Broughton break a scrum was formed and Sam James burst from the pack making good ground before passing to Harry in support, the centre flung a long, high pass to Wilson who *'with a great swerve, raced off down the field, Hogg, the wing threequarter in close attendance. The Salford full-back planted himself in Wilson's path and made ready to spring at Hogg. Wilson feinted to pass, and the full-back made his spring. Wilson safely dodged past and sped round to the back of the posts with a stream of discomfited red jerseys after him.'*

Willie James kicked the goal to give Rangers a 5-0 lead.

Moments later Wilson intercepted a pass between two Salford backs and flew down the right wing. This time the Salford full-back was more wary but once again Wilson beat him, this time sending a perfect pass to Hogg who scored with ease. Again Willie James converted.

Just before half-time Wilson was again racing down the right-hand side with only the full-back to beat. He fooled Smith completely with an outrageous dummy and scored his second try, which James converted.

In the second half Salford had plenty of the play but they very rarely got within reach of scoring, the backs letting them down by their sheer inability to grasp the situation. On one occasion Bone, the Salford right wingman, broke through the Rangers defence and had a clear field in front of him, but Widdeson, one of the smallest men on the pitch, sprinted back and hauled him down.

Wilson scored his hat-trick try with another dashing run which Oram converted. With around five minutes of play remaining Widdeson received the ball in his own half and dodged and weaved his way through a wall of red shirts until he at last sprinted clear and scored Broughton's fifth and final try. Willie James once again landed the conversion to give Broughton Rangers a 25-0 victory, the most decisive the competition had seen.

Northern Union Cup Results

First Round

Altrincham	12	Carnforth	4
Askham	0	Widnes	3
Aspatria	2	Rochdale H	4
Batley	8	Brighouse R	4
Castleford	15	Hebden Bridge	7
Dewsbury	10	Manningham	3
Halifax	0	Swinton	2
Heckmondwike	5	Birkenhead W	0
Holbeck	29	Alverthorpe	8
Huddersfield	22	Kendal Hornets	0
Hull	28	York	0
Hull KR	7	St Helens	0
Hunslet	37	Wath Brow	0
Keighley	7	Broughton R	15
Kirkstall	3	Eastmoor	0
Leigh	2	Runcorn	2
Maryport	0	Oldham	27
Ossett	5	Seaton	2
Otley	0	Leeds	5
Outwood Church	5	Morecambe	5
Penrith United	0	Whitehaven Rec	2
Radcliffe	6	Goole	7
Salford	28	Pontefract	2
South Shields	5	Bradford	23
Stockport	18	Liversedge	2
Todmorden	38	Featherstone	0
Wakefield T	5	Normanton	2
Warrington	6	Barrow	0
Werneth	4	Lancaster	6
Wigan	2	Bramley	0
Windhill	5	Millom	0

Walkover: Idle.
Featherstone and Kendal Hornets gave up ground advantage.

First Round Replays

Morecambe	15	Outwood Church	0
Runcorn	8	Leigh	0

Second Round

Altrincham	0	Batley	16
Broughton R	5	Stockport	0
Castleford	16	Wigan	0
Dewsbury	0	Salford	2
Goole	3	Kirkstall	3
Heckmondwike	7	Holbeck	5
Hull KR	5	Hull	10
Idle	5	Whitehaven Rec	5
Lancaster	2	Hunslet	7
Leeds	31	Windhill	0
Morecambe	6	Swinton	17
Ossett	15	Todmorden	2
Rochdale H	9	Huddersfield	19
Runcorn	10	Oldham	0
Warrington	0	Bradford	11
Widnes	16	Wakefield T	7

Windhill gave up ground advantage.

Second Round Replays

Kirkstall	0	Goole	3
Whitehaven Rec	6	Idle	3

Third Round

Batley	15	Bradford	10
Broughton R	13	Hull	2
Castleford	6	Runcorn	5
Heckmondwike	7	Ossett	4
Huddersfield	11	Leeds	0
Salford	67	Goole	0
Swinton	34	Whitehaven Rec	0
Widnes	5	Hunslet	5

Third Round Replay

Hunslet	21	Widnes	0

Fourth Round

Batley	21	Castleford	2
Broughton R	13	Swinton	0
Heckmondwike	2	Hunslet	2
Huddersfield	6	Salford	9

Fourth Round Replay

Hunslet	6	Heckmondwike	2

Semi-finals

Broughton R	9	Hunslet	5

At Belle Vue, Wakefield
Attendance: 10,500   *Receipts: £369*

Salford	8	Batley	0

At Watersheddings, Oldham
Attendance: 13,000

Final

Saturday, 26 April at The Athletic Ground, Rochdale

	T	G	P		T	G	P
Broughton R	5	5	25	**Salford**	0	0	0
J.Fielding				D.Smith			
A.Widdeson	T			E.J.Bone			
F.Harry				T.Williams			
B.Wilson	3T			D.Davies			
A.Hogg	T			H.Price			
W.James		4G		J.Lomas			
S.James				B.Griffiths			
H.Woodhead				J.Rhapps			
G.Whitehead				P.Tunney			
W.Winskill				G.Heath			
Stead				W.Brown			
W.Oram		G		H.Buckler			
J.W.Trotter				B.Shaw			
J.Garrety				J.Williams			
G.Thompson				M.Gledhill			

Referee: W.Robinson (Manningham)

Half-time: 15-0

Attendance: 15,006   *Receipts: £846*

Cup presented by Mrs Houghton, wife of the President of the Union.

1903 Halifax 7 Salford 0

SALFORD'S third Final in four years was, once again, a huge disappointment to the club and its followers. The Reds were beaten by a side which, on the day, were their complete masters and Salford were considered to be lucky to leave the field only seven points in arrears. The huge Headingley crowd of 32,507 created a new attendance record for the Northern Union.

From the kick-off it soon became obvious that the game was going to be dominated by forward play. One newspaper commented: *'It was decided in the first few minutes that no very finished or artistic football was going to be witnessed. The teams were too eager to carry out any nice passing movements or play with much thought.'*

Halifax began in a very determined mood and in the endless scrums they were by far the masters of the Salford pack, the *Manchester Guardian* reporting: *'Every now and then the blue and white forwards would come through the scrummage with the ball at their feet, sweep the scarlet Salfordians aside, and dash up the field in movements which gathered violence like a mountain torrent, with every yard of progress.'*

After about a quarter of an hour's play, and just after one of those Halifax rushes, the barriers suddenly gave way at one corner of the ground. Hundreds of supporters tumbled on to the playing surface, bringing the game to a standstill. The crowd were more than anxious not to cause any trouble and in a well-ordered exercise the majority walked to a position behind the Salford goal and watched the game from there.

On the resumption of play the Halifax side began to settle down and play with a little more thought, occasionally bringing their backs into the play. The threequarters were far too eager and over-excited by the occasion, however, and they soon squandered any chances they attempted to create. It was observed that their efforts at combined running were well below the high standard set by the Welsh backs playing in the Northern Union.

Despite all the wild attacks by Halifax, the first half was scoreless.

Halifax began the second half in their usual determined manner and, following a good run by Riley, finally crossed the Salford line. It was hardly a classic try, an eye-witness account describes the movement: *'The blue and white forwards again went off with a wild pell mell burst. All the efforts of the Salford defenders to fall on the ball were unavailing; it was driven over the line, a Yorkshire player and two Salfordians dropped on it in a heap, and the referee blew a decisive note on his whistle in announcement of a try.'*

Bartle was credited with the score and Hadwen converted. Following the try, it was just about all Halifax, but they could not breach the Salford line again. Hadwen added a penalty goal and Halifax were worthy 7-0 winners.

Halifax with the Cup at their Thrum Hall headquarters in 1903. Back row (left to right): Jones, Hammond, Bulmer, Swinbank, Summerskill. Standing: Dickenson, Mallinson, Langhorn, Ricketts (secretary), Winskill, Williams, Morton. Seated: Midgley, Wilson, Joe Riley, Rigg, Jitson, Wedgewood, Little, Morris. In front: Brown, Morley, Hadwen, Nettleton.

Northern Union Cup Results

First Round

Birkenhead W	15	Werneth	0
Bradford	10	Huddersfield	5
Bramley	10	Pontefract	5
Broughton R	0	Oldham	2
Castleford	2	Thrum Hall	0
Dewsbury	0	Leeds	15
Halifax	34	Salterhebble	0
Hull KR	2	York	6
Hunslet	18	Cleckheaton	5
Keighley	37	Heckmondwike	0
Kendal Hornets	3	Morecambe	5
Kinsley	0	Brighouse R	8
Leigh	0	Swinton	0
Manningham	0	Idle	0
Millom	10	Lancaster	0
Ossett	0	Otley	0
Parton	9	Workington	5
Rochdale H	33	Alverthorpe	0
Runcorn	7	Widnes	2
St Helens	6	Warrington	3
Seaton	2	Barrow	5
South Shields	58	St Paul's	0
Sowerby Bridge	5	Batley	14
Wakefield T	3	Holbeck	0
Wath Brow	5	Whitehaven Rec	0
Wigan	8	Stockport	0
Windhill	0	Normanton	8

Walkover: Hull, Hull Marlborough, Maryport, Outwood Church and Salford.
Stockport gave up ground advantage.

First Round Replays

Idle	0	Manningham	12
Otley	2	Ossett	0
Swinton	5	Leigh	7

Second Round

Barrow	15	Wath Brow	5
Bramley	0	Bradford	9
Brighouse R	12	South Shields	2
Castleford	0	Halifax	0
Hull	45	Hull Marlborough	0
Hunslet	7	Outwood Church	0
Keighley	12	Manningham	0
Maryport	2	Parton	2
Morecambe	0	Millom	0
Normanton	2	Batley	9
Oldham	4	Wigan	0
Runcorn	18	Birkenhead W	0
St Helens	2	Rochdale H	8
Salford	11	Leigh	0
Wakefield T	0	Leeds	13
York	17	Otley	2

Hull Marlborough, Outwood Church and Wath Brow gave up ground advantage.

Second Round Replays

Halifax	10	Castleford	3
Millom	10	Morecambe	2
Parton	0	Maryport	5

Third Round

Barrow	7	Batley	2
Bradford	0	Oldham	2
Halifax	0	Brighouse R	0
Hull	7	Millom	0
Hunslet	5	Leeds	2
Keighley	2	York	2
Rochdale H	0	Salford	15
Runcorn	17	Maryport	3

Millom gave up ground advantage.

Third Round Replays

Brighouse R	2	Halifax	8
York	12	Keighley	9

Fourth Round

Barrow	0	Hull	3
Oldham	8	Hunslet	0
Runcorn	0	Halifax	2
York	2	Salford	25

Semi-finals

Halifax	8	Hull	5

At Fartown, Huddersfield
Attendance: 17,500 *Receipts: £788*

Salford	0	Oldham	0

At Wheater's Field, Broughton
Attendance: 19,000 *Receipts: £793*

Semi-final Replay

Salford	8	Oldham	0

At Wheater's Field, Broughton
Attendance: 12,000 *Receipts: £419*

Final

Saturday, 25 April at Headingley, Leeds

	T	G	P		T	G	P
Halifax	1	2	7	**Salford**	0	0	0
W.B.Little				D.Smith			
W.B.Wedgewood				A.Norris			
W.W.Williams				R.Nesser			
J.A.Rigg				J.Lomas			
H.Hadwen		2G		T.G.Bell			
J.Morley				E. Harter			
Joe Riley				S.Griffiths			
Jack Riley				J.Williams			
I.Bartle	T			J.Rhapps			
F.Mallinson				P.Tunney			
J.Swinbank				G.Heath			
W.Morton				W.Brown			
F.Hammond				H.Buckler			
J.W.Bulmer				B.Shaw			
R.S.Winskill				H.Shore			

Referee: J.Bruckshaw (Stockport) *Half-time: 0-0*
Attendance: 32,507 *Receipts: £1,834*

Cup presented by Mrs Clifford, wife of the President of the Union.

1904 Halifax 8 Warrington 3

HALIFAX RETAIN THE CUP.

Joe Riley gets over for Halifax

Morley interrupts the progress of Fish

Hallam outwits the Halifax attack.

The Referee gets in the line of play.

Morley slips through the scrum and scores.

An artist's impression of the 1904 Final.

off it was all attack from Halifax and Warrington were forced to touch down behind their own line three times in as many minutes.

A bad mistake by Jack Fish gave Halifax a strong position near the Warrington line and from a scrummage Bulmer ran strongly before passing to Joe Riley who ran clear and scored a fine try under the posts. Hadwen missed the goal but Halifax continued their fierce onslaught to the line up to half-time.

Warrington started the second half well and their full-back Hallam saved a certain try when he dived at the feet of Bulmer and Bartle who were hurtling towards the line at the head of a furious forward rush. The Wire forwards improved dramatically after this and finally set their backs in motion. Jack Fish, who had seen little of the ball in the first half, was sent flying down the touchline in superb movement. Faced with the Halifax cover defence streaming across the field to tackle him, Fish hoisted the ball over their heads and

HALIFAX became the second side to win the Cup in consecutive seasons when they defeated Warrington in game that, while it lacked great skill, was never boring. The *Manchester Guardian* observed: '*The great achievement of the two sides playing on Saturday was that, while they failed to play brilliant football, they never for a moment failed to interest the people who were watching them.*'

Halifax controlled the scrums and loose forward play in their usual way, taking full advantage of the weight advantage their pack of eight had over the Warrington forwards. One newspaper described the Halifax players thus: '*Footballers in the town are as grim and sturdy as the rugged hills in which their habitation is surrounded. Halifax won largely by the method in which the forwards broke up the scrums, wheeled the ball on the Warrington backs, and thereby smashed up the latter's scoring combinations.*' From the kick-

Davies flashed past Billy Little to touch the ball down in the corner for a try. Jack Fish missed the conversion attempt.

With only two points the difference, Warrington tried hard for the last 20 minutes of the game, but they did not have the determination of the Halifax side. Towards the end of the game Halifax once again took complete control and Morley, their captain, scored a fine individual try direct from a scrum near the Warrington line. A newspaper account described the try: '*From the rear of the scrummage he shot past the opposition by sheer strength and speed, and if not one of those electrifying tries brought off by dazzling threequarters, it was none the less a point of real merit.*'

Hadwen missed the goal-kick when the ball hit an upright and rebounded into play. It was the last score of the game and Halifax had beaten Warrington 8-3 to collect the trophy for the second year running.

Northern Union Cup Results

Intermediate Round

Birkenhead	6	Marsh Hornets	0
Bramley	15	Hebden Bridge	8
Brighouse R	6	Otley	0
Brookland Rovers	2	Maryport	0
Castleford	5	York	5
Dewsbury	18	Beverley	10
Holbeck	11	Outwood Church	0
Lancaster	0	Morecambe	0
Millom	7	Parton	8
Normanton	2	Wakefield T	20
Pontefract	21	South Shields	2
Rochdale H	28	Rochdale Athletic	6
Roose	0	Barrow	34
St Helens	48	Highfield	5

Rochdale Athletic gave up ground advantage.

Intermediate Round Replays

Morecambe	4	Lancaster	13
York	2	Castleford	0

First Round

Barrow	10	Bramley	10
Batley	5	Oldham	0
Broughton R	26	Parton	0
Dewsbury	0	Hunslet	15
Halifax	15	St Helens	0
Holbeck	17	Birkenhead	0
Huddersfield	0	Wigan	7
Hull	9	Widnes	0
Hull KR	2	Leeds	3
Lancaster	0	Keighley	8
Pontefract	0	Brighouse R	0
Rochdale H	3	Leigh	10
Runcorn	0	Wakefield T	0
Salford	57	Brookland Rovers	0
Swinton	0	Warrington	0
York	0	Bradford	8

Brookland Rovers and Parton gave up ground advantage.

First Round Replays

Bramley	7	Barrow	7
Brighouse R	0	Pontefract	2
Wakefield T	5	Runcorn	7
Warrington	20	Swinton	0

First Round Second Replay

Barrow	14	Bramley	3

At Hanson Lane, Halifax

Second Round

Barrow	6	Halifax	11
Broughton R	11	Runcorn	0
Holbeck	0	Bradford	9
Hull	5	Salford	23
Leeds	13	Keighley	0
Leigh	0	Hunslet	8
Pontefract	9	Batley	3
Warrington	3	Wigan	0

Third Round

Broughton R	0	Bradford	0
Halifax	8	Leeds	2
Pontefract	4	Warrington	10
Salford	2	Hunslet	5

Third Round Replay

Bradford	0	Broughton R	0

Third Round Second Replay

Bradford	15	Broughton R	0

At Headingley, Leeds

Semi-finals

Halifax	7	Hunslet	2

At Belle Vue, Wakefield
Attendance: 21,000   *Receipts: £746*

Warrington	3	Bradford	3

At Wheater's Field, Broughton
Attendance: 13,000   *Receipts: £479*

Semi-final Replay

Warrington	8	Bradford	0

At Fartown, Huddersfield
Attendance: 10,000   *Receipts: £341*

Final

Saturday, 30 April at Weaste, Salford

Halifax	T	G	P	Warrington	T	G	P
Halifax	2	1	8	**Warrington**	1	0	3
W.B.Little				J.Hallam			
H.Hartley				J.Fish			
Joe Riley	T			D.Isherwood			
W.W.Williams				G.Dickenson			
H.Hadwen		G		E.Harris			
A.Nettleton				D.Davies	T		
J.Morley	T			T.Hockenhall			
I.Bartle				G.Thomas			
J.W.Bulmer				A.S.Boardman			
G.H.Langhorn				D.Morrison			
F.Mallinson				E.Lunt			
Jack Riley				G.Cook			
W.Morton				S.Jolley			
J.Swinbank				J.Edmonson			
R.S.Winskill				A.Naylor			

Referee: J.H.Smith (Widnes)   *Half-time: 5-0*
Attendance: 17,041   *Receipts: £936*

Cup presented by Mr F.Lister, Vice-President of the Union.

1905 Warrington 6 Hull Kingston Rovers 0

Warrington's 1905 Challenge Cup-winning side. Back row (left to right): Hackett (trainer) Harmer, Shugars, Preston, Boardman, Belton, Jolley, Heeson (trainer). Seated: Swift, Kenton, Dickenson, Hallam, Isherwood, Fish, Jenkins. Front: Thomas, Davies, Brooks, Naylor.

WARRINGTON were making their third appearance in a Final and had beaten a strong Bradford side 7-2 in the semi-final thanks to a brilliant interception try by Fish.

It was Hull Kingston Rovers' first Final and they had beaten Broughton Rangers 10-6 in the semi-final at Wakefield, helped by two tries from George 'Tich' West, their wingman who had scored 11 tries and ten goals in the first-round thrashing of Brookland Rangers.

A dull and showery day in Leeds reduced the attendance to just over 19,500 which was well short of the last Final to be held at Headingley, but still regarded as good and encouraging for the Northern Union.

The rains of the morning had softened the Headingley turf and the players soon churned up the field giving the heavier Hull Kingston pack a slight advantage in the initial stages of the game.

The play from the kick-off revolved almost entirely around the forwards and for the first 20 minutes the ball, with the exception of a solitary penalty attempt, never passed the two '25' yard lines. On the half-hour Jack Fish took a pass, lobbed more in hope than expectation, very well and set off on a clever zig-zag run towards the line. With the try line almost in sight, he slipped on the wet turf and although he struggled to his feet and carried on, a posse of Rovers defenders who he had passed once hauled him down again.

It was the only try scoring chance of the first half and the teams turned round for the last 40 minutes still deadlocked at 0-0.

Within three minutes of the restart, however, Warrington went ahead when Jack Fish scored a somewhat controversial try in the corner when he appeared to touch down after being held firm in a tackle.

His second try was free from doubt, however. An eyewitness described the events: '*Warrington, for the time being, were on the defensive, and from a scrummage in their own half Davies got the ball, and raced down the field, eventually passing to Isherwood, who entrusted the ball to Fish, who galloped away, and, beating all who tried to stop him, crossed the line and placed the ball between the posts amid terrific cheering from some thousands of deep-throated Lancastrians.*'

Hallam missed the easy kick and a few minutes later also fluffed a penalty attempt. The Rovers were now a well beaten side and although their backs attempted a late rally, were no match for Warrington.

The *Manchester Guardian* commented: '*Warrington won the day not by a large margin of points, but they won well and deservedly. They were far and away the better team, and showed a superiority which abundantly justified the predictions that they would probably have a margin of points in double figures.*'

Northern Union Cup Results

Intermediate Round

Barrow	11	Millom	0
Barrow St George's	2	Morecambe	8
Beverley	2	York	9
Bramley	0	Keighley	3
Brighouse R	6	Normanton	8
Brookland R	5	Maryport	10
Castleford	24	Lancaster	7
Huddersfield	20	Victoria Rangers	3
Ossett	5	Sharlston	0
Pontefract	2	Dewsbury	22
Rochdale H	2	Chadderton	0
Rochdale Rangers	10	Egerton	9
Seaton	3	Parton	5

Intermediate Round Replay

Brookland R	2	Maryport	0

Replayed due to Maryport fielding an ineligible player in the first tie.

First Round

Batley	13	Barrow	5
Bradford	42	Castleford	5
Broughton R	8	Runcorn	0
Halifax	2	Dewsbury	0
Huddersfield	5	York	0
Hull	52	Leigh Shamrocks	0
Hull KR	73	Brookland R	5
Keighley	8	Salford	0
Hunslet	22	Parton	3
Leeds	20	Ossett	0
Leigh	3	Wigan	0
Oldham	16	Normanton	3
St Helens	9	Rochdale R	2
Swinton	8	Rochdale H	3
Wakefield T	5	Widnes	3
Warrington	30	Morecambe	0

Brookland Rovers and Widnes gave up ground advantage.

First Round Replay

Wigan	5	Leigh	0

Replayed due to Leigh fielding an ineligible player in the first tie.

Second Round

Batley	10	Oldham	14
Broughton R	18	St Helens	0
Huddersfield	3	Wakefield T	3
Hull	5	Hunslet	7
Hull KR	3	Leeds	0
Swinton	0	Bradford	6
Warrington	3	Keighley	3
Wigan	5	Halifax	2

Second Round Replays

Keighley	0	Warrington	7
Wakefield T	7	Huddersfield	0

Third Round

Broughton R	16	Wakefield T	10
Hull KR	8	Hunslet	2
Oldham	0	Bradford	0
Warrington	13	Wigan	0

Third Round Replay

Bradford	8	Oldham	5

Semi-finals

Hull KR	10	Broughton R	6

At Belle Vue, Wakefield
Attendance: 12,859 *Receipts: £496*

Warrington	7	Bradford	2

At the Athletic Ground, Rochdale
Attendance: 15,000 *Receipts: £460*

Final

Saturday, April 29 at Headingley, Leeds

	T	G	P		T	G	P
Warrington	2	0	6	**Hull KR**	0	0	0
J.Hallam				H.Sinclair			
J.Fish	2T			W.Madley			
D.Isherwood				A.W.Robinson			
J.Dickenson				W.Phipps			
T.Kenyon				G.H.West			
D.Davies				J.Barry			
E.Brooks				J.Gordon			
A.S.Boardman				A.Starks			
G.Thomas				A.Kemp			
F.G.Shugars				W.T.Osborne			
G.Jolly				A.Spackman			
W.Belton				A.Windle			
A.Naylor				G.Ellis			
W.Swift				F.Gorman			
J.Harmer				D.Reed			

Referee: J.Bruckshaw (Stockport) *Half-time: 0-0*
Attendance: 19,638 *Receipts: £1,261*

Cup presented by Mrs Lister, wife of the President of the Union.

1906 Bradford 5 Salford 0

THE match between Salford and Bradford had generated a great deal of interest on both sides of the Pennines and the game was expected to create a new Challenge Cup Final attendance record.

However, atrocious weather conditions on the morning of the game soon dispelled any thoughts of a good crowd. Rain and sleet showers were driven across Leeds by a wind that at times reached gale force and effectively reduced the crowd to just under 16,000.

James Lomas, the Salford captain, won the all-important toss and elected to play with the advantage of the strong wind that was blowing straight down the pitch from the Kirkstall Road end.

Bradford kicked-off and George Marsden sent the ball sailing straight into touch for it to be brought back for a scrum on the centre spot. Salford, with the wind behind them, swept forward into the Bradford half and only some cool and clever defensive work by Gunn and Sinton prevented the Reds opening the score. With the wind in their favour Salford were quite content to hoist the ball high into the air and chase down into the Bradford half. Bradford, on the other hand, adopted far different tactics and despite playing into the gale, they kept the ball among their forwards using short passing movements, whenever possible, to gain valuable ground.

Shortly before half-time Thomas had a towering attempt at a drop goal but although the wind carried the ball toward the posts it hit an upright and bounced dead.

In the second half play became far more heated and aggressive and Greenwood, the Bradford forward, was cautioned for 'over zealous play'. Minutes later Dechan, the Bradford wingman, had his shirt ripped from his back while trying to force his way over in the corner. The niggling soon came to a head and Feather and Warwick began fighting and were immediately sent off.

With around 20 minutes of the match remaining Marsden, the Bradford captain, missed a simple shot at goal and the chance to give his side the lead. Minutes later Sammy Brear collected a loose ball and dodged his way past John, Preston and Lomas to dart over the line for a brilliant individual try. Marsden failed with the conversion attempt. Bradford sealed their hard-fought victory when Laidlaw kicked a penalty-goal from almost the exact spot where Marsden had missed earlier.

After the game James Lomas, the Salford captain, interviewed by the *Bradford Daily Argus* commented: *"Badford were just slightly the better team. A few of our men were not fit to start with."*

George Marsden said: *"I don't think the way we have played a team in the Union could beat us."*

Bradford's 1906 Cup-winning squad. Back row (left to right): Hoyle (secretary), Greenwood, Connell, Smales, Francis, Grayson, Walton, Mosby, Surman, Rees, Farrell (trainer). Middle row: Gunn, Sharratt, Dechan, Marsden, Turner, Laidlaw, Mann. Front row: Dunbavin, Hesletine, Brear.

Northern Union Cup Results

First Round

Batley	6	Warrington	5
Brighouse R	13	Morecambe	0
Broughton R	14	Barrow	5
Egerton	9	Leigh Shamrocks	0
Featherstone Rovers	16	Brookland R	5
Halifax	20	Hunslet	5
Hull	6	Runcorn	0
Hull KR	12	Dewsbury	5
Keighley	13	Egremont	0
Leeds	17	Normanton	0
Pontefract	0	Oldham	12
Rochdale H	0	Salford	6
Swinton	2	Leigh	4
Victoria Rangers	0	Widnes	0
Wakefield T	0	Bradford	5
York	5	Wigan	4

Egerton played at Salford and Victoria Rangers played at Bradford.

First Round Replay

Widnes	8	Victoria Rangers	3

Second Round

Batley	19	York	0
Bradford	15	Leigh	0
Brighouse R	0	Hull KR	0
Featherstone Rovers	23	Widnes	2
Hull	0	Keighley	5
Leeds	0	Broughton R	2
Oldham	2	Halifax	5
Salford	38	Egerton	5

Second Round Replay

Hull KR	29	Brighouse R	0

Third Round

Batley	15	Hull KR	0
Bradford	0	Halifax	0
Keighley	3	Featherstone Rovers	0
Salford	2	Broughton R	2

Third Round Replays

Halifax	2	Bradford	8
Broughton R	3	Salford	3

Third Round Second Replay

Salford	5	Broughton R	3

At Central Park, Wigan

Semi-finals

Bradford	11	Batley	3

At Fartown, Huddersfield
Attendance: 15,707   *Receipts: £895*

Salford	6	Keighley	3

At Wilderspool, Warrington
Attendance: 8,500   *Receipts: £246*

Final

Saturday, 28 April at Headingley, Leeds

	T	G	P		T	G	P
Bradford	1	1	5	**Salford**	0	0	0
G.Gunn				J.Cochrane			
W.Sinton				W.McWhirter			
J.Dechan				W.Thomas			
F.Heseltine				J.Lomas			
J.Connell				V.R.Hampson			
G.H.Marsden				W.D.John			
S.Brear	T			D.Preston			
H.Feather				J.Rhapps			
A.Laidlaw		G		E.J.Thomas			
H.Francis				D.Rees			
B.Smales				W.Brown			
H.Grayson				J.Spencer			
N.Greenwood				S.Warwick			
B.Sharratt				I.Lewis			
J.Turner				A.Foster			

Referee: W.McCutcheon (Oldham)   Half-time: 0-0
Attendance: 15,834   Receipts: £920

Cup presented by Miss Smith, daughter of the President of the Union.

1907 Warrington 17 Oldham 3

Warrington's 1907 Cup Final side with the trophy at Wilderspool. Directly behind the Cup is Jack Fish who scored a try and kicked four goals in the Final.

THE 1907 Final was the first to be played under the new rules of 13-a-side following the loss of two forwards. The introduction of a six-man pack of forwards had been designed to open out play and make the game faster and more attractive to the spectators. As a showpiece for the new rules, the Final was a failure. Both sides adopted kick and rush tactics and although as a spectacle the game was exciting, and played at a furiously fast pace, there were very few clever incidents or movements that involved much thought. The *Manchester Guardian* was scathing about the game commenting: '*The main idea seemed to be not to try to gain advantage by passing the ball from hand to hand, not to dribble if trickily forward with the toe, but to kick or punt it vigorously, and then to follow up and snatch any advantage that chance may provide.*'

The first half was played at a tremendous pace and consisted mainly of indiscriminate charging and rushing by two packs of forwards who seemed at times to be out of control. Oldham scored first when Lees broke clear of the Warrington defence and passed to Avery who crossed the line for a try. White failed with the goal attempt and then five minutes later, Jack Fish kicked a penalty for Warrington to make the half-time score 3-2.

After around 20 minutes of less frantic, but still far from

clever play, Warrington took the lead with a try scored in a somewhat bizarre incident. A desperate maul directly under the Oldham posts resulted in Warrington's Taylor and Sugar colliding with such force that they had to leave the field for treatment. From the resulting scrum, and with the two players still off the field, the ball was heeled by Warrington, Hockenhull flung the ball wide and following some frantic efforts by Fish and Isherwood, Lees hurled himself over the line for a try which Fish converted.

Oldham rallied well and launched a series of raids into Warrington territory that were only stopped by some cool and clever defensive work by Taylor. During one of these raids Irvin, the Oldham centre, threw a wild pass towards his wingman which landed straight into the arms of Jack Fish. Fish punted the ball upfield, chased after it and then dribbled the ball well clear of the Oldham defence and half the length of the field. With just Thomas to beat, Fish gathered the ball and swept round the full-back to ground the ball under the posts.

He converted the try to give Warrington a 12-3 lead. Minutes later Hockenhull gathered a loose ball and kicked over the heads of the Oldham defence. He quickly rushed through the melee of players and hacked the ball over the line for the final Warrington try, which Jack Fish converted.

Northern Union Cup Results

Intermediate Round

Barrow	24	Pemberton	0
Brighouse St James	15	Sharlston Rovers	0
Egerton	0	Radcliffe Rangers	14
Millom	14	Askham	5
Newington Rovers	3	York	3
Saville Green	10	Bramley	0
Workington	5	Maryport	4

Askham gave up ground advantage. Newington Rovers played at Craven Street, Hull and Egerton played at Salford.

Intermediate Round Replays

Maryport	6	Workington	8
York	13	Newington Rovers	13

Intermediate Round Second Replay

York	14	Newington Rovers	5

At The Boulevard, Hull.

First Round

Barrow	0	Dewsbury	0
Broughton R	38	Widnes	0
Halifax	45	Millom	3
Huddersfield	38	Brighouse St James	0
Hull	63	Liverpool City	2
Hull KR	9	Bradford	8
Keighley	18	Brookland R	0
Leeds	18	Rochdale H	11
Oldham	5	Runcorn	0
Radcliffe Rangers	0	York	13
Salford	10	Leigh	5
Swinton	16	St Helens	9
Warrington	34	Batley	9
Wigan	20	Hunslet	6
Whitehaven Rec	10	Saville Green	0
Workington	3	Wakefield T	3

Liverpool City and Millom gave up ground advantage.

First Round Replays

Dewsbury	16	Barrow	3
Wakefield T	16	Workington	5

Second Round

Broughton R	7	Leeds	11
Halifax	5	Oldham	10
Huddersfield	17	Hull KR	0
Salford	18	Wigan	5
Wakefield T	12	Dewsbury	12
Warrington	16	Hull	0
Whitehaven Rec	0	Keighley	14
York	3	Swinton	11

Second Round Replay

Dewsbury	5	Wakefield T	21

Third Round

Huddersfield	9	Warrington	15
Salford	12	Leeds	3
Swinton	22	Keighley	8
Wakefield T	10	Oldham	14

Semi-finals

Oldham	6	Salford	0

At The Athletic Ground, Rochdale
Attendance: 16,000   *Receipts: £540*

Warrington	21	Swinton	0

At Central Park, Wigan
Attendance: 12,000   *Receipts: £328*

Final

Saturday, 27 April at Wheater's Field, Broughton

	T	G	P		T	G	P
Warrington	3	4	17	**Oldham**	1	0	3
J.Tilley				L.Thomas			
J.Fish	T	4G		T.White			
I.Taylor				H.Irvin			
D.Isherwood	T			W.Dixon			
E.Brookes				G.Tyson			
T.Hockenhull	T			A.Lees			
S.Lees				M.Yewlett			
G.Heath				J.Ferguson			
A.S.Boardman				H.Topham			
G.Thomas				A.Smith			
F.H.Sugars				J.Vowles			
J.Belton				A.E.Avery	T		
A.Naylor				J.H.Wilkinson			

Referee: F.Renton (Hunslet)   *Half-time: 2-3*
Attendance: 18,500   *Receipts: £1,065*

Cup presented by Mrs Cooke, wife of the President of the Union.

1908 Hunslet 14 Hull 0

THE first Final to be held at Fartown since the Yorkshire Rugby Union Cup Final in 1892 was a memorable one if only for the weather conditions. Heavy snow showers had fallen during the morning and the entire second half of the game was played in a snowstorm. The snow and slush played havoc with the pitch and the conditions underfoot were appalling. Yet despite the weather, supporters of both clubs poured into Huddersfield, the London and North Eastern Railway ran seven special trains from Hull and at the kick-off there was a crowd of around 18,000 in the ground.

The poor state of the pitch dictated strategy from the kick-off and it soon became apparent that the team which mastered the conditions first would be winners. Both sides made many blunders in the atrocious conditions but Hunslet were able to recover better than Hull and when they had to, kicked with far better purpose and judgement. Hunslet's pack of forwards, who revelled in the nickname *The Terrible Six* were far from their awesome best but still had the power and mobility to dominate the scrums and loose play for much of the game.

With the possession the forwards gained, Albert Goldthorpe, the veteran Hunslet captain had the space and time do what he pleased with the ball. Hunslet opened the scoring after 20 minutes when, from a poor Hull clearance, Eagers dropped a goal. Five minutes from half-time Albert Goldthorpe passed to Fred Smith who dodged his way past Cottrell, Cook and Taylor to score a try which Goldthorpe converted with ease.

Hull started the second half the better side and, with the Hunslet forwards looking a little tired, gained some valuable possession from the early scrums. The ball gained was wasted by the over-eager backs and the defensive tenacity of the Hunslet threequarters prevented Hull from scoring. A weak and foolish kick by Wallace from behind his own line gave Hunslet a mark, and Albert Goldthorpe kicked a superb goal.

The score brought some life back into the Hunslet forwards and they once again began to dominate the play, their sweeping rushes causing havoc in the Hull defence. With minutes to go before the final whistle Walter Goldthorpe cross-kicked to the right, Eagers pounced on the ball and quickly transferred to Fred Farrar who strolled over for a simple try near the posts. Albert Goldthorpe, as ever, kicked the conversion to crown a performance which prompted the *Leeds Mercury* to write: '*One could not help admiring his artistry, some of his work did not make for an attractive game, but in everything he did there was method. It is indeed a pleasure to see a footballer who relies on his brains rather than mere speed and muscle, and Albert Goldthorpe once more stood out as the chief figure on the field.*'

Hunslet's famous 'All Four Cups' squad of 1908. Back row (left to right): J.T.Wray, W.Goldthorpe, Smales, Hannah (trainer), Cappleman, Randall, Jukes. Middle row: W.Wray, C.Ward, W.Ward, A.Goldthorpe, Batten, Place, Brookes, Higson. Front row: Hoyle, Whittaker, Smith, Eagers.

Northern Union Cup Results

First Round

Barrow	28	Millom	5
Batley	32	Barrow St George's	5
Beverley	3	Merthyr Tydfil	15
Dewsbury	2	Oldham	13
Half-Acre Trinity	2	York	7
Huddersfield	3	Broughton R	8
Hull	9	Swinton	5
Leeds	5	Hunslet	14
Leigh	18	Bradford N	3
Runcorn	12	Keighley	5
Salford	15	Widnes	2
Wakefield T	19	Hull KR	3
Warrington	11	Halifax	7
Whitehaven Rec	13	St Helens	8
Wigan	20	Rochdale H	3
Wigan Highfield	3	Bramley	3

First Round Replay

Bramley	8	Wigan Highfield	6

Second Round

Barrow	41	Bramley	3
Batley	4	Wakefield T	8
Broughton R	18	Wigan	6
Hull	15	Salford	9
Hunslet	15	Oldham	8
Leigh	16	York	11
Merthyr Tydfil	33	Whitehaven Rec	5
Runcorn	2	Warrington	6

Third Round

Barrow	0	Hunslet	8
Broughton R	7	Warrington	2
Hull	19	Wakefield T	0
Leigh	8	Merthyr Tydfil	2

Semi-finals

Hull	7	Leigh	0

At Thrum Hall, Halifax
Attendance: 8,296   *Receipts: £267*

Hunslet	16	Broughton R	2

At Central Park, Wigan
Attendance: 16,000   *Receipts: £430*

Final

Saturday, 25 April at Fartown, Huddersfield

	T	G	P		T	G	P
Hunslet	2	4	14	**Hull**	0	0	0
H.Place				W.H.Taylor			
F.Farrar	T			L.Parry			
W.J.Eagers		G		G.T.Cottrell			
W.Goldthorpe				J.Cook			
W.Batten				E.Rogers			
A.E.Goldthorpe		3G		H.Wallace			
F.Smith	T			W.Anderson			
H.Wilson				T.Herridge			
W.Brooks				J.Owen			
W.Jukes				G.Kilburn			
J.Randall				W.Carroll			
J.W.Higson				H.Fulton			
T.Walsh				W.Holder			

Referee: J.H.Smith (Widnes)   *Half-time: 7-0*
Attendance: 18,000   *Receipts: £906*

Cup presented by Mr H.Ashton, President of the Union.

An artist's impression of the 1909 Final.

WAKEFIELD Trinity won the Challenge Cup for the first time in their history with a superb display that prompted one newspaper to comment: 'As an exhibition of skill, intelligence and pluck, Wakefield's success deserves a flattering place in Northern Union history.'

Trinity's forwards dominated the game in general play but their real forté was in the scrums where they won the ball with a shrewd mixture of skill and brute strength. Heavy rain had fallen during the night and early morning and the pitch was soft and treacherous under foot, reducing any thoughts of an open passing game.

Despite the poor weather, a huge crowd assembled around the ground and with half an hour before kick-off the press near the bowling green was so great that the gates gave way and around a thousand people entered the ground without paying.

Wakefield won the toss and began to worry Hull straight from the kick-off, forcing full-back Taylor to touch the ball dead. Then they broke through the defensive line but Simpson failed to hold a pass that would have given a certain try in the corner. After five minutes play 'Trapper' Newbould gathered the ball from another successful Trinity scrum and fooled Wallace with a dummy before cutting inside to cross the line with three Hull men clinging to his back. Metcalfe failed with the conversion attempt.

At the restart it became obvious that the Wakefield forwards were far superior to the Hull six and they gained possession time after time from the scrums. Fifteen minutes after the first try the ubiquitous Slater, who had just made a superb try-saving tackle on Dechan, flung a well-judged pass out wide to create a huge opening for Sidwell to cruise over the Hull line for a try. Metcalfe once again missed the kick.

Trinity continued their dominance in the second half and when Connell misfielded a long kick, Taylor, on hand to help out, kicked the ball straight into the hands of the eager Bennett, who passed to Sidwell. He quickly gave the ball to the advancing Crosland who scored directly under the Airlie Birds posts. Metcalfe converted the try with ease.

Wakefield continued to attack and for a time play became so aggressive that the referee had to caution two or three players on each side for rough play.

From a scrum near the Hull line, the ball landed in the arms of Bennett who seized his opportunity well and romped over the line for a try. Within minutes of Hull restarting the game, they were on the defensive again and Simpson caught a well-directed cross-kick to cross the Hull line for Trinity's fifth and final try and a convincing victory over a strong Hull who had been considered favourites to capture the Cup for the first time.

Northern Union Cup Results

First Round

Barrow	36	Barrow St George	0
Bradford N	3	Wakefield T	13
Bramley	13	Broughton R	23
Beverley	7	Ebbw Vale	2
Halifax	15	St Helens	8
Huddersfield	25	Widnes	2
Hunslet	25	Mid-Rhondda	5
Leigh	6	Batley	5
Normanton	10	Hull	20
Oldham	8	Hull KR	7
Rochdale H	3	Swinton	3
Runcorn	23	Egremont	5
Pemberton	6	Keighley	41
Salford	28	Dewsbury	0
Warrington	3	Leeds	5
Wigan	20	York	7

Barrow St George and Widnes gave up ground advantage.

First Round Replay

Swinton	3	Rochdale H	0

Second Round

Broughton R	0	Salford	4
Halifax	53	Beverley	2
Huddersfield	34	Barrow	3
Hunslet	15	Leeds	9
Leigh	3	Wakefield T	9
Runcorn	9	Hull	11
Swinton	3	Oldham	3
Wigan	47	Keighley	0

Second Round Replay

Oldham	17	Swinton	3

Third Round

Huddersfield	10	Wigan	10
Oldham	6	Hull	13
Salford	7	Halifax	13
Wakefield T	19	Hunslet	0

Third Round Replay

Wigan	16	Huddersfield	3

Semi-finals

Hull	10	Halifax	4

At Fartown, Huddersfield
Attendance: 21,800   *Receipts: £768*

Wakefield T	14	Wigan	2

At Wheater's Field, Broughton
Attendance: 18,000

Final

Saturday, 24 April at Headingley, Leeds

	T	G	P		T	G	P
Wakefield Trinity	5	1	17	Hull	0	0	0
J.B.Metcalfe		G		W.H.Taylor			
E.W Bennett	2T			J.Dechan			
E.Sidwell				G.Connell			
W.Lynch				G.T.Cottrell			
W.G.Simpson	T			E.Rogers			
T.H.Newbould	T			W.Anderson			
H.Slater				H.Wallace			
A.K.Crosland	T			T.Herridge			
J.Auton				W.Holder			
G.Taylor				F.Boylen			
H.Beaumont				S.Britton			
J.Walton				H.Havelock			
H.Kershaw				W.Carroll			

Referee: K.H.Smirk (Wigan)   *Half-time: 6-0*
Attendance: 23,587   *Receipts: £1,489*

Cup presented by Mrs Nicholls, wife of the President of the Union.

1910 Leeds 26 Hull 12

(replay after a 7-7 draw)

AN unprecedented muddle in the usually streamlined and efficient arrangements for the Challenge Cup Final almost led to a postponement of the first match in 1910. By kick-off time neither team were at the ground and the Northern Union officials had little idea of their whereabouts. It was eventually discovered that the clubs were stuck in a huge tailback on the railway network between Leeds and Huddersfield. The sides finally arrived at Fartown and the game kicked off at 4.20pm, almost an hour late.

Leeds scored the first points after only two minutes, when Frank 'Bucket' Young, their Welsh full-back, kicked a penalty-goal. Fifteen minutes later Sanders, the Leeds half-back, was injured so badly that he left the field and was later taken home to recover. With a man down the Loiners shuffled their side around but their forwards lost none of the impetus and were the more aggressive towards the end of the game. Hull took advantage of their extra man and were leading 7-2 at half-time.

Leeds excelled in the second half and some good attacking play led to a fine try by Walter Goldthorpe. Young missed the conversion attempt but with around ten minutes of the game remaining landed an easy penalty to square the scores at 7-7. Despite several attempts at drop goals, the score remained even up to the final whistle and, for the first time in the history of the competition, the game was drawn.

Leeds were a far superior side to Hull in the replay at Fartown the following Monday and simply swept aside the challenge of the Airlie Birds. Playing with a stiff breeze in the first half, the Loiners adopted a kick-and-rush policy with very few passing movements in their play. They took the lead in the first five minutes when Young kicked a penalty-goal. Fifteen minutes later he added two more points when he dropped a superb goal from almost the centre of the field. Soon afterwards Ware burst over the line for the first try and then Topham charged down an attempted clearance to score another try. Young converted both tries to give Leeds a 16-point half-time lead.

Two converted tries by Goldthorpe and Rowe soon after the start of the second half gave Leeds a 26-point lead and the game as a contest seemed over. Hull, however, rallied well and in the last 20 minutes of the game, Connell and Walton scored tries and Rogers kicked three goals. In the final minutes, Fawcett, the Leeds wingman, was badly injured in some scrambled play and it was later found that he had broken his collar bone.

The end of the game was marred when the crowd invaded the pitch and one spectator made a rush at the referee, but was checked by the touch judge. He turned on the latter but was pushed aside by Topham, the Leeds forward, and then taken away by several policemen.

Leeds pose with the Cup in 1910. Back row (left to right): Morn (trainer), Goldthorpe, Barron, Topham, W.Ward, Biggs. Middle row: Sanders, Ware, Webster, Harrison, Whitaker, Rowe. Front row: Fawcett, Young, Gillie, Jarman.

Northern Union Cup Results

First Round

Barrow	0	St Helens	15
Bramley	3	Rochdale H	3
Dewsbury	3	Wakefield	8
Hull	10	Leigh	7
Hull KR	3	Leeds	5
Keighley	5	Broughton R	0
Merthyr Tydfil	7	Ebbw Vale	12
Millom	9	Brookland Rovers	4
Oldham	0	Huddersfield	2
Purston White Horse	10	Halifax	23
Runcorn	9	Bradford N	4
Salford	64	York Irish National League	0
Warrington	31	Wigan Highfield	3
Widnes	0	Hunslet	6
Wigan	16	Swinton	5
York	0	Batley	0

First Round Replays

Batley	3	York	3
Rochdale H.	11	Bramley	5

First Round Second Replay

Batley	8	York	0

Second Round

Batley	0	Hull	8
Halifax	21	St Helens	6
Huddersfield	3	Ebbw Vale	8
Hunslet	2	Wakefield T	2
Leeds	13	Rochdale H	3
Runcorn	3	Keighley	5
Salford	12	Wigan	5
Warrington	37	Millom	0

Second Round Replay

Wakefield T	2	Hunslet	5

Third Round

Hull	13	Halifax	7
Keighley	4	Leeds	7
Salford	8	Ebbw Vale	2
Warrington	7	Hunslet	0

Semi-finals

Hull	20	Salford	6

At Belle Vue, Wakefield
Attendance: 11,000   *Receipts: £380*

Leeds	11	Warrington	10

At Wheater's Field, Broughton
Attendance: 14,959   *Receipts: £403*

Final

Saturday, 16 April at Fartown, Huddersfield

	T	G	P		T	G	P
Leeds	**1**	**2**	**7**	**Hull**	**1**	**2**	**7**
W.F.Young		2G		W.H.Taylor			
J.Fawcett				G.T.Cottrell	T		
W.Goldthorpe	T			J.Devereux			
C.L.Gillie				A.D.Morton			
F.Barron				E.Rogers		G	
E.Ware				W.Anderson			
J.Sanders				H.Wallace		G	
W.Biggs				T.Herridge			
W.Jarman				W.T.Osborne			
F.Harrison				R.Taylor			
H.Topham				W.Holder			
F.Webster				G.Connell			
W.Ward				H.Walton			

Referee: J.Priestley (Broughton)   *Half-time: 2-7*
Attendance: 19,413   *Receipts: £1,102*

Final Replay

Monday, 18 April at Fartown, Huddersfield

	T	G	P		T	G	P
Leeds	**4**	**7**	**26**	**Hull**	**2**	**3**	**12**
W.F.Young		7G		E.Rogers		3G	
H.F.Rowe	T			G.T.Cottrell			
W.Goldthorpe	T			J.Devereux			
C.L.Gillie				A.D.Morton			
F.Barron				E.Atkinson			
E.Ware				G.Rogers			
J.Fawcett				H.Wallace			
F.Webster	T			T.Herridge			
F.Harrison				W.T.Osborne			
H.Topham	T			R.Taylor			
W.Ward				W.Holder			
W.Jarman				G.Connell	T		
S.Whittaker				H.Walton	T		

Referee: J.Priestley (Broughton)   *Half-time: 16-0*
Attendance: 11,608   *Receipts: £657*

Cup presented by Mrs Houghton, wife of the President of the Union.

THE heavy, and at times torrential, rain that had fallen on the Friday and Saturday had reduced the Weaste pitch to a dreadful, waterlogged morass, hardly fit for the most important game on the Northern Union calendar. The Wigan officials were so incensed at the state of the playing area that they lodged a complaint before the game and asked for a postponement. The Northern Union committee turned the request down, but it was felt by many that if there had not been so many spectators in the ground at the time of the request, the game could well have been cancelled.

The *Yorkshire Post* took a dim view of the protest by Wigan, commenting: *'Football is not a drawing room game, and England is blest with a climate, and player as well as spectator has to take things as they come.'*

In spite of the conditions the game was a good one, although almost all the play, as expected, was confined to the forwards.

For a few precious minutes after the kick-off it was possible for the players to handle the ball, but afterwards the only tactics that paid were kick, rush and dribble. From the onset the Wigan forwards gained possession from the majority of the scrums but were then more than content to hand the ball to the backs and let them attempt to do the hard work.

In the conditions the Wigan tactics were totally wrong.

Time after time the forwards would heel the ball cleanly from the scrum, Gleave and Thomas, the Wigan half-backs, would whip the ball out to the centres who would more often than not drop the ball. The most talented and skilful back division in the Northern Union were reduced to a group of muddied oafs who could only slip, slide and tumble their way around the pitch.

One newspaper account despaired at the Wigan methods: *'Had the Wigan forwards gone into the fray with as much zest as their opponents they would have done much better than they did. They beat the Rangers hollow in the scrimmages, but all the use that they made of the ball was to give it to the backs who could do nothing with it.'*

Broughton Rangers soon adapted to the conditions and their forwards were magnificent from start to finish. They all knew what was required of them and they did it. With the ball at their feet the Rangers forwards simply brushed past the Wigan defence in sweeping movements that would gain half the length of the field.

If it had not been for the brilliant defence of Sharrock, the Wigan full-back, the Rangers would have certainly crossed the Riversiders line.

The game was decided by two penalty-goals which Billy Harris, Broughton's best player on the day, kicked in the first half.

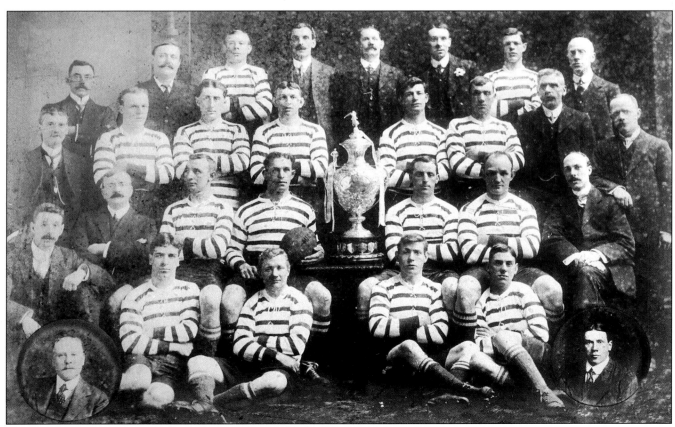

The Broughton Rangers 1911 Challenge Cup squad pose with the Cup.

Northern Union Cup Results

First Round

Barrow	7	Hull	0
Batley	7	Ebbw Vale	2
Broughton Moor	6	Runcorn	23
Coventry	10	Warrington	18
Dewsbury	47	York Grove United	0
Halifax	63	York	0
Hull KR	7	Oldham	9
Keighley	0	Salford	5
Leeds	8	Leigh	3
Normanton St John's	6	Broughton R	10
Pemberton	4	Bradford N	12
Rochdale H	11	Hunslet	5
St Helens	26	Bramley	7
Wakefield T	15	Swinton	0
Widnes	23	Lane End United	0
Wigan	18	Huddersfield	13

Lane End United gave up ground advantage.

Second Round

Barrow	5	Salford	6
Broughton R	9	Dewsbury	0
Halifax	5	Bradford N	7
Oldham	11	Wakefield T	3
Rochdale H	8	Widnes	0
Runcorn	3	Batley	9
St Helens	6	Leeds	11
Wigan	21	Warrington	2

Third Round

Broughton R	10	Bradford N	0
Leeds	4	Wigan	13
Oldham	8	Rochdale H	8
Salford	3	Batley	18

Third Round Replay

Rochdale H	4	Oldham	3

Semi-finals

Broughton R	12	Rochdale H	9

At Weaste, Salford
Attendance: 18,000   *Receipts: £520*

Wigan	4	Batley	2

At Fartown, Huddersfield
Attendance: 17,578   *Receipts: £652*

Final

Saturday, 29 April at Weaste, Salford

	T	G	P		T	G	P
Broughton R	0	2	4	**Wigan**	0	0	0
G.Davidson				J.Sharrock			
H.M.Bouch				J.Leytham			
A.G.Wild				B.Jenkins			
W.Harris		2G		L.B.Todd			
W.Scott				J.Miller			
W.H.Barlow				F.Gleave			
E.Jones				J.Thomas			
J.Gorry				C.Seeling			
A.Hirst				P.Williams			
W.Winskill				T.Whittaker			
G.Ruddick				W.Cheetham			
J.L.Clampitt				R.Silcock			
R.Clampitt				R.Ramsdale			

Referee: J.F.May (St Helens)   *Half-time: 4-0*
Attendance: 8,000   *Receipts: £376*
Cup presented by The Earl of Derby, President of the Union.

Dewsbury's 1912 Challenge Cup Final team pose with the trophy at their Crown Flatt base. Back row (left to right): Atkinson (physiotherapist), Abbishaw, Garnett, O'Neill, Hammill, Davies (trainer). Middle row: Evans, Ward, Rhodes, Richardson, Sharples, Ware, Jackett. Front row: Milner, Neary.

OLDHAM, by virtue of their superb victories over Wigan, Huddersfield and Wakefield Trinity, on their way to the Final, were considered by many to be firm favourites to take the Challenge Cup. The Roughyeds were expected to win with such ease that low attendance for the game was explained by many to be because a good number of the Oldham supporters decided against travelling to Leeds, thinking the game to be too much of a foregone conclusion.

From the onset of the match little unfashionable Dewsbury looked nothing like the underdogs they were thought to be and Oldham soon found themselves up against a team that were faster, stronger and cleverer that they anticipated. As with most successful sides it was the forwards who laid the foundations for the victory, one newspaper commenting: 'The pack are all a lusty, fast and enthusiastic lot and it is to their dashing qualities, which put the Oldham men off their game.'

Dewsbury won the toss and elected to play the first half with the advantage of a slight breeze that blew from the Kirkstall Road end of the ground. Oldham took the lead in the sixth minute when Ferguson kicked a penalty-goal after Richardson had been caught way offside. Three minutes later Dewsbury equalised when Neary dropped a clever goal from a scrum almost on the Roughyeds line.

The first quarter of the game was almost exclusively a forward battle with little headway made other than straight down the middle of the field and very few openings created for the backs.

On 20 minutes play Anlezark won possession from a scrum and passed immediately to Lomas who drew the defence around him and then released the ball to Davies. The centre whipped the ball to Deane who made ground, then passed to Cook who rounded Sharples and scored at the corner. Wood missed the conversion attempt.

Twenty minutes into the second half Dewsbury lost second-row forward Joe Hammill when a severe injury to his knee forced him to retire from the game. Within ten minutes the teams were numerically even again when, following an altercation at a scrum, Avery, the Oldham forward, was sent off, for 'being impertinent to the referee'.

With around eight minutes remaining Sharples, the Dewsbury wingman, was bundled into touch just inches short of scoring. From the ensuing scrum, however, Anlezark carelessly punted the ball straight into the hands of Rhodes who was standing completely unmarked. The wingman fielded the ball well and ran unopposed to score a try in the corner to level the scores. Ware missed the conversion.

Two minutes from time Milner collected the ball from a scrum and passed to Rhodes who managed to ground the ball over the line for a dramatic last-minute try. Ware failed with the goal attempt but it mattered little, for Dewsbury had pulled off a famous victory.

Northern Union Cup Results

First Round

Barrow	13	St Helens	3
Batley	22	Runcorn	0
Beverley	5	Hull KR	34
Bradford N.	0	Rochdale H	13
Broughton R	25	Bramley	3
Coventry	3	Oldham	21
Dewsbury	36	Lane End United	9
Halifax	10	Ebbw Vale	2
Huddersfield	30	Swinton	0
Hull	20	York	8
Leigh	13	Hunslet	0
Millom	0	Keighley	11
Normanton St John's	6	Warrington	6
Wakefield T	10	Leeds	2
Widnes	3	Salford	8
Wigan	35	Wigan Highfield	10

First Round Replay

Warrington	75	Normanton St John's	0

Second Round

Barrow	0	Batley	0
Halifax	19	Broughton R	8
Hull	27	Rochdale H	5
Hull KR	3	Warrington	3
Keighley	2	Wakefield T	13
Leigh	6	Huddersfield	33
Oldham	12	Wigan	8
Salford	8	Dewsbury	9

Second Round Replays

Batley	7	Barrow	5
Warrington	3	Hull KR	0

Third Round

Dewsbury	5	Batley	2
Hull	2	Halifax	11
Oldham	2	Huddersfield	0
Warrington	3	Wakefield T	3

Third Round Replay

Wakefield T	10	Warrington	5

Semi-finals

Dewsbury	8	Halifax	5

At Fartown, Huddersfield
Attendance: 18,271 *Receipts: £598*

Oldham	17	Wakefield T	0

At Wheater's Field, Broughton
Attendance: 11,000 *Receipts: £337*

Final

Saturday, 27 April at Headingley

	T	G	P		T	G	P
Dewsbury	2	1	8	**Oldham**	1	1	5
E.J.Jackett				A.E.Wood			
W.Rhodes	2T			G.Cook	T		
E.Ware				S.Deane			
E.Ward				E.Davies			
G.Sharples				T.J.Williams			
T.Milner				E.A.Anlezark			
J.Nearey		G		J.Lomas			
F.Richardson				J.Ferguson		G	
P.O'Neill				A.E.Avery			
G.A.Garnett				A.Smith			
J.Hammill				J.Wright			
A.V.Abbishaw				F.W.Wise			
A.Evans				J.Wiltshire			

Referee: B.Ennion (Wigan)   *Half-time: 2-5*
Attendance: 16,000   *Receipts: £853*

Cup presented by Mr A.H.Marshall, Member of Parliament for Wakefield.

HUDDERSFIELD'S first appearance in a Challenge Cup Final came as little surprise to followers of the Northern Union game. The club had recruited players from all over the world and the team assembled was one of the finest in the history of the game.

Led by their outstanding captain, Harold Wagstaff, '*The Prince of Centres*', they had perfected a scientific, passing game which was based on skill and speed, with a repertoire of moves that were quite bewildering and far advanced at the time. They also possessed one of the finest set of six forwards in the land which included Dougie Clarke, a Cumbrian wrestling champion, and ex-Welsh Rugby Union international Ben Gronow, who had been the first man to kick-off at the newly-opened Twickenham ground.

The day was a poor one for a Final. Heavy rain was accompanied by a strong, cold wind which blew straight down the ground.

The game was one of contrasting styles, Huddersfield's brilliant passing movements on all-out attack and the well-drilled, tenacious defence of Warrington. As an attacking force, Warrington were very weak and several chances they created went to waste. In defence, however, they were superb. Renwick, Tranter and Jolley were just as clever in defence as Wagstaff, Rosenfeld and Davies were in attack.

Warrington had the advantage of the wind in the first half and although they had few chances in attack, they scored first after 25 minutes. A huge touch-finding kick gave Warrington a platform well inside the Huddersfield half. From a scrum, Nicholas deceived Grey and transferred swiftly to Bradshaw who dummied the advancing Moorhouse and grounded the ball over the line despite the attentions of Holland whose tackle was just late. Ben Jolley judged the wind well and kicked the goal from the touchline to give Warrington a surprising, but well deserved 5-0 lead.

At the start of the second half Wagstaff broke free and passed to Moorhouse who kicked ahead and beat Jolley for the touchdown. The referee disallowed the try, however, penalising the Huddersfield winger for obstructing the full-back. A minute later Moorhouse was over the line for a try which stood, but Holland missed the conversion. Despite the setback, Warrington's defence still held firm and it was not until 15 minutes from the end of the game that Huddersfield took the lead, when Moorhouse raced over for a try. Two minutes later, a dazzling passing movement between Wagstaff and Holland put Moorhouse over for his hat-trick and the last points of the game.

Despite losing the game Warrington had plenty to be proud of. The *Daily News* commented: '*It was not the winners who took the eye of the impartial, but Warrington whose really wonderful display against such formidable opponents as Huddersfield contributed to the finest game I have ever seen in a Cup Final.*'

Huddersfield's 1913 squad with the Championship, Challenge Cup and Yorkshire League trophies. Players only, back row: Lee, Clarke, Swinden, Wrigley, Longstaff, Higson, Chilcott, Gronow. Middle row: Holland, Davies, Harold Wagstaff, Gleeson, Todd, Moorhouse. In front: Rosenfeld, Rogers.

Northern Union Cup Results

First Round

Barrow	16	Halifax	13
Bradford N	33	Pemberton	4
Bramley	5	Hull KR	18
Broughton R	59	Barton	0
Dewsbury	18	Runcorn	0
Elland	2	Wakefield T	15
Hull	24	Seaton	2
Keighley	0	Warrington	8
Normanton St John's	4	Oldham	17
Rochdale H	15	Featherstone R	3
St Helens	0	Huddersfield	19
Salford	34	Coventry	14
Swinton	0	Batley	3
Widnes	15	Leigh	3
Wigan	38	Leeds	0
York	2	Hunslet	0

Second Round

Barrow	5	Hull	8
Batley	2	Huddersfield	8
Broughton R	0	Salford	2
Dewsbury	10	Oldham	2
Rochdale H	0	Wigan	16
Wakefield T	6	Bradford N.	2
Warrington	13	Hull KR	6
York	10	Widnes	4

Third Round

Dewsbury	11	Hull	5
Salford	4	Warrington	7
Wakefield T	7	York	3
Wigan	5	Huddersfield	14

Semi-finals

Huddersfield	35	Wakefield T	2

At Thrum Hall, Halifax
Attendance: 22,000   *Receipts: £650*

Warrington	17	Dewsbury	5

At Watersheddings, Oldham
Attendance: 15,000   *Receipts: £425*

Final

Saturday, 26 April at Headingley, Leeds

	T	G	P		T	G	P
Huddersfield	3	0	9	**Warrington**	1	1	5
M.Holland				B.Jolley		G	
A.A.Rosenfeld				E.Brooks			
T.Gleeson				J.Tranter			
H.Wagstaff				A.G.Renwick			
S.Moorhouse	3T			B.Bradshaw	T		
T.H.Grey				J.Dainteth			
J.Davies				S.Nicholas			
J.W.Higson				G.Thomas			
A.Lee				J.Chesters			
D.Clark				A.Skelhorne			
B.Gronow				J.Fearnley			
F.Longstaffe				R.Thomas			
J.Chilcott				W.H.Cox			

Referee: J.F.May (St Helens)   *Half-time: 0-5*
Attendance: 22,754   *Receipts: £1,446*

Cup presented by Mr A.Sherwell, Member of Parliament for Huddersfield.

1914 Hull 6 Wakefield Trinity 0

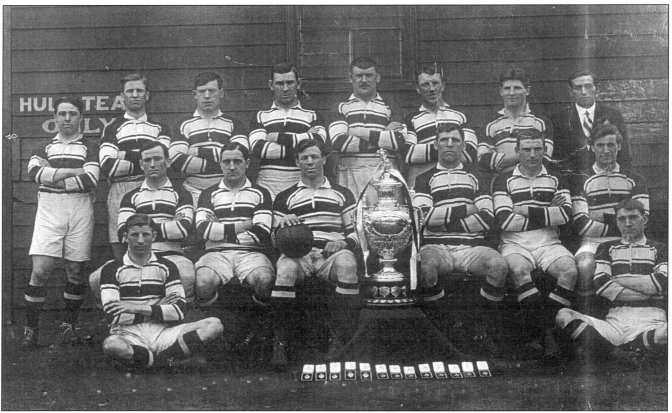

Hull with the Challenge Cup at the Boulevard in 1914. Seated on the left of the Cup is Australian captain Bert Gilbert and to the right is the famous Billy Batten.

HULL'S tremendous victory over the mighty Huddersfield in the semi-final had installed them as firm favourites to take the trophy and for their 11,000 fans who travelled to Halifax the game was thought to be a mere formality. Wakefield had other ideas, however, and played a far better game than most people had thought them capable of. Trinity were by far the better side in the first half and had they taken the chances they created, would have had the match won by half-time.

Wakefield opened the game with the advantage of a slight breeze and the sun at their backs. They soon had Hull on the defensive when a cleverly judged cross-kick found Johnson, but he somehow managed to step into touch when only yards from the line. Land and Lynch just missed with two well-struck drop goal attempts, then Beattie missed with a penalty shot after Hull had been caught obstructing.

Gradually Hull clawed their way into the game and Billy Batten began a series of strong assaults on the Wakefield line, only to be brought crashing to the ground by Land, Wakefield's diminutive full-back.

Five minutes into the second half Hubert Kershaw, the Trinity captain, was singled out by the linesman for kicking out at Francis and the referee had no hesitation in sending him off. The setback did little to dampen Wakefield's resolve and for a tremendous ten-minute spell their five-man pack of forwards monopolised the game both in the scrums and loose play.

Hull eventually broke through the Wakefield stranglehold when Taylor burst over the line for a 'try' but was called back by the referee, Darmody's pass being clearly a good yard forward.

After 72 minutes play, Anderson whipped the ball from a scrum and passed swiftly to Devereux. The Australian transferred to Gilbert who passed to the ever-eager Batten who galloped forward before passing to Jack Harrison. He beat the defence to score a brilliant try, although Rodgers failed with the goal-kick.

In the final minute of the game, Joe Hammill started a movement that was taken up by Anderson who passed to Gilbert. The Hull captain made good ground and passed to Francis, who scored right in the corner, too far out for the conversion attempt.

It had been an interesting but far from brilliant game with Billy Batten playing a tremendously important part in the Hull victory. The *Athletic News* singled Batten out for special praise: '*In the daring raids of Hull in the second half it was Batten who, with the ball under his arm, ploughed through the ranks of the defenders and left beaten opponents in his triumphal course. His courage and determination without doubt inspired his colleagues to rally round in the closing stages of the game.*'

Northern Union Cup Results

First Round

Barrow	6	Broughton R	11
Bramley	4	Halifax	13
Castleford	8	Wigan	27
Elland	2	Featherstone R	7
Huddersfield	119	Swinton Park	2
Hull	8	Salford	5
Hull KR	62	Millom	0
Leeds	39	Keighley	0
Leigh	0	Oldham	9
Rochdale H	9	Hunslet	3
Runcorn	16	Bradford N	6
St Helens	27	Wigan Highfield	4
Wakefield T	2	Swinton	0
Warrington	3	Batley	3
Widnes	16	Dewsbury	0
York	45	Glasson Rangers	0

First Round Replay

Batley	6	Warrington	5

Second Round

Broughton R	24	York	4
Featherstone R	3	Hull	27
Halifax	11	Batley	0
Hull KR	2	Huddersfield	17
Rochdale H	3	St Helens	3
Runcorn	2	Wigan	13
Wakefield T	9	Leeds	8
Widnes	8	Oldham	0

Second Round Replay

St Helens	0	Rochdale H	10

Third Round

Halifax	0	Hull	13
Huddersfield	21	Widnes	10
Rochdale H	7	Broughton R	9
Wakefield T	9	Wigan	6

Semi-finals

Hull	11	Huddersfield	3

At Headingley, Leeds
Attendance: 30,000 *Receipts: £1,441*

Wakefield T	3	Broughton R	3

At The Athletic Ground, Rochdale
Attendance: 10,000 *Receipts: £266*

Semi-final Replay

Wakefield T	5	Broughton R	0

At Fartown, Huddersfield
Attendance: 7,656 *Receipts: £255*

Final

Saturday, 18 April at Thrum Hall, Halifax

	T	G	P		T	G	P
Hull	2	0	6	**Wakefield Trinity**	0	0	0
E.Rogers				L.Land			
J.Harrison	T			B.Johnson			
W.Batten				W.Lynch			
H.Gilbert				T.W.Poynton			
A.J.Francis	T			B.A.Howarth			
J.Devereux				J.Parkin			
W Anderson				W.Milligan			
T.Herridge				A.Dixon			
W.Holder				A.K.Crosland			
R.Taylor				W.L.Beattie			
J.Hammill				H.Kershaw			
A.Grice				E.Parkin			
S.J.Darmody				A.Burton			

Referee: J.F.May (St Helens) *Half-time: 0-0*
Attendance: 19,000 *Receipts: £1,035*

Cup presented by Alderman W.H.Ingham, Mayor of Halifax.

1915 Huddersfield 37 St Helens 3

Huddersfield's 1915 'Team of all the Talent' pose with their 'All Four Cups' haul. Back row (left to right): Lee, Higson, Banks, Jones, Heyes, Longstaff, Clarke, Swinden. Seated middle: Habron, Holland, Moorhouse, Wagstaff, Gleeson, Gronow. In front: Ganley, Rosenfeld, Rogers.

HUDDERSFIELD'S *Team of all the Talent* became the second club in Northern Union history to collect *'All Four Cups'* when they trounced St Helens at Oldham's Watersheddings ground. St Helens offered only token resistance to the Huddersfield onslaught and were handicapped by the fact that a dressing-room squabble had only been resolved minutes before the kick-off. The St Helens players had received ten shillings for each of the games on the way to the Final and were expecting a bonus for playing in the Final itself. The Saints chairman, Tom Phillips, almost sparked off a players' strike when he told them there would be no bonus paid and it was only the intervention of captain Tom Barton whose passionate pre-match speech persuaded the team to take the field.

St Helens won the toss and elected to play with the wind and rain behind them. It mattered little, however, for within minutes of kicking-off Gleeson collected a perfectly-timed pass and with Rosenfeld lurking with intent at his side, the centre fooled the defence and doubled inside instead of passing and scored a clever try.

The early score against them spurred the Saints forwards on and a series of strong rushes, backed up well by half-backs Cleevy and Trenwith, caused havoc in the Huddersfield defence. The Saints threequarters were unable to match the clever work of their forwards and attack after attack broke down at crucial times.

In complete contrast the Fartowner's back division was in top form and Wagstaff swept majestically on to a pass from Gronow, which looked suspiciously forward, and scored a try which Gronow himself converted. The try all but shattered any further resistance from the Saints defence and Huddersfield crossed for three further tries before half-time.

In the opening minutes of the second half Gleeson, the Huddersfield full-back, moved forward into the attacking line and collected an inch-perfect pass to dodge through the St Helens defence to score a try. Gronow missed with the conversion attempt. A strong but somewhat dour rally by the Saints forwards kept the Huddersfield pack under control for around 20 minutes but they eventually tired and, once again, the Fartown back division took up the initiative.

Harold Wagstaff created a huge gap to send Moorhouse cantering over the line for a try, and then Gronow crossed for a try which he duly converted. Rodgers scored Huddersfield's ninth try with a swift and clever run from midfield.

In the final minutes of the game the St Helens forwards mounted their ultimate loose rush at the Huddersfield defence and in a melee almost on the Fartowners line, Davies picked up the ball and hurled himself over for a try which Barton failed to convert.

It was the last Final to be played for the duration of the Great War, many players enlisting immediately the season had finished.

44

Northern Union Cup Results

First Round

Barrow	15	Wakefield T	8
Bradford N	2	Batley	0
Brighouse R	0	Salford	26
Broughton Moor	6	Wardley	3
Broughton R	14	Runcorn	4
Featherstone R	0	St Helens	6
Halifax	6	Bramley	2
Hull	23	Dewsbury	2
Hull KR	10	Hunslet	0
Keighley	8	Askham	5
Leigh	0	Huddersfield	3
Oldham	5	Wigan	10
Warrington	5	Leeds	4
Widnes	13	St Helens Rec	4
Wigan Highfield	0	Swinton	2
York	0	Rochdale H	0

First Round Replay

Rochdale H	19	York	2

Second Round

Bradford N	3	Wigan	11
Broughton R	8	Hull KR	5
Hull	22	Halifax	0
Keighley	22	Barrow	8
Rochdale H	75	Broughton Moor	13
Swinton	0	St Helens	5
Warrington	2	Salford	11
Widnes	3	Huddersfield	29

Third Round

Huddersfield	33	Salford	0
Keighley	2	St Helens	3
Rochdale H	11	Hull	0
Wigan	11	Broughton R	5

Semi-finals

Huddersfield	27	Wigan	2

At Parkside, Hunslet
Attendance: 18,000 — *Receipts: £643*

St Helens	5	Rochdale H	5

At Wilderspool, Warrington
Attendance: 10,000 — *Receipts: £288*

Semi-final Replay

St Helens	9	Rochdale H	2

At Central Park, Wigan
Attendance: 10,000

Final

Saturday, 1 May at Watersheddings, Oldham

	T	G	P		T	G	P
Huddersfield	9	5	37	**St Helens**	1	0	3
M.Holland	T			H.Roberts			
A.A.Rosenfeld	T			T.Barton			
T.Gleeson	2T			J.Flanagan			
H.Wagstaff	2T			T.White			
S.Moorhouse	T			H.Greenall			
J.H.Rogers	T			F.Trenwith			
W.H.Ganley				M.Creevey			
H.Banks				S.Daniels	T		
D.Clark				T.Durkin			
B.Gronow	T	5G		G.Farrimond			
J.W.Higson				W.Myers			
A.Lee				W.Jackson			
F.Longstaff				J.Shallcross			

Referee: R.Robinson (Bradford) — *Half-time: 21-0*
Attendance: 8,000 — *Receipts: £472*

Cup presented by Mr J.H.Smith, Chairman of the Northern Union.

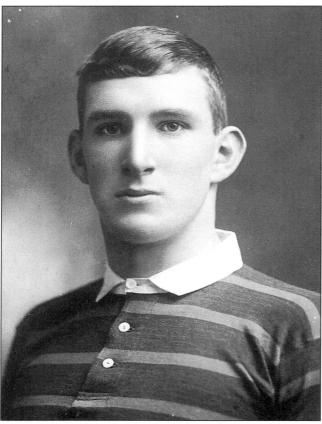

Douglas Clarke, the Cumbrian loose forward who scored a try in the 1920 Final.

Ben Gronow, Huddersfield's illustrious goal-kicker who landed three goals in the 1920 Final.

THE eagerly-awaited meeting of Huddersfield and Wigan was expected by many to produce one of the most interesting Finals of the modern times and, despite the day being marred by persistent and heavy rain showers, the match was indeed a well-fought and exciting encounter.

From the kick-off the pace of the game was usually fast and considering the heavy conditions underfoot, the players handled and fielded the ball with remarkable accuracy. Huddersfield had the better of the opening stages, despite an inability to secure possession from the scrummages, but had only a poor attempt at goal by Gronow to show for their efforts.

Wigan took the lead in sensational fashion midway through the half when Hall broke clear of the Huddersfield defence and punted the ball over the head of the advancing Holland. He rounded Holland and just as he was about to follow his kick towards the line, Pogson raced across and tackled him. The referee, who was close to the incident, had no hesitation in awarding an obstruction try, which Jolley easily converted. Many in the crowd thought the decision harsh, for although there was no doubt that Pogson had obstructed, Hall had still two men barring his path to line.

The setback spurred Huddersfield on and within minutes they equalised when a clever passing movement enabled Clarke to cross near the Wigan posts. Gronow converted the try but failed with another attempt just before half-time when a try by Pogson gave Huddersfield the lead.

Midway through the second half a loose rush by the Wigan forwards gave the ball to Shaw just on the Huddersfield '25' line. The wingman feigned to pass but instead lofted a neat kick over the head of the advancing Holland and Jerram, following up, just beat Pogson to the touchdown. Jolley kicked a magnificent goal from a very difficult angle to give Wigan a two point lead.

Huddersfield continued to play the more aggressive football and following a good run by Rogers the ball was passed to Hebron who burst through the Wigan defence and over the line for a try which Gronow converted. Within minutes the lead was extended when Todd charged down a poor kick by Smith and gathered the ball to score a try which Gronow once again converted.

With around five minutes remaining, Pogson crowned a superb performance with a fine swerving run that gave him a clever and well deserved individual try. Gronow sealed Wigan's fate with another well-struck goal.

Huddersfield's victory was a clever and confident one and prompted the *Yorkshire Post* to comment: '*Boldness of purpose carried out by accomplished methods in all departments of their play achieved a victory for Huddersfield, which adds one more to their laurels.*'

Northern Union Cup Results

First Round

Barrow	17	Hull KR	4
Batley	19	Salford	0
Bradford N	2	Oldham	2
Bramley	13	Wigan Highfield	0
Featherstone R	2	Broughton R	17
Halifax	55	Brookland Rovers	0
Huddersfield	19	Swinton	0
Hull	75	BOCM	2
Hunslet	0	St Helens Rec	9
Keighley	5	York	7
Leeds	44	Millom	5
Rochdale H	10	Dewsbury	7
St Helens	2	Wakefield T	2
Warrington	9	Askham in Furness	0
Widnes	3	Leigh	0
Wigan	64	Healey St Adults	3

Brookland Rovers and Millom gave up ground advantage.

First Round Replays

Oldham	28	Bradford N	3
Wakefield T	2	St Helens	2

First Round Second Replay

Wakefield T	12	St Helens	3

At Headingley, Leeds

Second Round

Bramley	5	Broughton R	3
Hull	29	Batley	10
Oldham	9	Warrington	0
Rochdale H	0	Leeds	5
St Helens Rec	9	Barrow	2
Wakefield T	2	Huddersfield	3
Widnes	4	Halifax	0
Wigan	35	York	5

Third Round

Bramley	0	Wigan	10
Huddersfield	2	St Helens Rec	2
Oldham	9	Leeds	0
Widnes	0	Hull	3

Third Round Replay

St Helens Rec	6	Huddersfield	8

Semi-finals

Huddersfield	17	Oldham	0

At Thrum Hall, Halifax
Attendance: 20,000   *Receipts: £2,000*

Wigan	12	Hull	5

At The Willows, Salford
Attendance: 22,000   *Receipts: £1,670*

Final

Saturday, 10 April at Headingley, Leeds

	T	G	P		T	G	P
Huddersfield	5	3	21	**Wigan**	2	2	10
M.Holland				W.Jolley		2G	
G.Todd	T			V.Smith			
T.Gleeson				F.Prescott			
H.Wagstaff				D.Hurcombe			
H.Pogson	2T			H.Hall	T		
J.H.Rogers				G.Hesketh			
R.Habron	T			S.G.Jerram	T		
A.Swinden				C.Seelong			
A.Sherwood				R.Ramsdale			
B.Gronow		3G		T.Prescott			
T.Fenwick				E.Shaw			
G.Naylor				A.P.Coldrick			
D.Clark	T			J.Lowe			

Referee: F.Mills (Oldham)   *Half-time: 8-5*

Attendance: 14,000   *Receipts: £1,935*

Cup presented by Mr J.H.Smith, President of the Union.

1921 Leigh 13 Halifax 0

THE game between Leigh and Halifax attracted tremendous interest and it soon became apparent that the choice of The Cliff, the home of Broughton Rangers, as the Final venue had been a poor one. Despite recent improvements and the estimations that the ground would hold at least 30,000, a good half-hour before the kick-off there was little room inside and thousands outside clamouring to gain admission. The frustration of the crowds locked out reached a peak and two gates were rushed with hundreds gaining free admission. It was only the swift and efficient action of the mounted police on duty that stopped the rush and prevented a disaster. Such was the crush that the majority who gained free admission soon turned round and left, unable to catch even a glimpse of the pitch. Many of those outside turned their attentions to a schoolboys' cricket match in an adjoining field.

The game kicked-off on time and after ten minutes even play, the Leigh forwards broke clear and charged down the field in a superb loose dribble. The movement was checked but from a scrum almost on the Halifax line, Mooney secured the ball and passed to Thomas who sprinted clear of the defence and scored under the posts. Five minutes later Parkinson baffled the Halifax defence and scored a try which Clarkson converted. Shortly before half-time Garforth, the

Halifax full-back, had an attempted clearance kick charged down and Thomas dashed over the line to score another try, giving Leigh an 11-0 lead. In the second half Clarkson added a penalty-goal to give Leigh a 13-0 and well-deserved victory.

The success of Leigh in their first-ever Final was due to a good all-round combination rather than any individual brilliance. It was the tackling of the Leigh players as much as anything that beat Halifax and in particular the marking and tackling of Ackroyd, the fastest player on the field. The Halifax centre was constantly caught with the ball, thanks to some brilliant work by Thomas and Heaton.

The Leigh forwards were superb with Darwell and Boardman playing leading parts in all aspects of the play. The two were always the first to break from the scrums and led many of the rushes and dribbles from the front of the pack.

The Halifax forwards were disappointing. They seemed strong enough to push the Leigh six all over the field but they allowed themselves to be out-manoeuvred far too often. The duel at half-back was won easily by Leigh, the *Manchester Guardian* commenting: '*Mooney had a splendid partner in Parkinson, and they varied their tactics so frequently that the Halifax backs were always in doubt as to their next line of attack, while Lloyd and Prosser were far too orthodox in their methods.*'

Leigh's Cup-winning team and the club officials at Sharples Hall, Bolton in May 1921.

Northern Union Cup Results

First Round

Askham	2	Bradford N	7
Dewsbury	12	Hull KR	0
Featherstone R	41	Pendlebury	0
Halifax	5	Batley	0
Hull	5	Warrington	5
Hunslet	7	Leeds	8
Keighley	5	Rochdale H	10
Leigh	0	York	0
Oldham	41	Elland Wanderers	5
St Helens	0	Bramley	7
St Helens Rec	9	Wigan	6
Salford	4	Barrow	0
Swinton	25	BOCM	5
Wakefield T	4	Huddersfield	8
Widnes	41	Dearham Wanderers	5
Wigan Highfield	10	Broughton R	15

First Round Replays

Warrington	16	Hull	5
York	0	Leigh	3

Second Round

Bradford N	7	Swinton	3
Bramley	4	Halifax	13
Broughton R	3	Rochdale H	5
Featherstone R	0	Dewsbury	22
Huddersfield	8	Oldham	3
Leigh	10	Warrington	10
St Helens Rec	0	Widnes	7
Salford	0	Leeds	21

Second Round Replay

Warrington	3	Leigh	8

Third Round

Dewsbury	0	Rochdale H	0
Halifax	5	Widnes	2
Huddersfield	5	Leeds	3
Leigh	7	Bradford N	0

Third Round Replay

Rochdale H	5	Dewsbury	2

Semi-finals

Leigh	10	Rochdale H	0

At Central Park, Wigan
Attendance: 20,000   *Receipts: £1,200*

Halifax	2	Huddersfield	0

At Headingley, Leeds
Attendance: 23,500   *Receipts: £3,084*

Final

Saturday, 30 April at The Cliff, Broughton

	T	G	P		T	G	P
Leigh	3	2	13	**Halifax**	0	0	0
T.Clarkson		2G		C.Garforth			
F.Hurst				R.Turnbull			
F.Heaton				A.W.Ackroyd			
E.Thomas	2T			J.C.Stacey			
C.C.Braund				F.Todd			
W.Parkinson	T			R.Lloyd			
W.Mooney				S.Prosser			
J.Winstanley				T.Gibson			
J.Cartwright				A.Milnes			
J.T.Prosser				I.Broadbent			
J.Darwell				J.Beames			
F.Coffey				J.Whiteley			
F.Boardman				T.Schofield			

Referee: F.Renton (Hunslet)   *Half-time: 11-0*
Attendance: 25,000   *Receipts: £2,700*

Cup presented by Mrs Fillan, wife of the Chairman of the Union.

1922 Rochdale Hornets 10 Hull 9

HEADINGLEY'S 35,000 capacity was taxed to the limit for the Final and at one point crush barriers gave way. There were no injuries, however, and the mounted police on duty at the ground prevented the crowd from encroaching onto the field. Hull were favourites for the game and even the official programme notes commented: *'The Hull side are reported to be in splendid condition and are popular favourites. Hornet's backs are generally supposed to be much weaker than the men from Hull.'*

The game was a fierce battle between two very powerful sets of forwards. Rochdale realised that their forwards had to do more than just beat their opponents, they had to out-think and out-manoeuvre them. They rose to the task well and the Hull six were beaten in the scrummages and often overwhelmed by the ferocity of the Hornets attack. The Rochdale pack repeatedly went away in a solid body and some fine and fierce dribbling put the Hull backs in serious difficulties. Indeed, had it not been for the brilliant defensive play of Billy Batten, the Airlie Birds would have been beaten by a much larger score. Batten's tackles broke up many of the Hornets' movements before they developed.

When the Hull forwards supplied their backs with the ball from the scrummages, the Rochdale six were there to tackle anything that moved towards them.

The opening stages were even, but at the end of ten minutes Kennedy, the Hull centre, charged down a wild clearance kick by Heaton and gathered the ball to score a try. His attempted conversion kick hit the post and rebounded back into play. Rochdale soon hit back and took the lead when Dicky Paddon, their Welsh forward, kicked two penalty-goals. They increased their lead soon after when Tommy Fitton squeezed in at the corner.

Padden missed the goal attempt and minutes later threw away a fine scoring chance when he placed the ball so close to his opponents that they were able to charge down the kick. Hull were penned in their own half for some time, but eventually Casewell broke clear and passed to Stone who drew the defence to him before throwing the ball to Billy Batten. Batten stormed forward and when Prescott closed in for the tackle, he jumped over the full-back and scrambled over the line for a fine try.

At the start of the second half Kennedy intercepted a wild Rochdale pass and got the ball to Morgan who dashed over the Hornets line, only to be brought back for stepping into touch. Rochdale rallied well and Fitton scored an unconverted try to give the Hornets a slender four-point lead. Hull second-row forward Bob Taylor scored a fine try near the end of the game but Billy Stone missed with the goal-kick and Rochdale hung on for a famous and well-deserved victory.

Rochdale Hornets team and officials pose with the Challenge Cup in 1922.

Northern Union Cup Results

First Round

Askham	15	Cadishead	5
Barrow	20	Salford	2
Batley	3	Featherstone R	5
Bradford N	0	Keighley	10
Broughton R	13	St Helens	0
Dewsbury	13	Warrington	2
Elland Wanderers	0	Oldham	29
Hull	24	Halifax	10
Hunslet	13	Bramley	0
Leigh	6	Huddersfield	10
Rochdale H	54	Broughton Moor	2
St Helens Rec	5	Leeds	20
Swinton	24	BOCM	5
Widnes	5	Wigan Highfield	5
Wigan	15	Wakefield T	6
York	2	Hull KR	4

First Round Replay

Wigan Highfield	4	Widnes	9

Second Round

Broughton R	11	Featherstone R	5
Hull KR	0	Hull	10
Keighley	15	Askham	0
Oldham	9	Huddersfield	5
Rochdale H	15	Leeds	7
Swinton	0	Dewsbury	3
Widnes	17	Barrow	10
Wigan	52	Hunslet	6

Third Round

Broughton R	2	Widnes	2
Dewsbury	4	Hull	9
Rochdale H	5	Oldham	2
Wigan	45	Keighley	0

Third Round Replay

Widnes	3	Broughton R	2

Semi-finals

Hull	18	Wigan	5

At Headingley, Leeds
Attendance: 16,685   *Receipts: £1,746*

Rochdale H	23	Widnes	3

At The Willows, Salford
Attendance: 10,000   *Receipts: £807*

Final

Saturday, 29 April at Headingley, Leeds

	T	G	P		T	G	P
Rochdale Hornets	2	2	10	**Hull**	3	0	9
F.Prescott				J.Holdsworth			
T.Fitton	2T			W.J.Stone			
F.Wild				J.E.Kennedy	T		
E.McLoughlin				W.Batten	T		
J.Corsi				T.E.Gwynne			
J.Eaton				A.E.Casewell			
J.Kynan				W.J.Charles			
T.H.Harris				J.Beasty			
J.Bennett				G.Oliver			
H.L.Paddon		2G		J.E.Wyburn			
T.Woods				D.E.Morgan			
D.Edwards				R.Taylor	T		
L.Corsi				H.Garrett			

Referee: R.Jones (Widnes)   *Half-time: 6-7*
Attendance: 34,700   *Receipts: £2,964*

Cup presented by Mrs Fillan, wife of the Chairman of the Union.

1923 Leeds 28 Hull 3

Leeds' 1923 Challenge Cup Final team with the trophy at Headingley. Back row (left to right): Ashton, Jackson, Dixon, W.Davies, Trusler, Thompson. Middle row: Bowen, Walmsley, Bacon, Lyons, Buck. Front row: Brittain, Binks.

FOR the first time in the competition's history, Wakefield Trinity's Belle Vue ground was chosen to host the Final.

From the kick-off the Leeds forward play was a revelation. In the scrums they held the heavier Hull pack and in the loose they worked together as a single unit. The Leeds six were constantly on the move and so complete was their domination that at times the Hull forwards were swept aside as the Loiners launched their driving raids deep into the Airlie Birds' territory. Behind this swift moving and deadly effective pack were Binks and Brittain, the hard-working half-backs who were always on hand to snatch a loose ball or tackle any Hull man in possession.

Hull held their line for 25 minutes then the Leeds forwards burst through the Hull defence and dribbled the ball deep towards the right wing. The ubiquitous Binks snapped up the ball, in an instance it went to Brittain, on to Bowen, and then to Buck who left the Hull defence baffled as he sped over the line. Joe Thompson kicked the goal. Minutes later a rush by Bacon took him to within yards of the Hull line, where a quick pass at just the right time saw Brittain and Ashton combine to send Bowen strolling under the posts for a try which Thompson converted with ease.

Hull rallied a little in the first five minutes of the second half but the defensive qualities of Brittain, Bacon and Bowen soon stopped any danger. Once again the Leeds pack began to dribble the ball to the Hull line and, led magnificently by Thompson and Davies, they were unstoppable. Davies scooped up a loose ball and, as if to demonstrate the pace of the Loiners forwards, sprinted clean through the Hull defence to score under the posts. Thompson kicked the goal and then added another following a try by Brittain. Hull were now a badly beaten side and Buck raced down his wing to toss an inside pass to Ashton who dived over the line despite a last-ditch tackle from Morgan who had chased back. Thompson's goal attempt hit the upright.

A rare mistake by Buck and Bowen, when they both failed to field a long kick, allowed Stone to gather the ball and pass to Kennedy who scored a belated try for Hull. The final try scored by Leeds was their finest, described thus: 'The full-back started to run in his own half. He and Buck went down the field passing and repassing, until finally the former Millom player made a big dash to score at the corner.'

Joe Thompson, the 20-year-old ex-Welsh international Rugby Union forward, kicked a superb conversion from the touchline, his fifth of the day, to complete the rout.

Rugby League Cup Results

First Round

Barrow	8	St Helens Rec	0
Batley	0	Oldham	0
Broughton R	0	Hull	13
Dewsbury	19	Bradford N	0
Keighley	2	Hull KR	0
Leigh	5	Leeds	11
Norwood	3	St Helens	29
Rochdale H	3	Huddersfield	5
Salford	16	Castleford	0
Swinton	4	Hunslet	2
Wakefield T	67	Hensingham	13
Warrington	3	Halifax	3
Widnes	2	Featherstone R	5
Wigan	47	Bramley	0
Wigan Highfield	16	Cadishead and Irlam	0
York	40	Millom	0

Hensingham gave up ground advantage.

First Round Replays

Halifax	16	Warrington	3
Oldham	14	Batley	0

Second Round

Dewsbury	21	Wigan Highfield	7
Featherstone R	13	Wigan	14
Keighley	0	Barrow	5
Leeds	19	Huddersfield	8
St Helens	3	Oldham	11
Salford	6	Wakefield T	0
Swinton	5	Hull	13
York	5	Halifax	0

Third Round

Barrow	12	Oldham	0
Salford	0	Hull	24
Wigan	20	Dewsbury	12
York	2	Leeds	10

Semi-finals

Hull	13	Wigan	9

At Fartown, Huddersfield
Attendance: 22,107 *Receipts: £1,961*

Leeds	0	Barrow	0

At The Cliff, Broughton
Attendance: 11,187 *Receipts: £790*

Semi-final Replay

Leeds	20	Barrow	0

At The Willows, Salford
Attendance: 9,000 *Receipts: £640*

Final

Saturday, 28 April at Belle Vue, Wakefield

	T	G	P		T	G	P
Leeds	6	5	28	**Hull**	1	0	3
S.O.Walmsley	T			F.Samuel			
H.Buck	T			J.Holdsworth			
W.Bowen	T			S.Whitty			
J.A.Bacon				J.E.Kennedy	T		
W.E.Lyons				W.J.Stone			
A.F.Binks				A.E.Caswell			
J.Brittain	T			E.Gwynne			
J.Dixon				G.Oliver			
G.Jackson				H.Bowman			
H.W.Trusler				J.Beasty			
W.Davies	T			E.Morgan			
J.F.Thompson		5G		R.Taylor			
J.A.Ashton	T			H.Garrett			

Referee: F.Mills (Oldham) *Half-time: 10-0*
Attendance: 29,335 *Receipts: £2,590*

Cup presented by Mr G.Ellis, MP for Wakefield.

1924 Wigan 21 Oldham 4

DESPITE a bitterly cold east wind and threatening grey skies, the game between Lancashire's finest sides aroused tremendous interest. A crowd of 10,000 gathered a good hour before the scheduled kick-off and this soon swelled to over 30,000, giving the organisers serious doubts as to Rochdale Hornets Athletic Ground's capacity. All seemed well until the police allowed a section of the crowd on the east terraces to climb the fences and take up positions on the cycle track that surrounded the pitch.

Within seconds control was lost, and the vast throng of people in other sections of the ground began to spill on to the track and the pitch itself. The almost total pandemonium that ensued was likened to the scenes at the first FA Cup Final to be held at Wembley the previous year. The police attempted to push the crowd back, and referee Chambers and several players from both sides appealed to the fans to retire.

Amazingly the game kicked-off only three minutes later, with the incredible scenes of mounted policemen galloping the length of the touchlines and the crowd surging around the Wigan goal posts.

Oldham took an early lead when Knapman kicked a long-range penalty-goal. Less than a minute later Wigan took the lead when a long scramble down the south touchline resulted in Brown tossing a pass to Roffey who crashed over the line for a try. The crowd had to be cleared from the pitch and the touchline before Sullivan could attempt the goal-kick, which he missed.

The Riversiders then began to take control of the game and Adrian Van Heerden, their South African winger, scored one of the most remarkable tries in the history of the Challenge Cup. Following up a crossfield kick at great speed and, while Corsi and Knapman were waiting for the ball to roll into touch, he snapped it up from almost under the prancing feet of a mounted policeman's horse to touch down under the posts. Sullivan converted the goal with ease.

The teams turned round without a break and, despite the game being stopped three times because of the crowd wandering on to the playing area, Wigan scored three more bizarre tries.

First Parker had to dive into the feet of the crowd on the try line, and then Price had to force his way through not only the Oldham defence but also the mass of spectators crowded on the line. Johnny Ring scored Wigan's last try and the police had to clear the pitch to enable Jim Sullivan to take the goal-kick. Sullivan kicked a late penalty-goal from almost on the half-way line to give Wigan a 21-4 victory and the Challenge Cup for the very first time. The official attendance for the game was 41,831, a new record for a Final.

The very first Wigan side to win the Challenge Cup, in 1924. Back row (left to right): McCarty (trainer), Coldrick, Hodder, Roffey, Jerrom, Van Rooyen, Hurst, Brown, Fishwick (trainer). Front row: Van Heerden,. Ring, Owens, Parker, Howley, Sullivan, Webster, Banks. Inserts: Price, Hurcombe.

Rugby League Cup Results

First Round

Barrow	67	Dearham Wanderers	3
Batley	19	Wigan Highfield	7
Bradford N	3	Dewsbury	13
Broughton R	34	Hull St Patrick's	0
Featherstone R	3	Swinton	5
Halifax	22	Hull	0
Huddersfield	19	Widnes	5
Hull KR	24	Castleford	2
Leeds	40	Bramley	0
Oldham	5	Rochdale H	0
St Helens Rec	0	Wakefield T	2
Salford	6	Hunslet	8
Wardley	0	St Helens	73
Warrington	46	Dalton	3
Wigan	7	Leigh	5
York	7	Keighley	3

Wardley played at Swinton. Dearham Wanderers gave up ground advantage.

Second Round

Barrow	17	Hull KR	9
Halifax	9	Batley	3
Huddersfield	24	St Helens	13
Hunslet	13	Swinton	2
Leeds	0	Wakefield T	6
Oldham	18	Dewsbury	0
Wigan	49	Broughton R	0
York	5	Warrington	7

Third Round

Barrow	34	Warrington	7
Huddersfield	7	Halifax	5
Hunslet	8	Wigan	13
Oldham	24	Wakefield T	10

Semi-finals

Oldham	9	Huddersfield	5

At Thrum Hall, Halifax
Attendance: 20,000   *Receipts: £1,750*

Wigan	30	Barrow	5

At The Willows, Salford
Attendance: 20,400   *Receipts: £1,600*

Final

Saturday, 12 April at The Athletic Ground, Rochdale

	T	G	P		T	G	P
Wigan	5	3	21	**Oldham**	0	2	4
J.Sullivan		3G		E.Knapman		G	
J.Ring	T			S.Rix			
T.Howley				W.Hall			
J.Parker	T			A.Woodward			
A.J.Van Heerden	T			J.A.Corsi			
S.G.Jerram				G.Hesketh			
D.Hurcombe				A.Bates			
A.Webster				J.Collins			
H.Banks				A.Baker			
G.Van Rooyen				A.Tomkins			
F.Brown				R.Sloman			
F.Roffey	T			A.Brough		G	
J.Price	T			H.Hilton			

Referee: Rev F.H.Chambers (Dewsbury)

Attendance: 41,831   *Half-time: 8-4*

Receipts: £3,712

Cup presented by Mrs Dannatt, wife of the Chairman of the Rugby League Council.

Oldham's 1925 squad with the Challenge Cup at the Watersheddings. Back row (left to right): Marlor, Rix, Carter, Collins, Sloman, Baker, Brough, Knapman. Middle row: Tompkins, Joe Corsi, Woodward, Hesketh, McCutcheon (chairman), Hilton, Davies, Farrar, Hall. Front row: Fisher, Benyon, Camm, Hurtley.

HULL Kingston Rovers' team of almost entirely Hull-born players was one of the finest in the club's history. Their success was based around a superb defence and it came as a great shock to their many fans to see them fail badly in the Challenge Cup Final.

Their normally sound and decisive tackling was hesitant and weak and it was only a brilliant display from full-back Laurie Osborne that saved the Rovers from a far heavier defeat.

In complete contrast Oldham were clever and capable footballers and above all were splendid tacticians. The Roughyeds had the advantage of the wind in the first half but seemed more content to let Rovers do the running so they could assess their strengths. The opening stages of the game were well contested and Hull KR, despite playing into a strong wind, threw themselves into attack and kept Oldham pinned down and on the defensive for some time.

Eventually Rix, who had been moved from the wing to the centre, broke through the Rovers line and gained several yards. He passed to Davies who held on to the ball just long enough to send Farrar away unopposed. Osborne came across to cover the danger but instead of tackling Farrar he tried to push him off the field and into touch. Farrar beat the somewhat foolish challenge well and ran on to dive over the

line for the first try. He converted the try himself to give Oldham a five-point lead at half-time.

The majority of the crowd, especially those from Hull thought Oldham's lead was far from enough to win the game and fully expected the Rovers to overwhelm the Roughyeds in the second half, when they had the aid of the wind.

Oldham must has sensed that they needed far more than five points to beat the still confident Hull men and started the second half at a great pace. A fine forward rush in the opening minutes drove the ball deep into Hull's half and Brough forced himself over for an unconverted try. Corsi added another try soon after and Farrar landed a goal to give Oldham a clear 13 point lead.

Despite looking weaker and weaker as the game wore on, Rovers fought back for a spell and Wilkinson scored a try. Oldham scored the final points however, when Davies scored his second try of the match.

Many of the newspaper reports of the game thought that the Hull Kingston forwards had had a good game, with Boagey, Bielby and Carmichael playing well, but the half-backs were the weak link and did little to combine with the threequarters as unit. Hesketh, the Oldham, half-back, had a brilliant game and had some superb support from Rix and Davies the two centres.

Rugby League Cup Results

First Round

Barnsley United	3	Dalton	3
Broughton R	0	Huddersfield	8
Halifax	0	Featherstone R	0
Hull KR	9	Bramley	0
Hunslet	25	Castleford	0
Keighley	4	Dewsbury	0
Leeds	27	Twelve Apostles	0
Leigh	0	Oldham	5
Rochdale H	7	Barrow	0
St Helens Rec	15	Hull	5
Swinton	2	Batley	3
Wakefield T	14	Salford	3
Warrington	11	Bradford N	3
Widnes	10	St Helens	8
Wigan	116	Flimby and Fothergill	0
York	3	Wigan H	8

Twelve Apostles gave up ground advantage. Barnsley United played at Hull.

First Round Replays

Dalton	3	Barnsley United	2
Featherstone R	2	Halifax	2

First Round Second Replay

Featherstone R	6	Halifax	2

At Headingley, Leeds

Second Round

Batley	30	Widnes	3
Featherstone R	6	Hunslet	2
Hull KR	13	Wigan H	5
Keighley	3	Wakefield T	0
Leeds	2	Wigan	0
Oldham	12	Warrington	7
Rochdale H	5	Huddersfield	0
St Helens Rec	74	Dalton	5

Dalton gave up ground advantage.

Third Round

Batley	4	Leeds	5
Keighley	0	Hull KR	5
Oldham	26	Featherstone R	0
Rochdale H	9	St Helens Rec	5

Semi-finals

Hull KR	7	Leeds	6

At Belle Vue, Wakefield
Attendance: 25,263   *Receipts: £2,115*

Oldham	9	Rochdale H	0

At Central Park, Wigan
Attendance: 26,208   *Receipts: £1,830*

Final

Saturday, 25 April at Headingley, Leeds

	T	G	P		T	G	P
Oldham	4	2	16	**Hull KR**	1	0	3
B.Knapman				L.Osborne			
R.Farrar	T	2G		L.Harris			
S.Rix				J.Cooke			
E.Davies	T			J.E.Hoult			
J.Corsi	T			G.Austin			
G.Hesketh				J.Raynor			
B.Benyon				J.McIntyre			
A.Tomkims				J.H.Wilkinson	T		
R.Marlor				F.Boagey			
J.Collins				J.R.Wilkinson			
R.Sloman				C.W.Westerdale			
A.Brough	T			F.Bielby			
J.Hilton				A.Carmichael			

Referee: R.Jones (Widnes)   *Half-time: 5-0*
Attendance: 28,335   *Receipts: £2,876*

Cup presented by Mrs Gale, wife of the Chairman of the Rugby League Council.

1926 Swinton 9 Oldham 3

Swinton's 1926 squad and directors with their three trophy haul. Back row (left to right): Turner, Beswick, Leigh. Third row: Kerns (trainer), Sulway, Fairhurst, Strong, Morris, Entwistle, Blewer, Halliwell. Seated: F.Evans, Pearson, J.Evans, Halsall, Brockbank, B.Evans, Pardon. Front: Atkinson, Rees.

CONDITIONS for the Final, at Rochdale Hornets Athletic Ground could hardly have been worse, heavy rain and a strong blustering wind making matters depressing for both spectators and players alike.

Swinton were without Halsall, their captain, who had still not recovered from the injury he received at Warrington the week before. Sulway took his place and played a good sound game, his tackling in particular being strong and sure.

Swinton won the toss and, as expected, chose to play with the wind behind them in the first half. Oldham's task in playing into the strong wind was highlighted from the start, when Knapman, their full-back, kicked to relieve his line and saw the ball blow back over his head into touch. Faced with such a problem, Oldham were for long periods pinned in their own half but did force their way to half-way with a series of forward rushes or short passing movements.

Swinton pressed the Oldham line for almost all of the first 15 minutes but missed their only real chance when F.Evans hesitated and was well tackled by Rix. Morris missed two easy attempts at goal, but finally succeed with his third. The Oldham forwards continued to force their way up the field and eventually Jones broke clear and was obstructed in the Swinton half. Knapman took the penalty, but against the wind he had little chance of scoring.

Swinton resumed their almost constant attacking and were rewarded with a bizarre try. Billo Rees took a drop at goal and the ball hit the crossbar and ricocheted straight into the arms of Blewer, who, hardly believing his luck, simply walked over the line to score. Morris converted and later kicked a tremendous penalty from the half-way line to give Swinton a 9-0 half-time lead.

The nine-point lead was considered far from enough and Oldham were expected to do much better with the wind behind them. But in the first few minutes of the second half they showed that the tremendous strain of the first part of the game was telling on them. They looked a tired team and their attack showed no aggression. At one point Brough actually crossed the Swinton line but allowed himself to be pushed into touch in goal. Their only points came when Corsi collected a poor clearance kick from Brockbank and raced over to score a try.

Swinton grew in confidence and Bryn Evans and Billo Rees combined superbly with the threequarters to set up some fine passing movements between Sulway and Brockbank which the Oldham backs were very lucky to stop.

Swinton were worthy winners of an interesting and well-fought game but many thought they had more than good fortune to win the toss on such a poor day.

Rugby League Cup Results

First Round

Barrow	44	Barrow Cambridge St	0
Bradford N	2	Keighley	2
Bramley	0	Rochdale H	11
Castleford	12	St Helens Rec	18
Featherstone R	7	Broughton R	8
Halifax	16	Dewsbury	0
Hensingham	0	Huddersfield	33
Hull	27	Pemberton R	3
Hull KR	28	Barnsley United	0
Hunslet	7	Warrington	11
Leigh	6	Oldham	18
Salford	2	Leeds	3
Swinton	19	Batley	9
Widnes	7	St Helens	10
Wigan	45	York	10
Wigan Highfield	7	Wakefield T	2

Bradford N played at Valley Parade. Barnsley United gave up ground advantage.

First Round Replay

Keighley	5	Bradford N	5

At Valley Parade, Bradford

First Round Second Replay

Bradford N	9	Keighley	4

At Headingley, Leeds

Second Round

Barrow	0	Halifax	3
Bradford N	3	Hull KR	6
Leeds	17	Wigan	10
Oldham	12	Rochdale H	3
St Helens	7	Hull	10
Swinton	8	Broughton R	8
Warrington	17	St Helens Rec	12
Wigan Highfield	5	Huddersfield	3

Second Round Replay

Broughton R	3	Swinton	20

Third Round

Hull	15	Warrington	2
Oldham	8	Halifax	5
Swinton	24	Hull KR	3
Wigan Highfield	11	Leeds	2

Semi-finals

Oldham	15	Wigan Highfield	6

At The Willows, Salford
Attendance: 18,290   *Receipts: £1,423*

Swinton	13	Hull	2

At Thrum Hall, Halifax
Attendance: 17,693   *Receipts: £1,367*

Final

Saturday, 1 May at The Athletic Ground, Rochdale

	T	G	P		T	G	P
Swinton	1	3	9	**Oldham**	1	0	3
J.Pearson				E.Knapman			
F.Evans				J.Corsi	T		
W.Sulway				A.Higgs			
J.Evans				S.Rix			
C.Brockbank				A.Brough			
W.Rees				G.Hesketh			
B.Evans				R.Jones			
M.F.Strong				R.Marlor			
H.Blewer	T			R.Lister			
H.E.Morris		3G		J.Read			
T.Halliwell				A.Baker			
E.Entwistle				P.Carter			
F.Beswick				R.Sloman			

Referee: A.Brown (Wakefield)   *Half-time: 9-0*
Attendance: 27,800   *Receipts: £2,537*

Cup presented by Mrs Whitaker, wife of the Chairman of the Rugby Football League.

1927 Oldham 26 Swinton 7

Oldham with the Cup at their Watersheddings base in 1927. Back row (left to right): Marsden (trainer), Brough, Rix, Comm, Foste. Middle row: Higgs, Marlor, Scaife, Read, Baker, Ashworth, Holliday. Seated: Jeremiah, Jones, Sloman, Hesketh, Johnson.

THE first Challenge Cup Final to be held at Wigan's Central Park was rewarded with one of the largest crowds for years.

Swinton were firm favourites for the Cup. They had beaten St Helens Recs the previous week in the Championship Final, at Warrington, and finished 18 points above Oldham in the League table. They were also the Challenge Cup holders, having beaten Oldham the previous season at Rochdale.

Swinton started so well that it looked as though they would beat Oldham in the first ten minutes of the game. Chris Brockbank opened the scoring when he dashed over the line for a try which Morris failed to convert. It was to be Swinton's only try, however. The superb ball-handling skills of their backs suddenly, and without explanation, deserted them and some of the finest threequarter backs in the League were reduced to a pitiful combination who seemed unable to hold even the easiest pass thrown towards them.

At one point Hector Halsall, the Swinton centre, sliced open a huge gap in the Oldham defence and with tremendous timing drew the defence to him before passing to Frank Evans, who, with the line totally undefended, fumbled the simplest of catches and dropped the ball. Minutes later Jack Evans created a similar chance and Frank Evans again failed to hold on to a perfect pass which a player of his ability should have caught with ease.

Johnson landed a penalty-goal for Oldham and then Morris did the same for Swinton. Just before half-time Holliday scored a try for Oldham which Johnson converted and the sides turned round with Oldham leading by a surprising two points.

Sensing they had more than an outside chance of victory, Oldham started the second half with a great surge towards the Swinton line. Swinton held out with some desperate scrambling defence for 15 minutes and then Hesketh sold Frank Evans an outrageous dummy to send Rix galloping over the line for a simple try. Brough converted the try, then minutes later Halsall, the Swinton captain, was so badly hurt he took no further part in the game.

From that moment, Swinton collapsed and seemed to have neither the energy nor will to attempt to play any further part in the game or prevent Oldham scoring. Oldham simply toyed with Swinton for the rest of the game and their forwards did as they pleased. Brough, Johnson, Sloman and Holliday scored tries for Oldham, and Morris kicked a solitary goal for Swinton.

The game, despite the high scoring, was a disappointing one and the *Manchester Guardian* commented: '*Everything was in perfect order for a game worthy to be classed in the front rank of Rugby League football but it was not produced. It was a Final in which, apart from Hesketh and Rees, few players showed any exceptional ability. Swinton played far below their form and thoroughly deserved defeat.*'

Rugby League Cup Results

First Round

Batley	32	Cottingham	5
Broughton R	18	Castleford	5
Dewsbury	20	Dearham Wanderers	5
Featherstone R	14	Barrow	0
Halifax	37	Bramley	5
Hull	6	St Helens Rec	5
Hull KR	22	Keighley	3
Hunslet	10	Bradford N	5
Oldham	8	Salford	0
Rochdale H	8	Leigh	2
Swinton	11	Huddersfield	2
Wakefield T	13	Wigan Highfield	5
Warrington	3	Leeds	12
Widnes	23	Pontypridd	2
Wigan	51	Pemberton R	11
York	9	St Helens	3

Dearham Wanderers gave up ground advantage.

Second Round

Batley	7	Featherstone R	0
Hull	29	Broughton R	15
Hunslet	3	Oldham	15
Leeds	13	Wigan	3
Rochdale H	0	Hull KR	14
Swinton	10	York	8
Wakefield T	7	Halifax	2
Widnes	2	Dewsbury	2

Second Round Replay

Dewsbury	13	Widnes	2

Third Round

Dewsbury	7	Hull KR	2
Leeds	5	Oldham	11
Swinton	19	Hull	2
Wakefield T	10	Batley	6

Semi-finals

Oldham 7 Wakefield T 3
At Central Park, Wigan
Attendance: 18,000 *Receipts: £1,199*

Swinton 10 Dewsbury 0
At Fartown, Huddersfield
Attendance: 24,227 *Receipts: £1,721*

Final

Saturday, 7 May at Central Park, Wigan

	T	G	P		T	G	P
Oldham	6	4	26	**Swinton**	1	2	7
H.J.Comm				E.Leigh			
A.Johnson		2G		F.Evans			
S.Rix	T			H.Halsall			
A.Higgs				J.Evans			
T.E.Holliday	3T			C.Brockbank	T		
G.Hesketh				W.Rees			
R.Jones				B.Evans			
J.Read				M.F.Strong			
J.M.Scaife				H.Blewer			
R.Marlor				H.E.Morris		2G	
R.Sloman	T			R.H.Cracknell			
F.W.Ashworth				T.Halliwell			
A.Brough	T	2G		F.Beswick			

Referee: R.Robinson (Bradford) *Half-time: 7-5*
Attendance: 33,448 *Receipts: £3,165*

Cup presented by Mrs Osborne, wife of the Chairman of the Rugby League Council.

1928 Swinton 5 Warrington 3

SWINTON collected the Cup for the third time in their history but the game was a poor one with one newspaper commenting: *'While Swinton were entitled to their victory, it is not possible to speak of the match as containing even a passable exhibition of the Rugby League code and one has to rummage a long way back in the memory of Cup Finals to find one in which the quality was so poor.'*

Warrington realised long before the kick-off that they could not compete with the talented Swinton backs and had decided to adopt a campaign that was based on full frontal assaults at the Lions defence. They mixed forward rushes with strong tackling and a kick-and-follow tactic that more often than not failed abysmally. The Wire's strategy might have worked if they had controlled themselves better and had not been almost constantly penalised by the referee for a series of scrummage infringements or straying offside when they were within yards of the Swinton line.

The *Yorkshire Post* was scathing in its condemnation of the Warrington methods: *'It is sheer stupidity to waste opportunities and surrender hard-won territory. Quite half a dozen times did Warrington contribute to their defeat by thus spoiling their own chances of a winning score.'*

From the kick-off, the play soon developed into a series of loose rushes and strong tackles which the heavier

Warrington forwards dominated but failed to capitalise upon. Swinton opened the scoring when J.Evans gave Brockbank a perfectly-timed pass to give the wingman the space to hurl himself over the line near the corner flag. Morris missed with the conversion attempt.

Early in the second half Warrington's half-back Kirk fell while attempting to avoid a tackle, hitting the ground with such force that he was knocked unconscious. He was carried from the field on a stretcher and was found to be suffering from severe concussion but recovered enough to be taken home later in the afternoon.

Warrington moved Davies to scrum-half and dropped Seeling back to cover the right wing. The weakened pack did far better in the scrums that followed and from one of the set pieces, Seeling forced his way over the line for a try which Rhodes failed to convert. Warrington attacked again but from a scrum Brockbank hoisted a huge kick up the field. The wind carried the ball over the head of Frowen and as he chased the ball back he played it before touching down over the line. The referee, who had followed play well, gave a five-yard scrum. Swinton's six heeled well and the ball was sent from Rees to J.Evans, who had the time and space to drop a superb goal and give the Lions a precious two-point lead and the Cup.

Swinton, the third and final team to win 'All Four Cups' in a single season, pose with their silverware in 1928.

Rugby League Cup Results

First Round

Barrow	20	York	5
Batley	31	Cottingham	2
Bradford N	17	Twelve Apostles	0
Bramley	2	Hull	5
Dewsbury	20	Broughton R	2
Featherstone R	28	Keighley	0
Halifax	4	Hunslet	4
Hull KR	19	Widnes	0
Oldham	15	St Helens	5
Rochdale H	5	Leigh	2
St Helens Rec	12	Wakefield T	0
Salford	3	Castleford	7
Warrington	43	Kinsley	2
Whitehaven Rec	0	Swinton	44
Wigan	2	Huddersfield	13
Wigan Highfield	2	Leeds	13

Kinsley gave up ground advantage.

First Round Replay

Hunslet	2	Halifax	16

Second Round

Barrow	8	Oldham	11
Batley	12	Bradford N	6
Castleford	3	Featherstone R	0
Dewsbury	7	Huddersfield	7
Halifax	2	Swinton	3
Hull KR	0	Warrington	5
Leeds	13	St Helens Rec	12
Rochdale H	3	Hull	3

Second Round Replays

Huddersfield	16	Dewsbury	8
Hull	16	Rochdale H	0

Third Round

Hull	0	Batley	0
Leeds	10	Oldham	5
Swinton	3	Castleford	0
Warrington	10	Huddersfield	3

Third Round Replay

Batley	0	Hull	0

Third Round Second Replay

Hull	6	Batley	2

At Headingley, Leeds

Semi-finals

Swinton	5	Hull	3

At Fartown, Huddersfield
Attendance: 12,000   *Receipts: £792*

Warrington	9	Leeds	2

At The Athletic Ground, Rochdale
Attendance: 22,000   *Receipts: £1,416*

Final

Saturday, 14 April at Central Park, Wigan

	T	G	P		T	G	P
Swinton	1	1	5	**Warrington**	1	0	3
W.Young				A.Frowen			
F.Evans				W.H.Rhodes			
H.Halsall				J.O.Meredith			
J.Evans		G		L.J.Perkins			
C.Brockbank	T			D.M.Davies			
A.Atkinson				T.Flynn			
W.Rees				W.Kirk			
M.F.Strong				W.Cunliffe			
H.Blewer				A.Peacock			
H.E.Morris				J.Miller			
M.Hodgsen				F.Willians			
R.H.Cracknell				J.Tranter			
F.Beswick				C.Seeling	T		

Referee H.Horsfall (Batley)   *Half-time: 3-0*
Attendance: 33,909   *Receipts: £3,159*

Cup presented by Mrs Preston, wife of the Chairman of the League.

1929 Wigan 13 Dewsbury 2

THE first Rugby League Challenge Cup Final to be held at the Empire Stadium, Wembley, was a resounding success and prompted one newspaper to comment: *'Most Rugby Union players will be grateful to the authorities for showing them the Rugby League Cup Final, even though it made the average southern game look rather weak and watery.'*

Wigan took the lead in the third minute when Jim Sullivan kicked the first-ever goal at Wembley following a penalty for a blatant piece of obstruction by Dewsbury's hooker, Percy Brown.

The renowned Dewsbury pack soon found their feet, however, and Wigan's line was saved by a series of clearances by full-back Sullivan. In the 14th minute, and against the run of play, Binks latched on to a hurried clearance by Dewsbury's full-back and passed to Abram who, although a good 40 yards from the line, outpaced the defence to score a great try.

Jim Sullivan, the Wigan captain, carries the Challenge Cup down the Wembley steps in 1929, following the first Final held at the Empire Stadium.

Rugby League Cup Results

First Round

Bramley	0	Oldham	16	
Bradford N	2	Halifax	5	
Broughton R	2	St Helens Rec	13	
Castleford	31	Whitehaven Rec	7	
Dewsbury	37	Cottingham	0	
Huddersfield	21	Widnes	11	
Hull	11	Wakefield T	5	
Hunslet	16	Hull KR	7	
Rochdale H	2	Barrow	6	
St Helens	32	Lindley	2	
Salford	5	Keighley	9	
Swinton	5	Leigh	2	
Warrington	8	Leeds	0	
Wigan	25	Batley	0	
Wigan H	45	Uno's Dabs	0	
York	0	Featherstone R	10	

Lindley gave up ground advantage.

Second Round

Castleford	8	Huddersfield	0
Dewsbury	14	Swinton	7
Featherstone R	0	St Helens Rec	13
Halifax	16	Barrow	0
St Helens	26	Keighley	5
Warrington	7	Oldham	0
Wigan	16	Hunslet	0
Wigan H	17	Hull	5

Third Round

Castleford	8	Wigan H	0
St Helens Rec	21	Halifax	0
St Helens	2	Wigan	2
Warrington	4	Dewsbury	10

Third Round Replay

Wigan	25	St Helens	5

Final

Saturday, 4 May at Wembley Stadium, London

	T	G	P		T	G	P
Wigan	3	2	13	**Dewsbury**	0	1	2
J.Sullivan		2G		J.Davies		G	
J.Ring				T.Bailey			
T.Parker				C.Smith			
R.Kinnear	T			H.Hirst			
L.Brown	T			H.Coates			
A.Binks				J.W.Woolmore			
S.Abram	T			J.Rudd			
W.Hodder				J.A.Hobson			
J.Bennett				P.Brown			
T.Beetham				W.Rhodes			
F.Stephens				H.Bland			
L.Mason				J.Malkin			
J.Sherrington				J.Lyman			

Referee: R.Robinson (Bradford)   *Half-time: 5-2*
Attendance: 41,600   *Receipts: £5,614*

Cup presented by Lord Daresbury.

Semi-finals

Dewsbury	9	Castleford	3

At Fartown, Huddersfield
Attendance: 25,000   *Receipts: £1,562*

Wigan	7	St Helens Rec	7

At Station Road, Swinton
Attendance: 31,000   *Receipts: £2,209*

Semi-final Replay

Wigan	13	St Helens Rec	12

At Mather Lane, Leigh
Attendance: 21,940   *Receipts: £1,437*

In the 33rd minute, Sullivan punted the ball upfield and Dewsbury's Welshman Jack Davies allowed the ball bounce, gathered it on the half-way line and taking careful aim kicked a superb goal to bring the Yorkshiremen back into the game.

At the start of the second half Dewsbury had near misses when first Lyman and then Coates were hauled down just short of the line. The brief spell of attacking was to be Dewsbury's last of the game, for Wigan's half-backs Abram and Binks took a vice-like grip on the game. The pair combined in the 60th minute to send Kinnear flying towards the line. The Scotsman was briefly checked by Smith, but shook the centre aside, brushed past Bailey and passed to Lou Brown, who scored a fine try. Sullivan missed the conversion.

With around ten minutes to the final whistle, Dewsbury's Herbert Hirst was carried from the field with an injury to his ribs and Joe Lyman took his place in the centre. Arthur Binks took full advantage of the missing man and soon carved out a huge gap for Roy Kinnear to charge over the line for a try which Sullivan converted with ease to give Wigan a 13-2 victory.

After the game it was revealed that an official of the Rugby League had visited the Dewsbury dressing-room before the game and asked that the Yorkshiremen adopt a more open method of play rather than use their usual tight, forward-dominated tactics. It is not know whether the players heeded his request but the Dewsbury pack was thought to be subdued and did not play their normal game.

The southern-based press, used to a diet of Rugby Union, did not know what to make of the game and one newspaper commented: '*It was rugger with the fun missing.*' Another commented: '*Several of the players engaged in this game would be welcomed anywhere.*'

1930 Widnes 10 St Helens 3

ST HELENS were installed as firm favourites to beat Widnes as soon as the Finalists were known, one newspaper writing: *'Given dry conditions, the chances are that the St Helens team, which is principally composed of international and county players, will have the pleasure of being presented with the handsome trophy by Lord Lonsdale.'*

The reporter went on to dismiss the thought of a Widnes victory: *'Widnes, though they think they play in the modern style, are not very skilful.'*

The Widnes side, with the exception of South African George Van Rooyen, who had found his way into the side more by accident than design, were all local players, whereas the Saints had nine Lancastrians, three New Zealanders and a Welshman in their team. Within six minutes of the kick-off, St Helens, as expected, swept into a 3-0 lead when an Alf Ellaby crossfield kick fooled Peter Topping and allowed prop forward Lou Houghton to swoop in and snatch a try. The score was against the run of play and instead of acting as a catalyst for the Saints, it infused the local lads of Widnes with an even greater team spirit.

From then on the script changed dramatically and Widnes, led from the front by the 37-year-old, 16st forward Van Rooyen, simply took control of the game. Just as the majority of the pre-match pundits had predicted, the Chemics were a commanding force in the scrummages, easily outplaying St Helens in the set pieces. They also – and this was certainly not predicted – controlled play in the loose as well. They were keener and quicker and seemed to be able to perform every task they undertook in half the time it took their hesitant opponents to accomplish the same feat.

Four minutes after the St Helens try, Widnes centre Albert Ratcliffe hoisted a harmless looking kick towards the Saints line. Full-back Charlie Crookes lost the flight of the ball and committed the cardinal sin of letting it bounce. Ratcliffe chased his kick at great speed and just as he looked likely to score, Crookes stepped in his path and obstructed him. Referee Peel had no option but to award a penalty try between the goals and Jim Hoey kicked the conversion to give Widnes a surprise 5-3 lead.

Just before half-time, a clever try by Jack Dennett increased the lead further and, with a minute of the first half remaining, Ratcliffe kicked a penalty-goal to score the final points of the match and give Widnes a 10-3 victory.

In many ways Widnes owed their success to the way they were able to settle down very early in the game. The *Manchester Guardian* remarked: *'Players with no big match experience were less unnerved by the occasion than those who played football in test matches at home and abroad.'*

The local lads of Widnes with the Cup at Wembley in 1930. Standing: Topping, Fraser, Douglas, Silcock, Van Rooyen, Hoey, Higgins, Lyons (trainer). Kneeling: Millington, Ratcliffe, Dennett, Owen, Laughton.

Rugby League Cup Results

First Round

Barrow	15	York	4
Batley	5	Hull KR	3
Castleford	11	Bramley	4
Dewsbury	24	Rochdale H	10
Halifax	74	Featherstone Juniors	9
Huddersfield	2	Warrington	5
Hull	44	Bickershaw Hornets	10
Hunslet	8	Oldham	3
Keighley	6	Great Clifton	5
Leeds	27	Featherstone R	5
Leigh	48	Cottingham	0
St Helens	9	St Helens Rec	7
Salford	0	Wigan H	5
Swinton	5	Wakefield T	5
Widnes	20	Bradford N	0
Wigan	19	Broughton R	7

Cottingham and Featherstone Juniors gave up ground advantage.

First Round Replay

Wakefield T	2	Swinton	7

Second Round

Barrow	7	Keighley	5
Castleford	3	Hull	6
Hunslet	15	Batley	0
Leeds	5	St Helens	18
Swinton	7	Widnes	7
Warrington	12	Leigh	3
Wigan	14	Halifax	5
Wigan H	0	Dewsbury	0

Second Round Replays

Dewsbury	7	Wigan H	5
Widnes	6	Swinton	5

Third Round

Barrow	13	Dewsbury	7
St Helens	22	Hunslet	7
Widnes	19	Hull	5
Wigan	16	Warrington	5

Semi-finals

Widnes	10	Barrow	3

At Wilderspool Stadium, Warrington
Attendance: 25,500   *Receipts: £1,630*

St Helens	5	Wigan	5

At Station Road, Swinton
Attendance: 37,169   *Receipts: £2,666*

Semi-final Replay

St Helens	22	Wigan	10

At Mather Lane, Leigh
Attendance: 24,000   *Receipts: £1,657*

Final

Saturday, 3 May at Wembley Stadium, London

	T	G	P		T	G	P
Widnes	2	2	10	**St Helens**	1	0	3
R.Fraser				C.E.Crooks			
H.Owen				R.A.Hardgrave			
R.Topping				G.Lewis			
A.Ratcliffe	T	G		W.Mercer			
J.Dennett	T			A.Ellaby			
P.Douglas				W.Groves			
J.Laughton				L.Fairclough			
F.Kelsall				L.Hutt			
G.Stevens				W.Clarey			
H.Silcock				L.Houghton	T		
G.Van Rooyen				B.Halfpenny			
H.Millington				E.T.Hall			
J.Hoey		G		R.Harrison			

Referee: F.Peel (Bradford)   *Half-time: 10-3*
Attendance: 36,549   *Receipts: £3,102*

Cup presented by Lord Lonsdale.

1931 Halifax 22 York 8

THE third Final to be held at the Empire Stadium produced a remarkable game that many in the crowd thought to be one of the finest games of rugby, of either code, seen in the capital for many years.

York, in their first and only appearance at Wembley, were by far the better side in the first half and it seemed almost inevitable that they would be the winners.

They took the lead after just two minutes play, when Pascoe kicked a goal from a penalty which had been awarded for a Halifax scrum infringement. Fifteen minutes later their captain, Billy Thomas, gathered the ball from a scrum in midfield and whipped a pass out to Lloyd who swept past Davies with a brilliant dummy and passed to Rosser. He continued the movement and side-stepped his way past the Halifax defence before handing to Harold Thomas who, *'like a hare in front of hounds'*, raced over for a superb try in the corner which Pascoe just failed to convert.

A defensive lapse allowed Bland to score a try for Halifax which Adams converted to level the scores. Despite the score against them, York were still by far the better side and just before half-time Harold Thomas scored his second try in the corner.

Led superbly by Dick Davies, Herbert Haigh and Dai Rees, Halifax were a different team after the interval, one

newspaper commenting: *'One really would have thought that the team's had exchanged jerseys in the second half.'*

The trio had played good solid football in the first 40 minutes but in the second they excelled. One account said: *'They twisted, they turned, they eluded the opposition when seemingly hemmed in by opponents, and even the York speedster Harold Thomas was not quick enough to catch Haigh or any of the Halifax threequarters who seemed to have doubled their speed.'*

The turnaround began when first Pascoe then Davies landed goals to nudge them just one point in front. A brilliant bout of quick and clever passing gave Ivor Davies a chance to score and only a blatant obstruction stopped him. Halifax were awarded a penalty try and Adams converted to give them a 14-8 lead. York were now a beaten side and a bad injury to their stand-off Lloyd, when he collided with a teammate, hardly helped.

In the 77th minute, Laurie Higgins burst through an attempted tackle by Harold Thomas and swept downfield at a tremendous pace to score a try which Adams converted. Two minutes later, Higgins was there again, dashing over the line for another try to give Halifax a 22-8 victory in one of the finest fight-backs the stadium has seen to this day.

Halifax with the Cup at Thrum Hall in 1931. Standing: Dick Davies, Renton, Norcliffe, Atkinson, Rawnsley, Bland. In front: Adams, Haigh, Hanson, Dai Rees, I.Davies, Higgs, Higgins.

Rugby League Cup Results

First Round

Bradford N	0	York	11
Bramley	7	Golden Lions	3
Broughton R	19	Hull KR	0
Castleford	0	Hull	0
Dewsbury	2	Halifax	3
Featherstone R	2	Swinton	7
Huddersfield	60	Brookland R	2
Hunslet	11	Wakefield T	0
Leigh	7	Leeds	24
Lindley	2	Rochdale H	13
Oldham	20	Widnes	5
St Helens	46	Keighley	4
St Helens Rec	19	Barrow	11
Salford	16	Batley	3
Warrington	16	Wigan	12
Wigan H	41	Featherstone Juniors	3

Golden Lions gave up ground advantage.

First Round Replay

Hull	4	Castleford	5

Second Round

Bramley	0	Oldham	11
Castleford	2	St Helens	8
Rochdale H	7	Broughton R	15
Salford	9	Leeds	0
Swinton	0	Halifax	2
Warrington	9	St Helens Rec	0
Wigan H	13	Hunslet	12
York	13	Huddersfield	2

Third Round

Broughton R	7	St Helens	8
Halifax	2	Oldham	2
Wigan H	3	Warrington	17
York	12	Salford	2

Third Round Replay

Oldham	2	Halifax	2

Third Round Second Replay

Halifax	5	Oldham	2

At Fartown, Huddersfield

Semifinals

Halifax	11	St Helens	2

At The Athletic Ground, Rochdale
Attendance: 21,674   Receipts: £1,498

York	15	Warrington	5

At Headingley, Leeds
Attendance: 32,419   Receipts: £2,329

Final

Saturday, 2 May at Wembley Stadium, London

	T	G	P		T	G	P
Halifax	4	5	22	**York**	2	1	8
R.Davies		G		E.J.Owen			
F.T.Adams		4G		H.Thomas	2T		
A.Higgs				M.A.Rosser			
H.Haigh				W.J.Davies			
L.Higgins	2T			J.W.Davies			
I.Davies	T			W.Thomas			
H.Hanson				A.C.Lloyd			
H.Bland	T			W.Davis			
A.Rawnsley				E.Myers			
W.Renton				D.Pascoe		G	
D.Rees				H.Davies			
E.Norcliffe				G.E.Layhe			
A.Atkinson				W.Johnson			

Referee: J.Eddon (Swinton)   *Half-time: 5-8*
Attendance: 40,368   *Receipts: £3,908*

Cup presented by Lord Derby.

THE 1932 Final had to be played earlier than usual due to the departure of Great Britain's tourists to Australia. Initially the Rugby League had attempted to book Wembley Stadium for 9 April, but that date was already selected for the England v Scotland soccer international. Several other dates were put forward, but finally the League announced that the game would be played at Wigan's Central Park.

The Final was a disappointing one for many of the spectators and little was seen of the superb football and handling skills of which both sides were capable. Both sides were, however, masters in defence as well as attack and neither of their lines had been breached in the rounds leading up to the Final.

Referee Peel, of Bradford, soon signalled his intentions to the players when he began to penalise both scrum halves at the set pieces. Bryn Evans, the Swinton scrum-half, certainly fell foul of Mr Peel's ideas of how the ball should enter the scrum and he was penalised on several occasions. Leeds took the lead with a penalty-goal in the eighth minute and Joe Thompson kicked three more in the following 11 minutes.

Swinton replied with a penalty shortly before the sides changed ends at half-time.

In the second half Adams was detected offside at a scrum by the ever-vigilant referee Peel, and Swinton's Hodgson kicked a superb goal from the resultant penalty.

The score gave the Lions fresh heart and they began a tremendous forward onslaught towards the Leeds line. But the Loiners held firm and found respite with a penalty-kick. Swinton soon had the ball back when they won a scrum on the half-way line. Bryn Evans scooped up the ball and passed to Billo Rees, whose wild pass to Green was snapped up by the ever-alert Moores. The Aussie centre passed to O'Rourke, who flipped the ball straight to the arms of Eric Harris on the wing.

Harris hared up the field, hugging the touchline, and slipped past Kenny, only to be faced with around half the field to go and Scott the advancing full-back. Harris stuck to the touchline – to cut inside would have proved fatal because the Swinton defence was streaming across to cover the break. Scott launched himself at the speeding wingman and just as

Joe Thompson, the Leeds forward who kicked four goals in the 1932 Final.

Rugby League Cup Results

First Round

Barrow	65	Lindley	5
Batley	12	Bramley	6
Castleford	6	Featherstone R	2
Dewsbury	27	Uno's Dabs	10
Great Clifton	2	Broughton R	20
Hull	2	Leeds	5
Hunslet	7	Huddersfield	5
Keighley	12	St Helens	6
Leigh	18	Wigan H	0
Oldham	8	Rochdale H	18
St Helens Rec	10	Salford	6
Wakefield T	26	Bradford N	8
Warrington	4	Hull KR	2
Widnes	2	Swinton	25
Wigan	10	York	4

Bye: Halifax. Uno's Dabs gave up ground advantage. Great Clifton played their tie at Workington.

Second Round

Dewsbury	14	Broughton R	0
Hunslet	7	Halifax	7
Leeds	36	Keighley	2
Leigh	14	Rochdale H	7
St Helens Rec	8	Castleford	11
Swinton	11	Batley	0
Wakefield T	15	Warrington	2
Wigan	34	Barrow	2

Second Round Replay

Halifax	16	Hunslet	2

Third Round

Castleford	2	Swinton	10
Dewsbury	7	Wakefield T	14
Leeds	21	Leigh	2
Wigan	2	Halifax	8

Semi-finals

Leeds	2	Halifax	2

At Fartown, Huddersfield
Attendance: 31,818   *Receipts: £2,456*

Final

Saturday, 9 April at Central Park, Wigan

	T	G	P		T	G	P
Leeds	1	4	11	**Swinton**	0	4	8
J.W.Brough				R.Scott			
E.Harris	T			F.Buckingham			
J.Moores				R.Green			
A.F.O'Rourke				H.Evans			
H.Goulthorpe				J.Kenny			
E.Williams				B.Evans			
L.Adams				W.Rees			
J.F.Thompson		4G		M.F.Strong			
J.Lowe				T.Armitt			
R.Smith				J.Wright			
J.Cox				M.Hodgson		4G	
J.Douglas				F.Beswick			
C.Glossop				F.Butters			

Referee: F.Peel (Bradford)   *Half-time: 8-2*
Attendance: 29,000   *Receipts: £2,479*

Swinton	7	Wakefield T	4

At The Athletic Ground, Rochdale
Attendance: 21,273   *Receipts: £1,369*

Semi-final Replay

Leeds	9	Halifax	2

At Belle Vue, Wakefield
Attendance: 21,000   *Receipts: £1,417*

he did, Harris accelerated to leave the full-back grasping at thin air while he dived in at the corner.

The score knocked Swinton off their stride for some time but encouraged by two penalty-goals from Hodgson, they once again attacked the Leeds line. The Leeds defence braced themselves for the final onslaught and some magnificent work by Adams, Williams and Moores kept the swarming Swinton backs at bay up to the final whistle.

HRH The Prince of Wales presents the Challenge Cup to Huddersfield captain Len Bowkett in 1933.

A BRILLIANT sunny day and the presence of the Prince of Wales combined to make a splendid setting for a game that was described by many critics as one of the most exciting Finals in years.

Warrington won the toss and from the kick-off their forwards began to dominate the game and put the Huddersfield defence under a 15-minute spell of intense pressure. With Warrington's pack in almost complete control, the backs had endless possession but the chances they created were wasted with a series of mishandled passes at crucial times. They seemed far too eager to beat the Huddersfield defence in the middle of the field and seemed reluctant to pass the ball out wide.

After absorbing the Warrington offensive for a full 20 minutes, Huddersfield took the lead when Len Bowkett kicked two fine penalty-goals. Three minutes later, Les Adams scooped up a loose ball just inside the Warrington half and swerved right and left through the ragged defence before turning inside full-back Holding to pass to Brindle who was racing up the centre of the field. Brindle took the pass well and outpaced the chasing threequarters to score a fine try under the posts, which Bowkett converted.

Two minutes later, Warrington struck back when Dingsdale, the centre, completely wrong-footed the Huddersfield defence and scored a great try which Holding converted. Eight minutes later Dai Davies showed his class when he slipped round the blind side of a scrum and scored a clever try. Holding kicked the extra two points and Warrington changed ends 10-9 in the lead.

At the start of the second half, Len Bowkett kicked another fine penalty-goal to give Huddersfield a slender lead. With 20 minutes remaining, a quick heel from a scrum and a clever kick by Les Adams found Stan Brogden, who raced forward, drew the defence and transferred to his wingman Ernie Mills, who scored a fine try a foot inside the line. Bowkett kicked a brilliant goal from the touchline to extend the lead to six points. Holding pulled two points back for Warrington with a penalty-goal.

With around six minutes remaining the ever alert Gwyn Richards intercepted a pass and after juggling with the ball, set off on an elusive run through the cover to score a fine try despite being tackled just on the line. Bowkett, as ever, landed the goal.

One last effort by the Warrington forwards gave Dai Davies a final chance to show his skills when he audaciously fooled the Huddersfield defence to prise open a meagre gap and cross for a brilliant individual try.

The *Manchester Guardian* summed the game up: '*So ended a game conspicuous for relentless tackling, fine backing up, and occasional flashes of real brilliance.*'

Rugby League Cup Results

First Round

Askern Welfare	0	Wigan	46
Barrow	19	Bramley	0
Batley	9	Featherstone R	6
Bradford N	3	St Helens	24
Broughton R	5	Wakefield T	6
Halifax	42	Uno's Dabs	5
Huddersfield	19	Dewsbury	7
Hull	37	Higginshaw	9
Hull KR	4	Keighley	4
Leeds	36	Wigan Highfield	0
Oldham	13	Rochdale H	8
St Helens Rec	5	Hunslet	19
Salford	11	Castleford	0
Swinton	5	Widnes	2
Warrington	34	Leigh	3
York	35	Barrow Marsh Hornets	6

First Round Replay

Keighley	23	Hull KR	7

Second Round

Barrow	0	Huddersfield	0
Batley	10	Warrington	20
Halifax	10	Keighley	0
Hull	9	Wakefield T	4
St Helens	14	Hunslet	3
Salford	3	Leeds	4
Wigan	5	Oldham	3
York	0	Swinton	3

Second Round Replay

Huddersfield	2	Barrow	0

Third Round

Leeds	12	Hull	0
St Helens	18	Halifax	3
Swinton	5	Huddersfield	12
Wigan	7	Warrington	9

Semi-finals

Huddersfield	30	Leeds	8

At Belle Vue, Wakefield
Attendance: 36,359   *Receipts: £2,299*

Warrington	11	St Helens	5

At Station Road, Swinton
Attendance: 30,373   *Receipts: £2,055*

Final

Saturday, 6 May at Wembley Stadium, London

	T	G	P		T	G	P
Huddersfield	3	6	21	**Warrington**	3	4	17
T.Scourfield				W.J.Holding		4G	
E.Mills	T			T.Blinkhorn			
S.Brogden				W.J.Shankland			
L.C.Bowkett		6G		W.Dingsdale	T		
R.T.Markham				T.Thompson			
G.Richards	T			J.Oster			
L.Adams				D.M.Davies	2T		
H.Sherwood				J.Miller			
S.C.Halliday				N.Bentham			
T.Banks				S.Hardman			
H.Tiffany				A.Evans			
F.Talbot				H.Smith			
F.Brindle	T			C.Seeling			

Referee: F.Fairhurst (Wigan)   *Half-time: 9-10*
Attendance: 41,874   *Receipts: £6,465*

Cup presented by HRH The Prince of Wales.

1934 Hunslet 11 Widnes 5

Hunslet half-backs Thornton and Todd chair captain Jack Walkington around Wembley Stadium following their 1934 victory over Widnes.

DESPITE being a tremendously exciting match, the Final was nevertheless a poor advertisement for the game of Rugby League and one newspaper was prompted to comment: *'The defences were magnificent, the forward play ferocious; and that was all. The Widnes backs did not know what to do with the ball when they had it, and their superb marking and tackling gave Hunslet hardly a chance of carrying out a clean threequarter movement. It would be hypocrisy to pretend that the match was not great fun, but one did wish at times for less wrestling and more football'.*

Widnes took the lead in the fifth minute when their second-row forward, Hugh McDowell, crashed over for a try directly from a scrum on the Hunslet line. Around ten minutes later, Mark Tolson kicked a penalty-goal for the Parksiders.

Widnes, clinging to their one-point lead, looked the better side until Hunslet finally launched an attack that showed the limitations of the Chemics. The move started from a scrum around half-way, Les White heeled swiftly and cleanly and Thornton scooped up the ball and passed straight to Todd who fired a pass into the hands of Walkington, bursting into the attack from full-back.

The very moment that Walkington held the pass, Widnes were doomed. His quick thinking and tremendous pace had created a two-man overlap and when the ball was transferred to Morrell, he crashed over the line to score a well-executed try. The score was important but proved to be very costly for Hunslet: Morrell had broken his collar bone in the act of scoring and despite attempting to play on, had to leave the field for the rest of the game. Facing the remaining minutes with a man down, Hunslet decided on a five-man scrum formation, dropping Beverley back into the centre.

Two minutes into the second half, Widnes drew level when Ratcliff kicked a penalty-goal, but the 12-man Hunslet side were playing the game of their lives and were threatening the Chemics defence with attack after attack. The veteran forward Frank 'Dolly' Dawson broke the deadlock in the 50th minute when he picked up the ball in a midfield melee and broke clear to lob a long and inspired pass out to Beverley, who galloped over the line for an unconverted try.

Hunslet kept up the pressure and only a bad pass at the critical moment spoiled an excellent movement by Winter and Broughton. Still Hunslet attacked and, following a series of scrums, almost on the Widnes line Todd and Dawson combined to create a chink in the Widnes armour. The ball was spun wide and prop forward Len Smith finally crashed over to score the final try of the match and give Hunslet an 11-5 victory in their first visit to Wembley.

Rugby League Cup Results

First Round

Batley	11	Halifax	12
Bradford N	6	St Helens	34
Bramley	20	Dearham Wanderers	11
Broughton R	3	Castleford	9
Featherstone R	4	Huddersfield	19
Hull	6	Rochdale H	5
Hull KR	18	Wigan Rangers	2
Keighley	4	Warrington	4
Leigh	6	Hunslet	8
London H	32	Hull St Mary's	2
Oldham	19	Dewsbury	2
St Helens Rec	32	Pendlebury Juniors	3
Salford	15	Barrow	2
Wakefield T	7	Wigan	14
Widnes	12	Leeds	3
York	0	Swinton	0

Hull St Mary's and Pendlebury Juniors gave up ground advantage.

First Round Replays

Swinton	5	York	15
Warrington	15	Keighley	9

Second Round

Bramley	17	St Helens	12
Castleford	4	Hunslet	4
Huddersfield	11	Hull	7
Hull KR	0	Widnes	10
London H	19	Warrington	5
St Helens Rec	7	Oldham	7
Salford	5	Halifax	9
Wigan	7	York	13

Second Round Replays

Oldham	18	St Helens Rec	5
Hunslet	23	Castleford	0

Third Round

Halifax	3	Widnes	5
Huddersfield	21	London H	2
Hunslet	2	York	0
Oldham	8	Bramley	6

Semi-finals

Hunslet	12	Huddersfield	7

At Belle Vue, Wakefield
Attendance: 27,450   *Receipts: £1,797*

Widnes	7	Oldham	4

At Station Road, Swinton
Attendance: 17,577   *Receipts: £1,050*

Final

Saturday, 5 May at Wembley Stadium, London

	T	G	P		T	G	P
Hunslet	3	1	11	**Widnes**	1	1	5
J.C.Walkington				W.Bradley			
G.Dennis				H.Owen			
C.Morrell	T			P.Topping			
E.Winter				P.Jacks			
G.Broughton				A.Gallimore			
G.Todd				T.Shannon			
W.S.Thornton				T.McCue			
L.Smith	T			N.Silcock			
L.L.White				J.Jones			
M.Tolson		G		A.Higgins			
F.Dawson				H.McDowell	T		
H.Crowther				A.Ratcliffe		G	
H.Beverley	T			H.Millington			

Referee: A.Holbrook (Warrington)   *Half-time: 5-3*
Attendance: 41,280   *Receipts: £4,686*

Cup presented by Lord Derby.

1935 Castleford 11 Huddersfield 8

Castleford skipper Arthur Atkinson is carried from the field by prop forward Brendon McManus after the 1935 Final. Also in the picture are Tom Taylor, Dennis Knowles (reserve forward), Tommy Askin and Harold Haley.

IN ONE of the finest Finals for many years, Castleford won the Challenge Cup for the first time with a superb tactical display in a fast and flowing match in which both sides produced some fine football. Castleford's strategy for the game was to prevent the ball reaching the classy Huddersfield backs and in particular Ray Markham, the free-scoring Australian wing. They did this in fine style, prompting one newspaper to comment: '*There was not a trace of luck about their victory; they were the better team throughout, spent nearly all the game in Huddersfield's half of the field, and dictated the play so that it should run in the only way which would enable them to win.*'

The Castleford forwards were superb: Haley hooked the ball in nine scrums out of ten; and Ted Sadler, at loose forward, was in brilliant form from start to finish. With such a platform created by his pack, Les 'Juicy' Adams had a superb game and set his backs going again and again.

With the wind behind them Castleford stormed into

attack from the kick-off and it was ten minutes before Huddersfield crossed the half-way line. Despite the pressure, Castleford put on the Huddersfield line it was the Fartowners who scored first. Davies cut through the Castleford defence a good 40 yards out and after some loose and scrambled play, Idris Towill bluffed the defence and scored in the corner.

Castleford were soon on the attack again and Atkinson kicked a penalty, having hit the posts with a far easier attempt moments earlier. Two minutes later Billy Davies collected the ball from a scrum just inside the Huddersfield '25' and managed to make a slight opening before passing to Jim Croston who dashed into space and transferred to Askin who forced his way over the line at the corner.

The second half started as the first had done and within five mniutes Castleford had increased their lead to five points. The try was described thus: '*Three of their forwards started a seemingly innocuous passing movement on the right,*

Rugby League Cup Results

First Round

Barrow	28	Sharlston Rovers	3
Castleford	33	Astley and Tyldesley Coll	4
Featherstone R	2	Broughton R	8
Hunslet	11	Hull KR	0
Keighley	24	Bramley	4
Leeds	3	Huddersfield	4
Leigh	0	Wigan	44
Manchester Ship Canal	9	Dewsbury	28
Oldham	3	St Helens	0
Rochdale H	28	Barrow Marsh Hornets	18
Salford	16	Halifax	11
Swinton	2	Liverpool S	10
Wakefield T	23	St Helens Rec	8
Warrington	11	Hull	11
Widnes	34	Batley	0
York	12	Bradford N	12

Manchester Ship Canal played at Runcorn. Astley and Tyldesley Collieries and Barrow Marsh Hornets gave up ground advantage.

First Round Replays

Bradford N	0	York	2
Hull	16	Warrington	2

Second Round

Barrow	17	York	5
Huddersfield	6	Oldham	0
Hull	21	Broughton R	0
Hunslet	22	Salford	2
Liverpool	2	Castleford	8
Wakefield T	18	Keighley	6
Widnes	13	Rochdale H	4
Wigan	25	Dewsbury	5

Third Round

Barrow	13	Wigan	4
Castleford	10	Hunslet	3
Huddersfield	4	Widnes	0

Final

Saturday, 4 May at Wembley Stadium, London

	T	G	P		T	G	P
Castleford	3	1	11	**Huddersfield**	2	1	8
G.Lewis				T.Scourfield			
B.Cunniffe	T			S.J.Mountain			
A.Atkinson		G		I.A.Towill	T		
A.J.Croston				A.E.Fiddes	T		
T.C.Askin	T			R.T.Markham			
L.Adams	T			G.Richards			
W.J.Davies				D.M.Davies			
P.B.McManus				H.Sherwood		G	
H.Haley				W.Watson			
T.Taylor				R.S.Roberts			
F.Smith				J.Fuller			
J.Crossley				H.Tiffany			
E.H.Sadler				F.Talbot			

Referee: A.E.Harding (Manchester)

Half-time: 5-3

Attendance: 39,000   *Receipts: £5,533*

Cup presented by Lord Cozens-Hardy.

Wakefield T	0	Hull	7

Semi-finals

Castleford	11	Barrow	5

At Station Road, Swinton
Attendance: 24,469   *Receipts: £1,534*

Huddersfield	21	Hull	5

At Headingley, Leeds
Attendance: 37,111   *Receipts: £2,753*

which suddenly became dangerous; Cunniffe took an inside pass and cross-kicked, and somehow the ubiquitous and invaluable Adams was there to recover the ball and dart over.'

Four minutes later a far more orthodox passing movement gave Cunniffe a half-chance and he galloped over the line with two defenders clinging to him.

With Castleford tiring rapidly, Huddersfield rallied and with eight minutes remaining Sherwood put them in striking distance with a well-struck penalty-goal. Huddersfield stormed forward and after holding firm under some intense pressure, the Castleford defence finally crumbled when Lewis fumbled a kick through by Alex Fiddes and allowed the Fartowners' Scottish captain the time to follow up and touch down for a try.

It was a fine, last-gasp effort but far too late and Castleford were worthy 11-8 winners.

1936 Leeds 18 Warrington 2

A WARM and sunny day and a huge crowd set the scene for the seventh Wembley Final, but for once the football was disappointing. Despite some superb tries the match never really got going and was thought by many to be one of the poorest seen at the Empire Stadium. Warrington, just as the pre-match pundits had predicted, were masters of the scrums, winning possession from 46 of the 64 set pieces. Yet despite this control of the ball, they were unable to cross the Loiners line for a try.

Leeds swept into a five-point lead in the seventh minute with one of the most controversial tries seen at Wembley. *'The Leeds backs opened out in their own half and got the ball to Eric Harris on the right wing. He made ground quickly but instead of kicking straight as he invariably does, he put the ball across the field to confound the Warrington defence sweeping across to cover. Isaac flashed into the picture, and went straight for the ball which was only a few yards from the Warrington line. He took the ball in his stride to dive over for the touch just wide of the posts.'*

The Warrington defenders close to the action had made no move to tackle Isaac. They had simply stood and waited for the referee to blow the whistle for offside. Mr Dobson, who had been in the perfect position to see the movement, blew his whistle, but it was for a try and he quickly dismissed the Warrington protests. Evan Williams converted the try and the Loiners were 5-0 up.

Warrington's Australian captain Bill Shankland landed a

Eric Harris, 'The Toowoomba Ghost', shows his remarkable ability to evade tackles as he rounds the attempted challenge of a Warrington defender in the 1936 Final. To the right is his centre partner, Fred Harris.

penalty-goal after 29 minutes play but the Wire could do little with the huge amount of possession they were winning from the scrums.

Four minutes later Fred Harris, the Leeds centre, scored a classic Wembley try that had skill, speed and judgement, and above everything else inspiration.

Fred Harris collected the ball around midfield and set off at great speed towards the touchline in an attempt to carve out space for his winger, Eric Harris. As the centre

Victorious Leeds parade the trophy.

Rugby League Cup Results

First Round

Acton and Willesden	0	Liverpool S	0
Barrow	8	Warrington	17
Batley	8	Bradford N	25
Bramley	0	Hunslet	13
Castleford	16	Rochdale H	3
Featherstone R	8	York	13
Halifax	10	Keighley	5
Huddersfield	12	Broughton R	11
Hull	16	St Helens	6
Hull KR	5	Streatham & Mitcham	18
Leeds	18	Dewsbury	7
Leigh	49	Seaton	4
Oldham	38	Higginshaw	2
Salford	20	St Helens Rec	3
Swinton	2	Wakefield T	9
Wigan	26	Widnes	9

Higginshaw gave up ground advantage.

First Round Replay

Liverpool S	29	Acton and Willesden	3

Second Round

Bradford N	0	Wakefield T	3
Castleford	8	Leigh	0
Halifax	2	Warrington	2
Huddersfield	8	York	2
Hull	9	Liverpool S	0
Hunslet	2	Salford	2
Oldham	4	Wigan	15
Streatham and Mitcham	3	Leeds	13

Second Round Replays

Salford	20	Hunslet	2
Warrington	18	Halifax	15

Third Round

Huddersfield	12	Wakefield T	0
Hull	4	Leeds	5
Salford	5	Castleford	4
Warrington	5	Wigan	2

Final

Saturday, 18 April at Wembley Stadium, London

	T	G	P		T	G	P
Leeds	4	3	18	**Warrington**	0	1	2
J.W.Brough				W.Shankland		G	
E.Harris	T			J.W.Garrett			
F.Harris	T			A.H.Hawker			
G.Parker	T			W.Dingsdale			
S.Brogden				G.Jenkins			
A.R.Ralph				J.Newcombe			
E.Williams		3G		P.J.Goodall			
S.J.Satterthwaite				S.Hardman			
J.Hall				D.Cotton			
H.Dyer				J.Miller			
K.Jubb				M.Flannery			
J.A.Casewell				J.Arkwright			
I.Isaac	T			J.Chadwick			

Referee: A.S.Dobson (Featherstone)

Half-time: 10-2

Attendance: 51,250   Receipts: £7,070

Cup presented by Lord Derby.

Semi-finals

Leeds	10	Huddersfield	5

At Belle Vue, Wakefield
Attendance: 37,906   Receipts: £2,456

Warrington	7	Salford	2

At Central Park, Wigan
Attendance: 41,538   Receipts: £2,796

---

approached the touchline Eric cut inside. The defence wavered slightly and Fred offered the ball to Eric but at the crucial moment tucked it into his chest and flew past the baffled defenders. With only Shankland blocking his path to the line, Harris chipped the ball over the full-back's head and darted round to re-gather and score a thrilling try.

The second half of the match was all Leeds and they added further points when Eric Harris, with a superb solo effort, during which he beat five men, and Gwyn Parker scored tries and Evan Williams kicked a solitary goal.

1937 Widnes 18 Keighley 5

WIDNES won their second Challenge Cup Final with a fine display of their own particular brand of forward-dominated football. The Chemics had many critics of their methods of play but found an enthusiastic supporter in the *Manchester Guardian* columnist: '*Nobody expected it to be great football, and it was not, but it was an admirable exposition of the Widnes style, which, to the true adorer of Rugby League football, has its own genuine interest. And whatever one may say against the sporting game, one never sees Widnes play without seeing great tackling and great combined forward play.*'

Both sides started nervously with plenty of tumbling and poor, aimless kicking but after eight minutes Tommy McCue, the Widnes scrum-half, gathered the ball from a scrum on the Keighley '25' and beat several men before passing to Shannon who after a moment's juggling with the ball crossed the line for a try. Topping kicked the extra two points with ease. A quarter of an hour later Keighley won a scrum in their own '25' and began a very slow and laboured passing movement, McCue, sensing the apathy of the Keighley players, stepped forward and calmly intercepted the ball. He side-stepped two men with ridiculous ease and scored a brilliant individual try.

A minute into the second half Widnes were caught offside and Sherburn landed a fine penalty-goal that gave Keighley the lift and confidence they were lacking. For a quarter of an hour they counter-attacked and posed all sorts of problems for the Widnes defence. A glorious chance to score was missed when Gwyn Parker held the ball for a split-second too long and was crashed to the ground by a posse of Widnes tacklers. And a minute later Lloyd was tackled inches short of the line.

The Widnes defence held firm, then struck back with a typical counter-blow. Bevan, the Keighley half-back, spilled the ball in a tackle and Barber snapped it up and dashed clean through the scattered defences to score a try which Topping converted.

Four minutes later, Millington caught the ball, wrong-footed two Keighley forwards and passed to the inevitable teammates who were backing up. The ball eventually landed in the hands of Nat Silcock, the 33-year-old 15st Widnes captain, who lumbered briskly over the line for a try that had the Chemics supporters baying with delight. Topping missed the goal-kick but landed his fourth of the afternoon when Shannon was obstructed in front of the posts.

With the luxury of a 16-point lead in a Wembley Final, Widnes eased off in the last ten minutes. Keighley took full advantage and, for once, Parker ran straight and passed perfectly to put 19-year-old Reg Lloyd in for a late consolation try at the corner.

The victorious Widnes side leave the Wembley pitch in 1937 with captain Nat Silcock holding the trophy.

Rugby League Cup Results

First Round

Batley	2	Castleford	2
Bradford N	39	Streatham & Mitcham	0
Bramley	0	Dewsbury	6
Goole	2	Broughton R	14
Halifax	8	Barrow	2
Hull KR	13	St Helens Rec	5
Hunslet	2	Keighley	5
Leigh	0	Liverpool S	28
Oldham	4	Wigan	15
Rochdale H	0	Hull	10
St Helens	4	Huddersfield	11
Salford	4	Warrington	10
Swinton	9	Newcastle	5
Wakefield T	2	Leeds	0
Widnes	39	Higginshaw	2
York	18	Featherstone R	4

Streatham & Mitcham gave up ground advantage.

First Round Replay

Castleford	8	Batley	4

Second Round

Bradford N	2	Huddersfield	12
Castleford	5	Wigan	5
Halifax	4	Wakefield T	5
Hull KR	2	Liverpool S	7
Keighley	11	Broughton R	5
Swinton	10	Hull	8
Widnes	8	Dewsbury	0
York	4	Warrington	5

The Bradford game was played at Valley Parade. The game at Widnes was abandoned at half-time.

Second Round Replays

Widnes	12	Dewsbury	7
Wigan	13	Castleford	6

Third Round

Huddersfield	7	Wigan	8
Liverpool S	2	Keighley	7
Wakefield T	5	Warrington	0
Widnes	7	Swinton	2

Semi-finals

Keighley	0	Wakefield T	0

At Headingley, Leeds
Attendance: 39,998   *Receipts: £2,793*

Widnes	13	Wigan	9

At Wilderspool Stadium, Warrington
Attendance: 29,260   *Receipts: £1,972*

Semi-final Replay

Keighley	5	Wakefield T	3

At Fartown, Huddersfield
Attendance: 14,000   *Receipts: £1,052*

Final

Saturday, 8 May at Wembley Stadium, London

	T	G	P		T	G	P
Widnes	4	3	18	**Keighley**	1	1	5
W.Bradley				I.Herbert			
A.Evans				J.Sherburn		G	
K.Barber	T			I.A.Towill			
P.Topping		3G		G.Parker			
F.Whyte				K.Lloyd	T		
T.Shannon	T			L.Bevan			
T.McCue	T			D.M.Davies			
N.Silcock	T			J.Traill			
J.Jones				H.C.Halliday			
A.Higgins				H.Jones			
H.McDowell				F.Talbot			
R.Roberts				C.Dixon			
H.Millington				J.Gill			

Referee: P.owell (Warrington)   *Half-time: 8-0*
Attendance: 47,699   *Receipts: £6,579*

Cup presented by Lord Cozens Hardy.

1938 Salford 7 Barrow 4

Harold Thomas and Gus Risman carry the Cup in 1938 with Barney Hudson following behind.

THE strength and superb tactics of the Barrow forwards dominated a game that many described as the worst ever seen at Wembley. Barrow's strategy was simple – they had to control and contain the game with their mighty pack and do their utmost to throw the clever and confident Salford back division out of gear. The Barrow pack monopolised the ball in the first half so successfully that, to some extent, they spoilt the match as spectacle and little was seen of the finer points of the game. The full-backs on each side handled well but were guilty of some very poor, almost aimless kicking for touch, and only very rarely did they start a passing movement. French, the Barrow full-back, handled faultlessly but constantly kicked into touch on the full. One newspaper was scathing in its criticism of the match: '*The game was smash and grab, crash and bang, ten yards run, tackle and play the ball and hardly one concerted movement.*'

The showpiece started with a very poor attempt at goal from Gus Risman, following a penalty against Barrow. After eight minutes play Fred French put Barrow ahead from a successful penalty-kick.

Gus Risman put Salford on level terms with a penalty-goal and on the half-hour collected a loose ball well and made himself the space and time to drop a good goal to put the Reds in front.

For the first 30 minutes of the second half, each side attacked furiously but incoherently. Barrow had the best of the play but were unable to score and missed one of the best chances of the game when Cumberbatch was stopped, despite two Salford players lying injured on the ground. With 14 minutes to play, Billy Little collected the ball from a scrum on the Salford '25' and dropped a brilliant goal with his left foot.

The surprise score was the catalyst for a tremendous burst of play from each side and with about a minute remaining, Barrow were penalised on the half-way line. Risman found touch ten yards from the Barrow line with a long, raking kick. One account describes the last few dramatic moments of the game: '*Five or six men jumped for the ball when it came out of the scrum, and there was a fine confused melee, in the course of which it was fumbled and juggled across the field in front of the Barrow goal posts until, finally, Gear dashed in, took the ball on the bounce, forced his way past two tacklers, and threw himself over the line with three men hanging on to him.*'

The goal-kick was missed but the try was enough, for there was not even enough time left to restart the game.

Rugby League Cup Results

First Round

Barrow	83	Maryport	3
Bradford N	7	Featherstone R	2
Bramley	23	Leigh	5
Castleford	18	Newcastle	9
Halifax	4	Warrington	4
Huddersfield	2	Broughton R	0
Hull KR	0	Keighley	2
Leeds	27	Wigan	4
Liverpool S	6	Hunslet	5
Oldham	7	Batley	8
Rochdale H	50	Glass Houghton	2
St Helens	39	Pendlebury Juniors	0
St Helens Rec	11	Dewsbury	10
Salford	38	Hull	2
Wakefield T	7	Widnes	3
York	2	Swinton	12

Glass Houghton gave up ground advantage.

First Round Replay

Warrington	9	Halifax	16

Second Round

Barrow	26	Bramley	4
Batley	8	Keighley	6
Castleford	18	St Helens	2
Halifax	5	Bradford N	5
Leeds	11	Huddersfield	7
Liverpool S	3	Salford	11
St Helens Rec	18	Rochdale H	10
Swinton	10	Wakefield T	5

Second Round Replay

Bradford N	2	Halifax	10

Third Round

Barrow	7	Leeds	5
Batley	3	Swinton	9
Castleford	7	Halifax	7
Salford	19	St Helens Rec	0

Third Round Replay

Halifax	11	Castleford	7

Semi-finals

Barrow	4	Halifax	2

At Fartown, Huddersfield
Attendance: 31,384 *Receipts: £2,431*

Salford	6	Swinton	0

At Belle Vue Stadium, Manchester
Attendance: 31,664 *Receipts: £2,396*

Final

Saturday, 7 May at Wembley Stadium, London

	T	G	P		T	G	P
Salford	1	2	7	**Barrow**	0	2	4
H.Osbaldestin				F.French		G	
B.Hudson				V.Cumberbatch			
R.Brown				J.Higgin			
A.Gear	T			D.McDonnell			
A.S.Edwards				J.Thornburrow			
A.J.Risman		2G		I.Lloyd			
W.Watkins				W.Little			
H.A.Williams				G.A.Rawlings			
H.C.Day				D.McKeating			
D.M.Davies				W.J.Skelly			
H.Thomas				L.A.Troup			
P.Dalton				R.Ayres			
J.Feetham				A.E.Marklew			

Referee: F.Peel (Bradford)   *Half-time: 4-2*
Attendance: 51,243   *Receipts: £7,474*

Cup presented by Donald Bradman, the Australian Test batsman.

A RECORD attendance of 55,453 witnessed a brilliant exhibition of Rugby League football that many of the critics described as one of the best games to have been played at Wembley. From the onset both sides set out to entertain the crowd with some superb and intricate passing movements that at last showed the suspicious Londoners in the stadium how fast and skilful this game of Rugby League could be.

It was expected that Salford, with their classy backs, would provide the bulk of the entertainment, but surprisingly it was Halifax who excelled, playing a clever and expansive attacking game that was a delight to watch. Beverley, at loose forward, was an important and dangerous part of the Halifax attack, his quick and clever ball-handling creating space galore for the centres Smith and Treen.

Halifax scored in the fifth minute when, from a scrum in the Salford half, Goodhall gave the ball to Beverley, who switched the direction of the attack with a short pass to Todd. The stand-off threw a sloppy pass out to Smith who somehow managed to scoop up the ball and simply walk over the line for a try which Lockwood converted.

Salford struck back and twice Kenny was hauled down yards from the line. Halifax then conjured up one of the best movements of the afternoon when a sweeping attack put Cox over the line for a 'try', which was disallowed for a forward pass.

A few moments later Smith crashed through a Salford tackler and although falling, managed to pass to Treen who was, as ever, backing up. Smith's fine pass had

given Treen just the half-yard advantage over Miller he needed and he raced over the line unopposed. Lockwood again converted the try.

Four minutes into the second half Salford struck back when Watkins burst away from a scrum, passed to Kenny who transferred to Risman who crossed for a try. Risman missed the conversion attempt.

Just under ten minutes later Salford were shaken when their full-back Harold Osbaldestin was carried from the field with a severe injury to his Achilles tendon. The Reds shuffled their team and continued to press the Halifax defence, but could do little better than get near to scoring.

With around 30 minutes to play, Jack Treen broke through the first line of defence and totally dumbfounded Feetham with a dummy before passing inside to George

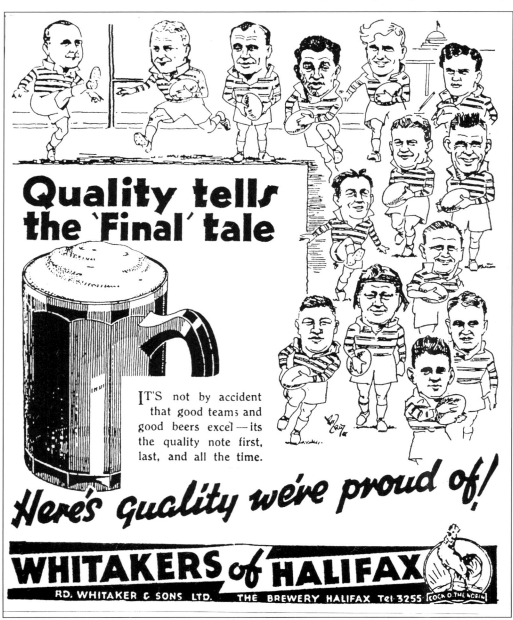

A local Halifax brewery celebrate the 1939 Wembley victory over Salford.

Rugby League Cup Results

First Round

Bradford N	37	Seaton	7
Broughton R	5	Wakefield T	5
Featherstone R	3	Batley	0
Halifax	8	Barrow	3
Hull KR	8	Hull	5
Hunslet	48	United Glass Blowers	5
Keighley	11	York	9
Leeds	9	Huddersfield	2
Liverpool S	2	St Helens Rec	2
Oldham	10	Castleford	3
Rochdale H	3	Warrington	29
Salford	11	St Helens	0
Sharlston Rovers	5	Bramley	23
Swinton	46	Higginshaw	3
Widnes	10	Dewsbury	5
Wigan	33	Leigh	0

Higginshaw gave up ground advantage.

First Round Replays

St Helens Rec	12	Liverpool S	3
Wakefield T	23	Broughton R	5

Second Round

Bradford N	2	Oldham	0
Halifax	6	Hull KR	2
Keighley	10	Featherstone R	0
Leeds	6	Widnes	2
St Helens Rec	3	Wigan	8
Salford	18	Hunslet	2
Swinton	0	Bramley	5
Wakefield T	7	Warrington	2

Third Round

Keighley	0	Leeds	2
Salford	20	Bramley	0
Wakefield T	5	Halifax	5
Wigan	7	Bradford N	0

Third Round Replay

Halifax	15	Wakefield T	12

Final

Saturday, 6 May at Wembley Stadium, London

	T	G	P		T	G	P
Halifax	4	4	20	**Salford**	1	0	3
H.Lockwood		4G		H.Osbaldestin			
J.Bevan	T			B.Hudson			
C.Smith	T			S.Miller			
J.H.Treen	T			A.J.Risman	T		
A.Bassett				A.S.Edwards			
G.Todd	T			T.Kenny			
J.Goodall				W.Watkins			
G.Baynham				J.Bradbury			
H.Field				H.C.Day			
H.Irving				D.M.Davies			
J.Chadwick				P.Dalton			
J.Cox				H.Thomas			
H.Beverley				J.Feetham			

Referee: G.S.Phillips (Widnes)   *Half-time: 10-0*
Attendance: 55,453   *Receipts: £7,813*

Cup presented by Earl De La Warr.

Semi-finals

Halifax	10	Leeds	4

At Odsal Stadium, Bradford
Attendance: 64,453   *Receipts: £3,645*

Salford	11	Wigan	2

At The Athletic Grounds, Rochdale
Attendance: 40,000   *Receipts: £2,154*

Todd who scored under the posts. Once again Lockwood converted with ease.

Salford continued to attack and Miller, Hudson and Edwards were all tantalisingly close to scoring, but it was Halifax who had the final say three minutes from time.

George Todd hoisted the ball high into the air above the Salford line and Edwards completely missed the flight and saw it bounce in favour of Bevan, who snapped it up and scored a try. Hubert Lockwood converted.

A very rare photograph of the 1941 Final shows the teams lining up before the game at Odsal Stadium, Bradford.

Rugby League Cup Results

First Round

Featherstone R	5	Castleford	8
Halifax	24	Broughton R	12
Hunslet	18	Leigh	8
Oldham	9	Dewsbury	13
Wakefield T	25	Keighley	0

Byes: Batley, Bradford N, Bramley, Huddersfield, Hull, Leeds, Liverpool S, St Helens, Swinton, Wigan and York.

Second Round

Batley	9	Hull	8
Bradford N	25	Swinton	8
Castleford	21	St Helens	13
Dewsbury	5	Leeds	6
Huddersfield	60	Bramley	7
Hunslet	64	Liverpool S	5
Wakefield T	22	Wigan	0
York	6	Halifax	13

Third Round

Batley	0	Wakefield T	22
Bradford N	18	Castleford	4
Halifax	10	Huddersfield	5
Hunslet	10	Leeds	17

Semi-finals, First Leg

Halifax	11	Wakefield T	2
Attendance: 7,752		*Receipts: £377*	
Leeds	10	Bradford N	10
Attendance: 16,000		*Receipts: £835*	

Semi-finals, Second Leg

Wakefield T	10	Halifax	5
Attendance: 7,000		*Receipts: £405*	
Bradford N	2	Leeds	12
Attendance: 22,500		*Receipts: £1,212*	

Final

Saturday, 17 May at Odsal Stadium, Bradford

	T	G	P		T	G	P
Leeds	5	2	19	**Halifax**	0	1	2
C.Eaton		2G		A.Bassett			
E.Batten*				J.Bevan			
C.Evans				C.Smith			
V.J.Hey	2T			F.Rule			
J.Lawrenson*	2T			A.E.Doyle			
O.Morris				G.Todd			
D.Jenkins	T			T.McCue*			
D.R.Prosser				F.Osborne*			
C.Murphy				A.M.Meek		G	
E.Bennett*				H.Irving			
S.Satterthwaite				H.Millington*			
B.Pearson*				C.Brereton			
E.Tattersfield				H.Beverley			

Referee: P.Cowell (Warrington)   *Half-time: 5-2*
Attendance: 28,500   *Receipts: £1,703*

*Guest players: Batten and Bennett (Hunslet); Lawrenson (Wigan); Pearson (Bramley), Osborne (Salford); McCue and Millington (Widnes).

THE Rugby Football League suspended the Challenge Cup competition when war broke out in September 1939. After missing one season the League decided to run a Challenge Cup tournament at the end of the 1940-41 League campaign. The event was played along similar lines to the restricted League season and clubs were allowed to play several 'guest' players from other teams.

The Finalists would not be presented with the traditional medals but the winners would receive four War Saving Certificates and the losers three. The Final was held at Odsal Stadium, Bradford, where, considering the problems with travelling, a good crowd of 29,000 witnessed the game.

Both sides included guest players in their teams: Halifax had Osborne from Salford and the Widnes pair of McCue and Millington; the Loiners acquired the services of Batten and Bennett from Hunslet, Pearson from Bramley and Wigan's Lawrenson.

In a game that was thought by many to have far too much 'needle' Leeds defeated Halifax 19-2 thanks to tries from Hey (2), Lawrenson (2) and Jenkins and a brace of goals from full-back Charlie Eaton.

Jim Brough, who captained Leeds in 1942, shows his kicking prowess.

Rugby League Cup Results

First Round, First Leg

Featherstone R	11	St Helens	21
Wakefield T	7	Batley	4

First Round, Second Leg

St Helens	8	Featherstone R	3
Batley	2	Wakefield T	5

First round byes: Bradford N, Bramley, Castleford, Dewsbury, Halifax, Huddersfield, Hull, Hunslet, Keighley, Leeds, Oldham, Swinton, Wigan and York.

Second Round, First Leg

Bradford N	18	Keighley	0
Halifax	14	Huddersfield	5
Hull	34	Bramley	0
Hunslet	16	St Helens	3
Oldham	14	Castleford	3
Swinton	29	York	5
Wakefield T	3	Leeds	0
Wigan	6	Dewsbury	4

Second Round, Second Leg

Keighley	6	Bradford N	17
Huddersfield	10	Halifax	10
Bramley	8	Hull	17
St Helens	21	Hunslet	14
Castleford	0	Oldham	10
York	7	Swinton	15
Leeds	8	Wakefield T	0
Dewsbury	12	Wigan	14

The Keighley game was played at Bradford.

Third Round, First Leg

Bradford N	11	Halifax	10
Leeds	22	Hull	8
Oldham	29	Hunslet	0
Swinton	0	Wigan	9

Third Round, Second Leg

Halifax	21	Bradford N	16
Hull	12	Leeds	7
Hunslet	18	Oldham	17
Wigan	12	Swinton	17

Final

Saturday, 6 June at Odsal Stadium, Bradford

	T	G	P		T	G	P
Leeds	3	3	15	**Halifax**	0	5	10
J.W.Brough				H.Lockwood		5G	
A.S.Edwards*	2T			J.Bevan			
A.J.Risman*		3G		C.Smith			
V.J.Hey				F.Rule			
C.Evans				A.E.Doyle			
O.Morris	T			G.Todd			
D.Jenkins				T.McCue*			
D.R.Prosser				C.Brereton			
C.D.Murphy				C.Jones*			
S.Satterthwaite				H.Irving			
F.Gregory*				H.Millington*			
G.Brown*				M.A.Meek			
E.Tattersfield				J.Dixon			

Referee: P.Cowell (Warrington)   *Half-time: 11-6*

Attendance: 15,250   *Receipts: £1,276*

*Guest players: Edwards and Risman (Salford); Gregory (Warrington); Brown (Batley); McCue, Jones and Millington (Widnes).

Semi-finals, First Leg

Halifax	10	Wigan	0
Leeds	5	Oldham	2

Semi-finals, Second Leg

Wigan	16	Halifax	16
Oldham	3	Leeds	12

LEEDS and Halifax met again in a re-run of the previous year's Final which was once again held at Bradford's Odsal Stadium.

Both sides took full advantage of the relaxed restrictions on players and fielded some notable guests. Leeds acquired the services of Edwards and Risman from Salford, Gregory of Warrington and Batley's Brown. Halifax had the Widnes trio of McCue, Jones and Millington.

Despite a strong offensive from Halifax's sturdy pack of forwards, the Leeds six held firm and gained sufficient possession to feed their talented back division. It was primarily the Loiners backs that won the game, Alan

Edwards and Gus Risman were superb and Jim Brough, the 39-year-old full-back, rolled back the years with a stunning display. Brough's fielding was faultless. He kicked with power and skill and was constantly moving forward to link up with his threequarters.

Salford's Edwards opened the Loiners scoring when he sprinted to collect a cross-kick, caught the ball and dived over at the corner. Welsh stand-off Oliver Morris scored the second Leeds try when he collected a clever kick from Dai Jenkins and scampered over for a try. Shoddy defence from Halifax gave Edwards a gift of a try which Risman converted to give Leeds a 15-10 victory, their sixth win in six Finals.

1943 Dewsbury 16 Leeds 15

(aggregate score after two-legged Final)

LEEDS made their third successive appearance in a wartime Final and faced League Champions and Yorkshire Cup holders Dewsbury who took full advantage of the guest player rule and fielded eight visitors, including Alan Edwards who had helped Leeds win the Cup the previous season. They were managed by the young, ambitious Eddie Waring who saw the opportunity to field guest players, many who were actually staying at an army camp about a mile from Dewsbury's ground.

Almost 11,000 turned up to witness the first leg at Crown Flatt, a game dominated by the Dewsbury backs, who with the exception of Royal were all guesting. Leeds lacked power and pace in the midfield and Dewsbury soon took full advantage of the weakness to gain a confidence boosting 16-9 victory.

Two days later 16,000 saw the Leeds forwards play a magnificent game and pave the way for a 6-0 win, just short of forcing a replay. Despite the brilliant display from the Loiners' six and scrum-half Dai Jenkins, Leeds once again lacked the pace and power to penetrate the Dewsbury defence and all their points were scored from goal-kicks. So for the first time since 1912 the Challenge Cup made its way back to Dewsbury's Crown Flatt headquarters.

Dewsbury's victorious 1943 team line-up with the Cup and their talented young manager Eddie Waring.

Rugby League Cup Results

Rugby League Cup

First Round, First Leg

Batley	3	Keighley	7
Featherstone R	11	Wakefield T	12
Halifax	2	Huddersfield	0
Hull	0	Dewsbury	21
Leeds	18	York	0
St Helens	13	Barrow	2
Wigan	6	Bradford N	5

Bye: Oldham

First Round, Second Leg

Keighley	15	Batley	0
Wakefield T	10	Featherstone R	0
Huddersfield	7	Halifax	2
Dewsbury	21	Hull	12
York	7	Leeds	14
Barrow	4	St Helens	0
Bradford N	18	Wigan	3

Second Round, First Leg

Huddersfield	8	Dewsbury	10
Keighley	2	Bradford N	0
Oldham	17	St Helens	12
Wakefield T	5	Leeds	8

Second Round, Second Leg

Dewsbury	15	Huddersfield	10
Bradford N	6	Keighley	7
St Helens	5	Oldham	20
Leeds	10	Wakefield T	8

Semi-finals, First Leg

Keighley	5	Leeds	3
Oldham	3	Dewsbury	25

Semi-finals, Second Leg

Leeds	27	Keighley	0
Dewsbury	43	Oldham	5

Final

First Leg
Saturday, 24 April

	T	G	P		T	G	P
Dewsbury	4	2	16	**Leeds**	1	3	9
G.Bunter*				J.C.Walkington*			
B.Hudson*				C.Eaton	T	3G	
A.S.Edwards*	T			S.Rookes*			
J.Robinson*	T			D.Warrior			
R.Lloyd*				C.Callaghan			
T.Kenny*	T			C.Evans			
T.H.Royal				D.Jenkins			
H.Hammond				D.R.Prosser			
G.Curran*				C.D.Murphy			
J.Gardner*				S.Satterthwaite			
G.Kershaw				K.Jubb			
F.Smith				F.Gregory*			
C.Seeling	T	2G		E.Tattersfield			

Referee: G.S.Phillips (Widnes)   *Half-time: 13-5*
Attendance: 10,470   *Receipts: £823*

*Guest players: Bunter (Broughton R); Hudson, Edwards, Kenny, Curran and Gardner (Salford); Robinson and Lloyd (Castleford); Walkington and Rookes (Hunslet); Gregory (Warrington).

Second Leg
Monday, 26 April

	T	G	P		T	G	P
Leeds	0	3	6	**Dewsbury**	0	0	0
J.C.Walkington*		G		G.Bunter*			
E.Batten*				B.Hudson*			
D.Warrior				A.S.Edwards*			
C.Eaton		G		J.Robinson*			
C.Callaghan				R.Lloyd*			
C.Evans				T.Kenny*			
D.Jenkins		G		T.H.Royal			
D.R.Prosser				H.Hammond			
C.D.Murphy				G.Curran*			
S.Satterthwaite				J.Gardner*			
K.Jubb				G.Kershaw			
F.Gregory*				F.Smith			
E.Tattersfield				C.Seeling			

Referee: G.S.Phillips (Widnes)   *Half-time: 6-0*
Attendance: 16,000   *Receipts: £1,521*

*Guest players: Walkington and Batten (Hunslet); Gregory (Warrington); Bunter (Broughton R); Hudson, Edwards, Kenny, Curran and Gardner (Salford); Robinson and Lloyd (Castleford).

1944 Bradford Northern 8 Wigan 3

(aggregate score after two-legged Final)

A CROWD of 22,000 witnessed the first leg of the Final at Central Park, an awesome struggle of two resolute defences. Northern's game plan was simple – they set out to contain the famous Wigan side as much as they could. Their plan worked well, clever marking and a tremendous display of tackling keeping Wigan down to a 3-0 victory. The second leg attracted another huge crowd, almost 30,000 packing into the enormous Odsal bowl.

Bradford attacked from the kick-off and after 11 minutes play their expansive tactics worked when Eric Batten snatched up a loose ball and dived over for a try.

In the second half Carmichael kicked a 30-yard penalty to give Northern a precious two-point lead. Bradford pressurised the Wigan line for long periods of the second half and in the final minute of the game their efforts were rewarded when Whitcombe crashed over the line to give Northern an 8-0 victory and the Cup for the first time since 1906.

Eric Batten, a try scorer for Bradford Northern, in the second leg of the 1944 Final.

Frank Whitcombe, Bradford's powerful prop forward.

Rugby League Cup Results

Rugby League Cup

First Round, First Leg

Bradford N	15	Wakefield T	2
Dewsbury	43	St Helens	7
Halifax	13	Hunslet	2
Huddersfield	13	Hull	0
Keighley	13	Barrow	7
Leeds	12	Featherstone R	9
Oldham	5	Wigan	8
York	11	Batley	10

First Round, Second Leg

Wakefield T	7	Bradford N	5
St Helens	15	Dewsbury	33
Hunslet	13	Halifax	12
Hull	5	Huddersfield	0
Barrow	6	Keighley	10
Featherstone R	2	Leeds	7
Wigan	25	Oldham	3
Batley	3	York	0

Second Round, First Leg

Halifax	13	Batley	4
Huddersfield	8	Leeds	14
Keighley	9	Bradford N	18
Wigan	14	Dewsbury	3

Second Round, Second Leg

Batley	8	Halifax	8
Leeds	2	Huddersfield	7
Bradford N	17	Keighley	5
Dewsbury	2	Wigan	11

Semi-finals, First Leg

Halifax	5	Bradford N	2
Leeds	10	Wigan	5

Semi-finals, Second Leg

Bradford N	7	Halifax	0
Wigan	11	Leeds	4

Final

First Leg
Saturday, 15 April 15

	T	G	P		T	G	P
Wigan	1	0	3	**Bradford N**	0	0	0
J.Sullivan				G.Carmichael			
J.H.Lawrenson				E.Batten			
W.Belshaw*				G.M.Bennett			
J.R.Maloney*				E.Ward			
E.J.Ashcroft				W.Best			
M.Ryan				W.T.H.Davies			
H.Gee				D.Ward			
K.Gee				F.W.Whitcombe			
J.Egan				V.J.Darlison			
J.Blan				L.Higson			
J.J.Featherstone	T			L.Roberts			
E.Watkins				W.Hutchinson			
J.Bowen				A.Marklew*			

Referee: S.Adams (Hull)   *Half-time: 3-0*
Attendance: 21,500   *Receipts: £1,663*

*Guest Players: Belshaw (Warrington); Maloney (Liverpool S); Marklew (Barrow).

Second Leg
Saturday, 22 April

	T	G	P		T	G	P
Bradford N	2	1	8	**Wigan**	0	0	0
C.Carmichael		G		J.Jones			
E.Batten	T			J.H.Lawrenson			
J.Kitching				W.Belshaw			
E.Ward				J.R.Maloney			
E.Walters				E.J.Ashcroft			
G.M.Bennett				M.Ryan			
D.Ward				H.Gee			
F.W.Whitcombe	T			K.Gee			
V.J.Darlison				J.Egan			
L.Higson				J.Blan			
T.Foster				J.J.Featherstone			
L.Roberts				E.Watkins			
W.Hutchinson				J.Bowen			

Referee: A.Cowell (Warrington)   *Half-time: 3-0*
Attendance: 30,000   *Receipts: £2,061*

*Guest Players: Belshaw (Warrington); Maloney (Liverpool S).

1945 Huddersfield 13 Bradford Northern 9

(aggregate score after two-legged Final)

Huddersfield with the Challenge Cup in 1945.

THE last two-legged Final of the war years pitted Bradford Northern against Huddersfield. The first game was at Fartown, where a crowd of just over 9,000 braved a cold day and intermittent wintry showers.

Bradford were League leaders and firm favourites to beat a Huddersfield side which had struggled around mid-table all season. On the day, however, Northern were missing key men and a stunning display of tackling from Huddersfield gave them a well deserved 7-4 victory.

A crowd of 17,500 gathered to witness the second leg at Odsal, despite a torrential downpour just before the kick-off and a constant drizzle throughout the game. The atrocious conditions reduced the notorious Odsal pitch to a quagmire and dispelled any thoughts of open, attractive play from either side.

Just as they had done in the first leg, Huddersfield adapted to the conditions far faster than Northern and they were comfortable 6-5 winners, taking the Cup on a 13-9 aggregate for the two games.

Rugby League Cup Results

Preliminary Round, First Leg

Castleford	5	Halifax	8

Preliminary Round, Second Leg

Halifax	8	Castleford	3

First Round, First Leg

Batley	7	Wakefield	10
Featherstone R	4	Oldham	18
Halifax	10	Wigan	11
Hull	13	Dewsbury	18
Keighley	11	Hunslet	8
Leeds	5	Huddersfield	21
St Helens	8	Bradford N	15
York	12	Barrow	21

First Round, Second Leg

Wakefield T	24	Batley	12
Oldham	8	Featherstone R	7
Wigan	6	Halifax	21
Dewsbury	23	Hull	9
Hunslet	4	Keighley	2
Huddersfield	17	Leeds	3
Bradford N	34	St Helens	13
Barrow	19	York	5

Second Round, First Leg

Bradford N	18	Wakefield T	8
Dewsbury	5	Halifax	11
Huddersfield	13	Barrow	3
Keighley	11	Oldham	0

Second Round, Second Leg

Wakefield T	10	Bradford N	3
Halifax	19	Dewsbury	5
Barrow	6	Huddersfield	9
Oldham	8	Keighley	9

Semi-finals, First Leg

Halifax	6	Huddersfield	0
Keighley	5	Bradford N	0

Semi-finals, Second Leg

Bradford N	35	Keighley	3
Huddersfield	10	Halifax	3

Final

First Leg

Saturday, 28 April

	T	G	P		T	G	P
Huddersfield	1	2	7	**Bradford N**	0	2	4
W.Leake				E.Ward		2G	
O.Peake*	T			E.Batten			
A.E.Fiddes				A.S.Edwards*			
R.D.Lewis*				J.Kitching			
J.Bawden		2G		W.Best			
T.L.Grahame				G.Bennett			
A.J.Pepperell				D.Ward			
J.Bradbury*				F.W.Whitcombe			
H.Whitehead				V.J.Darlison			
J.Miller*				L.Higson			
K.Mallinson				L.Roberts			
L.Baxter				A.Marklew			
A.Givvons				W.Hutchinson			

Referee: F.Fairhurst (Wigan) *Half-time: 7-2*
Attendance: 9,041 *Receipts: £1,184*

*Guest Players: Peake and Miller (Warrington); Lewis (Swinton); Bradbury and Edwards (Salford).

Second Leg

Saturday, 5 May

	T	G	P		T	G	P
Bradford N	1	1	5	**Huddersfield**	2	0	6
E.Ward		G		W.Leake			
E.Batten	T			O.Peake*			
A.S.Edwards*				A.E.Fiddes			
J.Kitching				R.D.Lewis*			
W.Best				J.Bawden	2T		
W.T.H.Davies				T.L.Grahame			
D.Ward				A.J.Pepperell			
F.W.Whitcombe				K.Mallinson			
V.J.Darlison				H.Whitehead			
L.Higson				J.Miller*			
L.Roberts				A.Givvons			
H.Smith				J.Aspinall			
W.Hutchinson				L.Baxter			

Referee: G.S.Phillips (Widnes) *Half-time: 0-0*
Attendance: 17,500 *Receipts: £2,050*

*Guest Players: Edwards (Salford); Peake and Miller (Warrington); Lewis (Swinton).

A joyous Wakefield Trinity carry their captain Billy Stott around Wembley after the 1946 Final. Oldham-born Stott was the first player to be awarded the Lance Todd Trophy for man of the match.

THE arrangements for the first British Lions tour to Australasia since the war had left both sides lining up at Wembley missing key players. Trinity were without Harry Murphy, but Wigan had four players, Martin Ryan, Ken Gee, Joe Egan and Ted Ward sailing for Australia.

Trinity missed the first scoring chance when Stott failed to kick an early penalty. Seven minutes into the game the Wigan forwards rushed down the field and some weak defending by Wakefield let Jack Blan in for the first try. For a full 15 minutes after the score, Trinity seemed totally unsure of how to combat the quick-moving Wigan side and following a lightning break by centres Ratcliff and Ashcroft, the ball was passed to Nordgren. The strong-running New Zealander accelerated away from the cover then brushed aside a tackle as he sprinted clear to touch down in the corner. He failed to convert his own try.

The score jolted Wakefield into life and following a sustained attack, Rylance slipped the ball to Billy Stott who, from 15 yards out, hurled himself and Cunliffe, the Wigan full-back, over the line for a try. He missed the kick but ten minutes later landed a penalty to put Wakefield within one point of Wigan.

Trinity started the second half with a series of attacks and despite being well positioned to score on more than one occasion, the fast Wigan backs were always there to cover. On 57 minutes a Wakefield attack broke down just inside the Wigan half. Stan Jolley scooped up the loose ball and sped toward the try line. Wakefield had neither a player near enough or fast enough to stop him and from the second he collected the ball it was a sure try. Nordgren missed the goal attempt but the Riversiders were 9-5 in the lead.

Again Wakefield came back at Wigan, Goodfellow cutting through the Wigan defence with such ease that he could have scored himself. Instead he passed to Stott on the wing, who made no mistake to score his second try. Stott missed with his conversion attempt and when Nordgren scored Wigan's fourth try a little later, all seemed lost for Wakefield. They stuck to their task, however, and nine minutes from time Wigan-born Jim Croston pierced the Riversiders defence and squeezed over the line with a Wigan defender still clinging to

Rugby League Cup Results

First Round, First Leg

Bradford N	11	Hull	0
Castleford	10	St Helens	4
Dewsbury	0	Hunslet	5
Featherstone R	7	Halifax	10
Higher Ince	3	Widnes	30
Huddersfield	3	Wakefield T	14
Hull Juniors	0	Bramley	29
Hull KR	18	Langworthy Juniors	0
Keighley	5	Liverpool S	0
Kells	0	Warrington	3
Leeds	10	Batley	2
Rochdale H	9	Barrow	11
Salford	8	Oldham	3
Sharlston Rovers	12	Workington T	7
Swinton	5	Wigan	4
York	6	Broughton R	13

The Higher Ince game was played at Wigan.

First Round, Second Leg

Hull	2	Bradford N	0
St Helens	14	Castleford	5
Hunslet	0	Dewsbury	2
Halifax	18	Featherstone R	15
Widnes	42	Higher Ince	3
Wakefield T	5	Huddersfield	2
Bramley	51	Hull Juniors	3
Langworthy Juniors	7	Hull KR	14
Liverpool S	7	Keighley	5
Warrington	27	Kells	0
Batley	8	Leeds	29
Barrow	21	Rochdale H	5
Oldham	2	Salford	3
Workington T	16	Sharlston Rovers	2
Wigan	14	Swinton	2
Broughton R	14	York	2

The Langworthy game was played at Salford.

Second Round

Barrow	5	Bradford N	0
Bramley	8	Warrington	2
Hull KR	0	Salford	0
Hunslet	18	Broughton R	2
St Helens	6	Workington T	13
Wakefield T	10	Halifax	0
Widnes	8	Leeds	2
Wigan	37	Keighley	0

Second Round Replay

Salford	38	Hull KR	6

Third Round

Barrow	3	Wigan	13
Bramley	5	Widnes	11
Salford	8	Hunslet	15
Wakefield T	14	Workington T	4

Semi-finals

Wakefield T	7	Hunslet	3

At Headingley, Leeds
Attendance: 33,000   *Receipts: £4,991*

Wigan	12	Widnes	5

At Station Road, Swinton
Attendance: 36,976   *Receipts: £4,746*

Final

Saturday, 4 May at Wembley Stadium, London

	T	G	P		T	G	P
Wakefield T	3	2	13	**Wigan**	4	0	12
W.Teall				J.Cunliffe			
R.Rylance				B.C.Nordgren	2T		
W.Stott	2T	2G		G.W.Ratcliffe			
A.J.Croston	T			E.J.Ashcroft			
D.Baddeley				G.Jolley	T		
J.Jones				R.D.Lowry			
H.Goodfellow				T.Bradshaw			
H.Wilkinson				G.W.Banks			
L.Marston				J.Blan	T		
J.Higgins				F.Barton			
G.H.Exley				E.Watkins			
W.L.D.Howes				H.Atkinson			
L.Bratley				W.Blan			

Lance Todd Trophy: W.Stott

Referee: A.Hill (Leeds)   *Half-time: 5-6*

Attendance: 54,730   *Receipts: £12,013*

Cup presented by The Rt Hon C.R.Atlee, Prime Minister.

---

him. The atrocious exhibition of goal-kicking seen all afternoon continued when Stott missed the conversion attempt.

Wigan closed ranks on their '25' line and checked a last-gasp Trinity attack. Then, with only 90 seconds remaining, a Wigan player obstructed and Wakefield were awarded a penalty. Stott steadied himself, stepped back slowly and then launched the ball in a perfect arc straight through the uprights. His dramatic kick won Trinity the match and Stott the first-ever Lance Todd trophy for Man of the Match.

1947 Bradford Northern 8 Leeds 4

LEEDS were installed as 6/4 favourites to take the Cup, thanks mainly to the media attention their pack had been given in the build- up to the Final. Northern had a good squad and were led by captain Ernest Ward and coached by Dai Rees, the master tactician who had tasted victory at Wembley as a player with Halifax in 1931.

Both sides were affected by a tension at the start of the match but despite this, Leeds attacked from the kick-off and did everything but score. Their famous pack was in fine form and, led by Owens, the six tried every trick and movement they knew to try and break the Northern defence. They used short inside passes from scrums, they tried reverse passes, back-flicked passes, scissors movements and feints and dummies galore, but nothing could beat the superb Bradford defence.

The Loiners were out-thought by Frank Whitcombe and Trevor Foster, who conceived a defence which met the clever tactics with sound commonsense. The giant prop Whitcombe and his front row partners met everything that Leeds threw at them down the middle of the field and Foster and his second rowers and half-backs stopped the movements that were designed to open the play out wide. Between them they created a huge shield and this, coupled with a tremendous tackling stint, proved just too much for the Leeds attack.

Bert Cook, the diminutive New Zealander, had given Leeds a 2-0 half-time lead with a well-struck penalty goal, but in the 49th minute Bradford struck when their classy centres, Ward and Kitchen, set up a clever try. Ernest Ward broke through the Loiners lines and swept across the field before being tackled just short of the line. A quick play-the-ball sent the ball back across the field and Kitchen drew his man before passing to Walters who dived over the line for a try in the corner. Within two minutes Leeds had grabbed the lead back when Cook kicked a penalty goal.

Bradford's back attacked again and from a scrum Darlison heeled quickly and cleanly and the ball was whipped to Kitchen who was tackled as he tried to cut inside. The ball ran loose and Ernest Ward, hovering at the edge of the action, picked it up and created himself just enough space to drop a beautiful goal to give Bradford the lead again.

Bradford had a grip of the game by now and almost the whole of the final 15 minutes were played in the Loiners '25' as the rampant Northern swarmed around desperate for that final killer try. Leeds held out well, but with a minute before the final whistle, Bert Cook made a rare mistake when he fumbled a harmless punt by Carmichael. The ball ran loose and Trevor Foster simply picked it up and trotted over the line for a try to give Bradford an 8-4 victory.

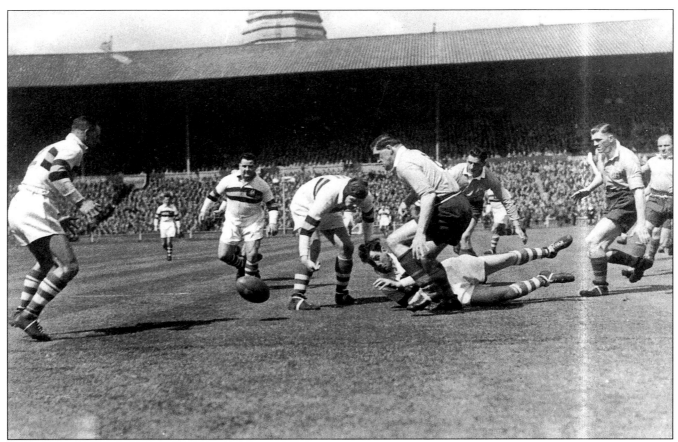

A tense moment for Bradford Northern as the ball spills from the grasp of their Welsh forward Trevor Foster in the 1947 Final.

Rugby League Cup Results

First Round, First Leg

Castleford	19	Swinton	2
Dewsbury	0	Huddersfield	3
Hull	11	Bramley	3
Hunslet	2	Hull KR	3
Leeds	12	Barrow	0
Leigh	3	Wakefield T	3
Liverpool S	27	Pemberton Rovers	6
Oldham	3	Belle Vue R	10
St Helens	17	Keighley	7
Salford	5	Bradford N	2
Warrington	46	Brookland Rovers	3
Wheldale Colliery	0	Halifax	25
Widnes	13	Rochdale H	2
Wigan	24	Featherstone R	11
Workington T	48	Widnes Dragons	0
York	3	Batley	6

The Liverpool S game was played at Warrington. The Wheldale Colliery game was played at Castleford.

First Round, Second Leg

Swinton	8	Castleford	7
Huddersfield	3	Dewsbury	0
Bramley	2	Hull	28
Hull KR	0	Hunslet	6
Barrow	0	Leeds	6
Wakefield T	5	Leigh	0
Pemberton Rovers	5	Liverpool S	20
Belle Vue R	0	Oldham	0
Keighley	8	St Helens	5
Bradford N	10	Salford	0
Brookland Rovers	3	Warrington	32
Halifax	20	Wheldale Colliery	10
Rochdale H	0	Widnes	11
Featherstone R	7	Wigan	13
Widnes Dragons	45	Workington T	21
Batley	11	York	0

Bramley's game and Barrow's game were played at Leeds. The Pemberton Rovers game was played at Wigan. Belle Vue's game and Rochdale's game were played at Salford. Keighley's game and Halifax's game were played at Hunslet. The Brookland Rovers game was played at Warrington. The Widnes Dragons game was played at Widnes. The Batley game was played at Dewsbury.

Second Round

Batley	2	Castleford	13
Halifax	3	Workington T	10
Huddersfield	0	Bradford N	8
Leeds	5	Hunslet	0
Liverpool S	10	Hull	5
Wakefield T	8	Widnes	5
Warrington	24	St Helens	2
Wigan	12	Belle Vue R	5

Third Round

Bradford N	10	Workington T	3
Wakefield T	15	Liverpool S	0
Warrington	5	Castleford	0
Wigan	0	Leeds	5

Semi-finals

Bradford N	11	Warrington	7

At Station Road, Swinton
Attendance: 33,474 *Receipts: £4,946*

Leeds	21	Wakefield T	0

At Fartown, Huddersfield
Attendance: 35,136 *Receipts: £6,339*

Final

Saturday, 3 May at Wembley Stadium, London

	T	G	P		T	G	P
Bradford N	2	1	8	**Leeds**	0	2	4
G.Carmichael				H.E.Cook		2G	
E.Batten				A.T.Cornelius			
J.Kitching				G.M.Price			
E.Ward		G		T.L.Williams			
E.Walters	T			E.C.Whitehead			
W.T.H.Davies				R.Williams			
D.Ward				D.Jenkins			
F.W.Whitcombe				C.Brereton			
V.J.Darlison				C.D.Murphy			
H.Smith				D.R.Prosser			
B.Tyler				A.Watson			
T.J.F.Foster	T			A.Clues			
H.Evans				I.A.Owens			

Lance Todd Trophy: W.T.H.Davies.

Referee: P.Cowell (Warrington) *Half-time: 0-2*
Attendance: 77,605 *Receipts: £17,434*

Cup presented by HRH The Duke of Gloucester.

1948 Wigan 8 Bradford Northern 3

Wigan's 1948 Wembley heroes celebrate with the trophy.

A WORLD record crowd of 91,465 flocked to Wembley confident of seeing a game of open, exciting football between two of the finest exponents of attacking play in the League. For the followers of both sides there was plenty of excitement, although most of it was in the form of horror at missed opportunities and narrow escapes in defence.

A chilly, showery day did little to help the players, making the thick, lush turf greasy and treacherous underfoot. These conditions, coupled with the League's decision to play with the dreaded new ball that had caused problems all season, soon dispelled the teams' ideas of playing an expansive attacking game. Instead both sides chose the tactics of containment and seemed be in awe of each other's powers, seemingly content to mark and tackle their way through the full 80 minutes.

Wigan took the lead after 20 minutes when, according to one account: '*A harmless kick through in the Wigan half was badly fumbled by Batten; Hilton was on him in a flash, got the ball, kicked past Leak, and dived for the touch.*'

Edward Ward kicked the conversion and Wigan, it seemed, were on their way. Within minutes of the restart it was the Riversiders' handling that was to let them down. An inoffensive-looking cross-kick caused Wigan's Gordon Ratcliffe all sorts of problems and he eventually spilled the ball into the path of Alan Edwards who seized his chance and scored in the corner. Ernest Ward missed the kick and the rest of the half was keen and fast but still scrappy with Wigan holding their slender lead when Ward once again missed a relatively easy shot at goal.

The second-half was almost a carbon copy of the first, relentless marking and sloppy, erratic tackling – exciting for the fans of Wigan and Bradford but poor unattractive fare for the many neutrals in the vast crowd. Ernest Ward was given two chances to make amends for his first-half misses but the usually reliable goal-kicker failed with both attempts. Bradford rallied well in the final ten minutes and their attack, led from the front by the 18st prop Frank Whitcombe, whose sure handling and shrewd kicking earned him the Lance Todd Trophy, was only just denied by a desperate Wigan defence.

In the last minute of the game a last-ditch attack from the Riversiders forced Northern's full-back Bill Leake to fumble badly over his own line but recover in time to touch the ball down. The resultant drop-out from under the sticks was dreadfully short and with one triumphant surge Wigan forced the ball over the line for Barton to get the touch for a try. Edward Ward missed the conversion attempt but Wigan were home, if not dry, 8-3.

Rugby League Cup Results

First Round, First Leg

Barrow	18	Halifax	4
Batley	0	Dewsbury	2
Bramley*	3	Vine Tavern	3
Featherstone R	3	Leigh	18
Huddersfield	6	Bradford N	2
Hull	23	Swinton	2
Hull KR	12	Oldham	5
Keighley	11	Risehow and Gillhead	0
Leeds	23	York	9
Liverpool S	0	Belle Vue R	9
Rochdale H	13	Pemberton Rovers	0
St Helens	48	Buslingthorpe Vale	0
Salford	2	Wakefield T	13
Warrington	10	Workington T	0
Widnes	5	Hunslet	3
Wigan	27	Castleford	0

*Abandoned after 43 minutes

First Round, First Leg Replay

Bramley	10	Vine Tavern	2

First Round, Second Leg

Halifax	17	Barrow	4
Dewsbury	10	Batley	4
Vine Tavern	6	Bramley	17
Leigh	10	Featherstone R	6
Bradford N	15	Huddersfield	2
Swinton	12	Hull	2
Oldham	22	Hull KR	4
Risehow and Gillhead	10	Keighley	2
Belle Vue R	10	Liverpool S	8
York	0	Leeds	13
Pemberton R	0	Rochdale H	11
Buslingthorpe Vale	2	St Helens	13
Wakefield T	20	Salford	15
Workington T	0	Warrington	7
Hunslet	5	Widnes	3
Castleford	7	Wigan	19

The Buslingthorpe Vale game was played at Leeds. The Pemberton Rovers game was played at Wigan. The Risehow and Gillhead game was played at Workington. The Vine Tavern game was played at St Helens.

First Round Replay

Widnes	0	Hunslet	3

Second Round

Barrow	2	Keighley	6
Dewsbury	2	Hunslet	2
Hull	22	Bramley	0
Oldham	5	St Helens	0
Rochdale H	3	Belle Vue R	2
Wakefield T	3	Bradford N	3
Warrington	8	Leigh	2
Wigan	17	Leeds	3

Second Round Replays

Bradford N	9	Wakefield T	2
Hunslet	11	Dewsbury	0

Third Round

Bradford N	30	Oldham	0
Hunslet	5	Hull	0
Keighley	4	Rochdale H	6
Warrington	10	Wigan	13

Semi-finals

Bradford N	14	Hunslet	7

At Headingley, Leeds
Attendance: 38,125   *Receipts: £7,500*

Wigan	11	Rochdale H	0

At Station Road, Swinton
Attendance: 26,004   *Receipts: £4,210*

Final

Saturday, 1 May at Wembley Stadium, London

	T	G	P		T	G	P
Wigan	2	1	8	**Bradford N**	1	0	3
M.Ryan				W.Leake			
G.W.Ratcliffe				E.Batten			
E.H.Ward		G		D.Case			
E.J.Ashcroft				E.Ward			
J.Hilton	T			A.S.Edwards	T		
C.R.Mountford				W.T.H.Davies			
T.Bradshaw				D.Ward			
K.Gee				F.W.Whitcombe			
J.Egan				V.J.Darlison			
F.Barton	T			H.Smith			
L.White				T.J.F.Foster			
W.Blan				B.Tyler			
W.Hudson				K.Traill			

Lance Todd Trophy: F.W.Whitcombe

Referee: C.S.Phillips (Widnes)   *Half-time: 5-3*
Attendance: 91,465   *Receipts: £21,121*

Cup presented by HM King George VI.

1949 Bradford Northern 12 Halifax 0

Action from Bradford's third successive Wembley Final, in 1949, as the ball spins loose.

BRADFORD became the first club to play in three successive Finals and a new record crowd of over 95,000 basked in brilliant sunshine on a warm spring day.

Northern's side contained many tactical and technical masters and under the guidance of the astute Dai Rees the players were expected to provide a real spectacle. But, as in many previous Finals, the great play never really materialised and the Bradford players seemed so be afflicted by a fit of bad handling that clever, completed passing movements were few and far between. When the ball was not dropped or passed forward, a midfield player would hold on far too long and either try to beat one man too many or completely ignore precious overlaps created on the wings. So great was Bradford's advantage in the scrums that with the gifted players they had in the side, they should have scored 30 to 40 points.

For the Northern fans in the crowd, ever ready to boast to the sprinkling of Rugby Union followers present how good was the League code, the game was a let-down and an insipid reflection of the titanic struggles witnessed every week in Yorkshire and Lancashire.

Bradford took the lead after eight minutes play when Ernest Ward chipped the ball delightfully over the Halifax left wing and centre, and Eric Batten, who had run outside his opposite number, gathered a fortunate bounce and crossed in the corner. Batten's try was a courageous one, for the winger had broken his collar-bone in the first minutes of the game but played on for the full 80 minutes. Ward added the two points from the conversion, but moments later missed a relatively easy penalty attempt.

The remainder of the first half was a series of sporadic attacks by Bradford, with occasional counter-attacks from Halifax when Northern either spilled the ball or gave away needless penalties at set-pieces. Halifax came close to scoring when Daniels broke through but lost the ball when Leake attempted to cut him off, and when McDonald beat Batten on the wing and punted the ball across to find there was not one Halifax player in support.

The second half was almost one continual Bradford attack but they constantly lost the ball, gave away penalties and failed to take chances that they created. On the hour, Ernest Ward kicked a penalty after a rare Halifax infringement.

The Halifax defence, despite taking a pounding from the Bradford forwards, held firm until the 72nd minute when Donald Ward and Ken Traill at last contrived to create a gap and Trevor Foster dummied, side-stepped and finally strolled over the line for a brilliant try. Ernest Ward kicked the conversion with ease.

The *Manchester Guardian* summed up the game: '*So Bradford won, but they did not enhance their own reputation nor that of the game.*'

Rugby League Cup Results

First Round, First Leg

Bradford N	3	St Helens	4
Castleford	10	Bramley	2
Dewsbury	9	Barrow	6
Huddersfield	4	Rochdale H	5
Hull	4	Halifax	0
Hunslet	22	Salford	0
Leeds	16	Batley	2
Liverpool S	3	Wakefield T	32
Normanton	4	Belle Vue R	9
Oldham	30	Broughton Moor	0
Swinton	15	Featherstone R	2
Vine Tavern	4	York	11
Warrington	17	Hull KR	7
Whitehaven	0	Keighley	0
Wigan	11	Leigh	12
Workington T	6	Widnes	7

The Normanton game was played at Wakefield. The Vine Tavern game was played at St Helens.

First Round, Second Leg

St Helens	0	Bradford N	5
Bramley	2	Castleford	10
Barrow	13	Dewsbury	9
Rochdale H	0	Huddersfield	11
Halifax	10	Hull	0
Salford	11	Hunslet	10
Batley	4	Leeds	7
Wakefield T	41	Liverpool S	12
Belle Vue R	12	Normanton	0
Broughton Moor	2	Oldham	35
Featherstone R	13	Swinton	10
York	17	Vine Tavern	3
Hull KR	5	Warrington	28
Keighley	19	Whitehaven	9
Leigh	4	Wigan	5
Widnes	0	Workington T	10

The Broughton Moor game was played at Workington.

First Round Replay

Leigh	4	Wigan	10

The first round second leg was declared void because no extra-time was played.

Second Round

Barrow	13	Keighley	2
Belle Vue R	8	Warrington	3
Bradford N	11	Castleford	5
Halifax	5	Swinton	0
Huddersfield	3	Workington T	0
Leeds	14	Hunslet	8
Wigan	37	Wakefield T	2
York	3	Oldham	4

Third Round

Barrow	8	Wigan	7
Bradford N	8	Belle Vue R	7
Leeds	9	Huddersfield	20
Oldham	2	Halifax	7

Semi-finals

Bradford N	10	Barrow	0

At Station Road, Swinton
Attendance: 26,900   *Receipts: £4,653*

Halifax	11	Huddersfield	10

At Odsal Stadium, Bradford
Attendance: 64,250   *Receipts: £8,608*

Final

Saturday, 7 May at Wembley Stadium, London

	T	G	P		T	G	P
Bradford N	2	3	12	**Halifax**	0	0	0
W.Leake				D.Chalkley			
E.Batten	T			A.H.Daniels			
J.Kitching				P.J.Reid			
E.Ward		3G		G.M.Price			
A.S.Edwards				E.McDonald			
W.T.H.Davies				G.Kenny			
D.Ward				S.Keilty			
F.W.Whitcombe				M.J.Condon			
V.J.Darlison				A.Ackerley			
R.Greaves				J.W.Rothwell			
T.J.F.Foster	T			D.Healy			
B.Tyler				J.S.Pansegrouw			
K.Traill				F.Mawson			

Lance Todd Trophy: E.Ward

Referee: C.S.Phillips (Widnes)   *Half-time: 5-0*
Attendance: 95,050   *Receipts: £21,930*

Cup presented by HRH Prince Philip, the Duke of Edinburgh.

1950 Warrington 19 Widnes 0

Warrington's Australian captain Harry Bath is carried shoulder-high around Wembley Stadium in 1950. Lance Todd Trophy winner Gerry Helme is content to carry the base of the Cup.

WARRINGTON'S first Challenge Cup Final victory since 1907 was a well-deserved one. They were by far the better side, controlling the game straight from the kick-off and easily outplaying a poor Widnes side. The Wire were more alert, decisive, faster, and by far fitter than Widnes, who seemed to lack direction and creativity in much of their play. When the Chemics did mount an attack, all too often the man with the ball would waste precious minutes twirling round to seek either a new line of attack or support from colleagues who were generally never there. Warrington enjoyed a 2-1 advantage in the scrums and with the possession his forwards created for him, scrum-half Gerry Helme played one of the finest games of his career, his performance earning him the Lance Todd trophy.

Warrington scored their first points in the 16th minute when Palm dropped a neat goal from loose play in front of the Widnes posts. Two minutes later, he added a further two points with a tremendous touchline penalty-kick. Before Widnes could compose themselves, Australian loose-forward Harry Bath led a series of battering ram assaults at the Chemics line and he eventually scored himself, crashing through a quartet of would-be tacklers for a try which Palm converted with almost arrogant ease.

Widnes rallied briefly and some fine forward play from Rowbottom and Leigh established a fragile bridgehead deep into Wire territory. From this platform the backs created a series of superb overlaps but, as usual, they let themselves down, dropping and tumbling passes that they should have taken in a deep sleep. Warrington did not relent and before half-time scored a further five points when Ron Ryder showed the Widnes defence just what to do with an overlap when he scorched over the line for a try created from a play-the-ball and Palm added another well-struck penalty goal.

Many sides in Widnes' position might have been routed in the second half, for Warrington started in rampant fashion, swarming towards the try-line like a colony of ants on the move. The Chemics, however, were made of sterner stuff and every man stuck to his task well and between them they held firm for 22 minutes. And even then it was a penalty goal from Palm that increased Warrington's lead to 16-0.

Rugby League Cup Results

First Round, First Leg

Barrow	5	Hull	10
Batley	10	Castleford	9
Belle Vue R	20	Whitehaven	2
Broughton Moor	5	Wakefield T	28
Cardiff	10	Salford	15
Featherstone R	19	Bramley	2
Huddersfield	6	Dewsbury	9
Hull KR	2	Warrington	12
Leeds	14	Leigh	7
Oldham	5	Bradford N	16
St Helens	10	Halifax	6
Swinton	24	Liverpool S	10
Widnes	15	Rochdale H	2
Workington T	0	Keighley	5
Worsley Boys' Club	7	Hunslet	45
York	2	Wigan	38

The Broughton Moor game was played at Workington and the Worsley Boys' Club game at Wigan.

First Round, Second Leg

Hull	0	Barrow	11
Castleford	6	Batley	6
Whitehaven	12	Belle Vue R	0
Wakefield T	73	Broughton Moor	3
Salford	20	Cardiff	5
Bramley	5	Featherstone R	2
Dewsbury	4	Huddersfield	2
Warrington	24	Hull KR	4
Leigh	7	Leeds	2
Bradford N	6	Oldham	8
Halifax	2	St Helens	0
Liverpool S	9	Swinton	25
Rochdale H	0	Widnes	27
Keighley	4	Workington T	3
Hunslet	18	Worsley Boys' Club	9
Wigan	65	York	15

Second Round

Barrow	6	Featherstone R	2
Batley	4	Widnes	12
Belle Vue R	6	Hunslet	17
Bradford N	13	Keighley	2
Leeds	7	Wigan	2
Salford	2	St Helens	9
Wakefield T	2	Dewsbury	2
Warrington	17	Swinton	2

Second Round Replay

Dewsbury	10	Wakefield T	15

Third Round

Leeds	14	Wakefield T	8
St Helens	0	Bradford N	0
Warrington	21	Hunslet	7
Widnes	12	Barrow	7

Third Round Replay

Bradford N	11	St Helens	0

Semi-finals

Warrington	16	Leeds	4

At Odsal Stadium, Bradford
Attendance: 70,198 *Receipts: £9,957*

Widnes	8	Bradford N	0

At Central Park, Wigan
Attendance: 24,783 *Receipts: £3,896*

Final

Saturday, 6 May at Wembley Stadium, London

	T	G	P		T	G	P
Warrington	3	5	19	**Widnes**	0	0	0
L.Jones				F.Bradley			
B.Bevan				J.Parkes			
R.Ryder	T			C.Hutton			
A.Naughton				T.Sale			
A.E.Johnson				A.Malone			
B.Knowelden	T			J.Fleming			
G.J.Helme				H.Anderson			
W.Derbyshire				R.Rowbottom			
H.H.Fishwick				R.Band			
R.Fisher				C.Wilcox			
A.H.Bath	T			F.Leigh			
G.Lowe				J.Naughton			
H.Palin		5G		C.Reynolds			

Lance Todd Trophy: G.J.Helme

Referee: A.S.Dobson (Pontefract) *Half-time: 14-0*
Attendance: 94,249 *Receipts: £24,782*

Cup presented by The Rt Hon C.R.Attlee PC MP.

With 13 minutes remaining, Warrington's persistence paid off and they scored a classic Wembley try. One account described it: '*There was a scrum some ten yards from the line and 15 yards from Warrington's right-hand touchline. Anderson put the ball in from the open side. Fisher timed his strike perfectly and the heel was smooth. Helme snatched the ball up and burst for the corner flag on the blind side. Knowelden came racing in support, between him and the scrum, the inside pass was a model and Knowelden was over for as fine a try of its kind as one could desire.*'

It was the final score of the match. Warrington had beaten Widnes 19-0.

1951 Wigan 10 Barrow 0

WIGAN won the Challenge Cup with a deserved ten-point margin but never once reached anything like their best form.

Heavy, intermittent rain showers fell during the game and ruined any chances of open football. The conditions were ideally suited to the strong Wigan pack and they dominated the game throughout. There was a great deal to admire in the superb, strong tackling of both defences and in Willie Home's marking of Cec Mountford. The game on the whole was a dour and drab affair, however, and prompted one newspaper to comment: *'It was not the sort of stuff which has made Rugby League a fine and thrilling spectacle so often in the north.'*

One of the basic problems with the game in the first half was the close marking at the play the ball set-pieces and the near-obsessive way that players held on to the ball, fearful of losing any ground gained by the monotonous advance by the forwards. Barrow's tactics of tight marking and either one-man rushes or slow, short passes, were perfectly correct in the circumstances but their inability to attempt to move the ball around the field stifled play. Wigan, in the first half at least, were just as bad, the self-proclaimed champions of open play did little to demonstrate their awesome array of clever little through kicks and swift flicked passes that could prise open any defence.

The Riversiders had one clear chance in the first half. Blan broke through in the middle of the field, found himself without support, chipped the ball delicately over the full-back and was promptly floored, quite illegally, behind the referee's back. In the eighth minute Gee kicked a good goal but then missed with three far easier attempts.

The second half was a little more open and after 20 minutes play Wigan finally crossed the Barrow line. Bradshaw broke quickly from a scrum in midfield and changed direction to throw a long looping pass to Mountford, who combined with Broome to give Hilton the room to just evade Stretch's high tackle and cross the line in the corner. With ten minutes remaining Nordgren burst through a tackle and flew to the line, only to be held yards short.

From the play of the ball, Ken Gee got possession, fiented to pass out and saw the Barrow defence open in front of him *'like a windjacket that has been unzipped'*. The mighty prop took three huge strides and plunged over the line with two Barrow defenders clinging to him for a brilliant opportunist try. Lance Todd Trophy winner Cec Mountford stepped forward to kick the conversion and seal Wigan's victory. Barrow refused to give in and only a superb covering tackle by Broome on Castle prevented the Cumbrians scoring late in the game.

Wigan celebrate with the Challenge Cup at Wembley in 1951.

Rugby League Cup Results

First Round, First Leg

Batley	41	Broughton Moor	3
Belle Vue R	8	Castleford	5
Bradford N	11	St Helens	6
Featherstone R	9	York	5
Halifax	17	Hunslet	4
Hull KR	7	Dewsbury	13
Leeds	23	Oldham	5
Leigh	43	Latchford Albion	0
Liverpool S	5	Workington T	25
Llanelli	9	Barrow	23
Rochdale H	0	Wigan	32
Salford	16	Wakefield T	10
Swinton	25	Bramley	4
Warrington	25	Hull	9
Whitehaven	2	Huddersfield	7
Widnes	8	Keighley	3

First Round, Second Leg

Broughton Moor	0	Batley	36
Castleford	2	Belle Vue R	5
St Helens	4	Bradford N	0
York	5	Featherstone R	4
Hunslet	2	Halifax	0
Dewsbury	19	Hull KR	3
Oldham	13	Leeds	10
Latchford Albion	0	Leigh	19
Workington T	28	Liverpool S	8
Barrow	39	Llanelli	5
Wigan	18	Rochdale H	5
Wakefield T	2	Salford	6
Bramley	7	Swinton	14
Hull	3	Warrington	5
Huddersfield	21	Whitehaven	9
Keighley	6	Widnes	0

The Broughton Moor game was played at Whitehaven. The Latchford Albion game was played at Warrington.

Second Round

Barrow	12	Workington T	5
Belle Vue R	12	Huddersfield	14
Bradford N	14	Swinton	4
Keighley	6	Halifax	7
Leeds	20	Leigh	3
Salford	6	Dewsbury	0
Warrington	18	Featherstone R	6
Wigan	16	Batley	8

Third Round

Barrow	5	Bradford N	4
Leeds	15	Halifax	7
Salford	4	Warrington	8
Wigan	2	Huddersfield	0

Semi-finals

Barrow	14	Leeds	14

At Odsal Stadium, Bradford
Attendance: 57,729   *Receipts: £8,236*

Wigan	3	Warrington	2

At Station Road, Swinton
Attendance: 44,621   *Receipts: £7,358*

Semi-final Replay

Barrow	28	Leeds	13

At Fartown, Huddersfield
Attendance: 31,078   *Receipts: £5,038*

Final

Saturday, 5 May at Wembley Stadium, London

	T	G	P		T	G	P
Wigan	2	2	10	**Barrow**	0	0	0
J.Cunliffe				H.Stretch			
J.Hilton	T			J.Lewthwaite			
J.Broome				P.Jackson			
G.Roughley				D.Goodwin			
B.C.Nordgren				F.Castle			
C.R.Mountford		G		W.Horne			
T.Bradshaw				E.Toohey			
K.Gee	T	G		F.Longman			
G.Curran				J.McKinnell			
F.Barton				R.Hartley			
N.Silcock				J.Grundy			
E.Slevin				H.H.Atkinson			
W.Blan				H.McGregor			

Lance Todd Trophy: C.R.Mountford

Referee: M.Coates (Pudsey)   *Half-time: 2-0*
Attendance: 94,262   *Receipts: £24,797*

Cup presented by HRH The Duke of Gloucester.

At the age of 41 – and 14 years after his first Wembley success – Gus Risman holds the Challenge Cup aloft following the victory over Featherstone Rovers in 1952.

LED superbly by Gus Risman, their 41-year-old captain and coach, Workington won a fine game which was described by many as one of the best seen in the south for years. Workington thoroughly deserved their victory but were given a much sterner challenge than had been expected.

Featherstone Rovers played a superb game but were beaten almost everywhere for speed, yet they never gave up and stuck to their task well. Their veteran player-coach Eric Batten led his men by example, his quick clever tackling of Gibson, which prevented the ball from reaching the speedy George Wilson, inspiring the rest of the Rovers defence.

With barely a minute played, Featherstone's John Daly strayed offside and Risman opened the scoring with a good goal from the penalty. Ten minutes later Rovers full-back Miller hit the post with a penalty attempt when Workington

had been penalised at a play the ball. Sixteen minutes into the game, Workington heeled well from a scrum and Iveson was away, beating Evans, Cording and Lambert before passing to Lawrenson. The wingman kicked ahead, rounded Miller, collected the ball and was tackled inches short of the line. Despite a huddle of Featherstone players around him, he regained his feet, played the ball to himself and burrowed through a mass of legs to score a hard-won try. Risman added the two points. Featherstone hit back with two well-struck goals from Miller and had a 'try' disallowed when the touch judge ruled that Batten had stepped into touch in the act of scoring.

Three minutes into the second half a huge kick by Miller found touch fifteen yards from the Workington line and from the scrum Rovers won possession. The ball flashed along the

Rugby League Cup Results

First Round, First Leg

Batley	9	Bramley	9
Bradford N	6	Doncaster	5
Cardiff	7	Dewsbury	7
Castleford	4	Swinton	5
Huddersfield	5	Halifax	13
Hull	8	Oldham	6
Leeds	44	Hull KR	14
Leigh	11	Keighley	4
Rochdale H	7	Featherstone R	8
St Helens	6	Belle Vue R	5
Salford	13	Hunslet	6
Wakefield T	18	Wigan	13
Warrington	28	Liverpool C	4
Whitehaven	16	Rylands Recreation	0
Widnes	5	Barrow	5
York	7	Workington T	18

First Round, Second Leg

Bramley	0	Batley	9
Doncaster	4	Bradford N	7
Dewsbury	16	Cardiff	0
Swinton	2	Castleford	9
Halifax	5	Huddersfield	5
Oldham	24	Hull	0
Hull KR	3	Leeds	5
Keighley	0	Leigh	8
Featherstone R	17	Rochdale H	2
Belle Vue R	4	St Helens	9
Hunslet	6	Salford	3
Wigan	40	Wakefield T	3
Liverpool C	6	Warrington	6
Rylands Recreation	9	Whitehaven	9
Barrow	8	Widnes	2
Workington T	42	York	5

The Rylands game was played at Warrington.

Second Round

Batley	4	Featherstone R	11
Castleford	6	Leigh	7
Leeds	12	Oldham	9
Salford	6	Barrow	11
Warrington	26	Dewsbury	9
Whitehaven	7	Halifax	5
Wigan	28	Bradford N	12
Workington T	15	St Helens	4

Third Round

Featherstone R	14	Wigan	11
Leigh	9	Leeds	5
Whitehaven	2	Barrow	10
Workington T	14	Warrington	0

Semi-finals

Featherstone R	6	Leigh	2

At Headingley, Leeds
Attendance: 33,926   *Receipts: £6,671*

Workington T	5	Barrow	2

At Central Park, Wigan
Attendance: 31,200   *Receipts: £4,782*

Final

Saturday, 19 April at Wembley Stadium, London

	T	G	P		T	G	P
Workington T	**4**	**3**	**18**	**Featherstone R**	**2**	**2**	**10**
A.J.Risman		3G		F.Miller		2G	
J.H.Lawrenson	2T			E.Batten	T		
A.H.Paskins				D.Metcalfe			
E.Gibson				A.Tennant			
G.Wilson	T			N.Mitchell			
J.H.Thomas				R.Cording			
A.J.Pepperell				R.Evans	T		
J.A.Hayton				K.Welburn			
V.McKeating				W.Bradshaw			
J.V.Wareing				J.C.Daly			
J.R.Mudge	T			F.Hulme			
B.Wilson				L.Gant			
W.H.Ivison				C.Lambert			

Lance Todd Trophy: W.H.Ivison

Referee: C.F.Appleton (Warrington)

Half-time: 7-4

Attendance: 72,093   *Receipts: £22,374*

Cup presented by The Rt Hon Anthony Eden, Secretary of State for Foreign Affairs.

---

line to Gant, who switched the direction of the attack and passed to Metcalfe, the centre flicked the ball to the eager Batten who just made it to the corner to score. Featherstone attacked strongly and only some desperate scrambling defence from Risman and Lawrenson kept them out.

Rovers were still pressing hard when Iveson burst through the centre and faced with only Miller, stumbled when the full-back managed to tap his ankle. Two minutes later Iveson repeated the move and this drew Miller before passing to Mudge who raced 45 yards for a try. A minute after that, a far too optimistic pass from Daly was intercepted by John Lawrenson and the wingman swept down the field for a glorious try which Risman converted to give Workington a 15-7 lead.

Tony Paskins made a fine break to put George Wilson through for Town's final try on 66 minutes. The last score went to Featherstone who never gave up and were rewarded with an excellent try from Ray Evans following a clever break and fast diagonal run to the line.

The victorious 1953 Huddersfield team carry their captain Russ Pepperell (with Cup) and Lance Todd Trophy winner Peter Ramsden.

HUDDERSFIELD'S first visit to Wembley since 1933 ended in triumph in a game that provided thrills galore and some very dubious tactics from firm favourites St Helens. The Saints never really got into their stride and adopted the somewhat strange tactics of trying to charge their way through the middle of the field. The strategy not only starved their backs of the ball but also led to some particularly nasty incidents which earned the displeasure of the Huddersfield fans and referee alike.

Large sections of the vast crowd were so incensed at some of the Saints tactics that they vented their anger with a round of booing. The *Manchester Guardian* commented on the scenes: '*The crowd booed the St Helens side for some time and it renewed its signs of disapproval when the St Helens players were receiving their medals. At Wembley above all places, such a scene was regrettable – as regrettable as the tactics that prompted it.*'

The game was almost half an hour old when 19-year-old Peter Ramsden blasted through the St Helens defence and, despite being tackled by Alan Prescott, dived over the line for a try. The St Helens players claimed that the young stand-off had grounded the ball short but referee Phillips awarded the try and Devery kicked the goal. Despite winning the majority of the scrums, including 12 in a row, Saints continued to hog the middle of the field and dropped or mishandled far too often.

In the 39th minute Saints scrum-half, George Langfield pulled two points back when he landed a penalty and then right on the stroke of half-time Llewellyn finally received a pass out on the wing and scored an unconverted try.

Eighteen minutes into the second half Saints delighted their followers when they finally expanded their game beyond the forwards and George Langfield finished a fluid 75-yard movement with a brilliant try. He failed with the goal-kick that would have opened up a five-point lead. Within minutes victory seemed impossible for Huddersfield. Three points adrift, they had full-back Hunter carried from the field after being tackled off the ball by St Helens wingman Stuart Llewellyn.

Huddersfield stuck to their task, however, and from a

Rugby League Cup Results

First Round, First Leg

Barrow	20	Featherstone R	8
Batley	6	Bradford N	15
Belle Vue R	10	Keighley	2
Halifax	14	Dewsbury	7
Huddersfield	36	Castleford	14
Hull KR	12	Doncaster	0
Hunslet	14	Workington T	12
Leigh	34	Bramley	10
Liverpool C	3	Swinton	26
St Helens	20	Oldham	4
Salford	24	York	14
Wakefield T	9	Leeds	33
Warrington	46	Orford Tannery	2
Whitehaven	13	Hull	6
Widnes	28	NDLB	0
Wigan	27	Rochdale H	7

Orford Tannery gave up ground advantage.

First Round, Second Leg

Featherstone R	5	Barrow	15
Bradford N	17	Batley	3
Keighley	7	Belle Vue R	0
Dewsbury	2	Halifax	16
Castleford	2	Huddersfield	6
Doncaster	5	Hull KR	5
Workington T	12	Hunslet	8
Bramley	3	Leigh	11
Swinton	12	Liverpool C	4
Oldham	5	St Helens	5
York	3	Salford	8
Leeds	32	Wakefield T	9
Warrington	46	Orford Tannery	8
Hull	14	Whitehaven T	9
NDLB	3	Widnes	22
Rochdale H	15	Wigan	24

The NDLB game was played at Hull KR.

Second Round

Bradford N	18	Salford	4
Huddersfield	21	Barrow	7
Hull KR	14	Swinton	3
Leeds	26	Widnes	17
Leigh	7	Halifax	7
St Helens	28	Belle Vue R	0
Warrington	10	Workington T	2
Wigan	18	Hull	10

Second Round Replay

Halifax	4	Leigh	7

Third Round

Bradford N	7	Huddersfield	17
Leigh	3	St Helens	12
Warrington	25	Leeds	8
Wigan	25	Hull KR	6

Semi-finals

Huddersfield	7	Wigan	0

At Odsal Stadium, Bradford
Attendance: 58,722   *Receipts: £10,523*

St Helens	9	Warrington	3

At Station Road, Swinton
Attendance: 38,059   *Receipts: £7,779*

Final

Saturday, 25 April at Wembley Stadium, London

	T	G	P		T	G	P
Huddersfield	**3**	**3**	**15**	**St Helens**	**2**	**2**	**10**
J.C.H.Hunter				A.G.Moses			
P.Henderson				S.M.Llewellyn	T		
G.R.Pepperell				D.Greenall			
P.C.Devery		G		D.Gullick			
L.W.Cooper		2G		S.McCormick			
P.Ramsden	2T			J.Honey			
W.M.Banks	T			G.Langfield	T	2G	
E.Slevin				A.G.Prescott			
G.Curran				R.E.Blakemore			
J.Bowden				G.Parr			
J.Brown				G.Parsons			
J.Large				W.Bretherton			
D.D.Valentine				W.R.Cale			

Lance Todd Trophy: P.Ramsden
Referee: G.S.Phillips (Widnes)   *Half-time: 5-5*
Attendance: 89,588   *Receipts: £30,865*

Cup presented by His Grace The Duke of Norfolk.

---

scrum Welsh scrum-half Billy Banks darted over the line for a try. Cooper kicked the all-important conversion and the Tykes were back in the lead.

Seven minutes later it was all-square again when Langfield dropped a goal. With barely five minutes remaining, forwards Bowden and Valentine combined to create a tiny gap which Peter Ramsden sailed through to race half the length of the field for a fine try. Australian Lionel Cooper made no mistake with the conversion kick and Huddersfield, after surviving many shocks and set backs, were worthy 15-10 victors.

Young Ramsden celebrated his 19th birthday in style when he was awarded the Lance Todd Trophy.

1954 Warrington 8 Halifax 4

(after a replay)

WEMBLEY'S first-ever drawn Final, a drab 4-4 affair, led the way to a game that is part of Rugby League's heritage. Officially, 102,575 paid to see the replay at Odsal Stadium, Bradford, but several over-eager fans broke through fences and it was estimated that as many as 120,000 were in the huge natural bowl for the game.

At Wembley, Tuss Griffiths kicked two first-half penalty goals to give Halifax the lead but these were cancelled out in the second half when Harry Bath landed two penalties to level the scores.

At Odsal, Halifax tore into Warrington from the kick-off and it was only an excellent touch-finding kick by Stan McCormick that relieved the pressure in the first few minutes. Warrington held their attacking position from the scrum and then settled themselves for a series of assaults on the Halifax line. After eight minutes a passing move developed on the right, Harry Bath changed the direction with a simple reverse pass that completely wrong-footed the Halifax defenders who were closing in, and Lowe continued the move with a lobbed pass to Challinor who dived in at the corner.

Shortly before half-time Halifax pressed hard near the Wire line and Lynch finally pierced the Warrington line, but his pass from Daniels was ruled a fraction forward. The pressure eventually told and Halifax scored, but only through a Griffiths penalty goal after Naughton had been caught offside.

Warrington pushed strongly at the opening stages of the second half and Brian Bevan, with one of characteristic weaving runs, came inches short and then Heathwood was crashed into touch at the corner. In the 57th minute, Halifax were caught offside and Bath kicked the penalty from a good 35 yards out. Four minutes later Griffiths brought Halifax back to within a point when he landed a penalty following McCormick's obstruction of Daniels.

Eventually Warrington's superior handling and the speed of their backs began to punch holes into the Halifax defence. In the 68th minute Gerry Helme collected the ball in midfield and, 40 yards from the line, he accelerated, beat three men with pace alone, then dummied to pass to the supporting McCormick. The trick worked and he ducked under the tackle of the advancing Griffiths to score in the corner.

Halifax responded well but despite being camped in the Wire '25' for the final ten minutes, they lacked the telling thrust down the middle to penetrate the Warrington defence. In the final emotion-charged minute, Keilty launched a high kick toward the line, Daniels caught the ball and at the exact same moment was tackled by Frodsham. In the ensuing melee the wingman appeared to ground the ball but the referee disallowed the 'try', despite the strong protests of the Halifax players. It was to be Halifax's last chance of a truly memorable game.

Wakefield-based referee Ron Gelder leads the touch judges and players from the field after the 2-2 draw in 1954. The players in the immediate foreground are Ken Dean of Halifax and Warrington's Gerald Lowe.

Rugby League Cup Results

First Round, First Leg

Belle Vue R	15	Huddersfield	20
Bramley	5	Warrington	30
Castleford	8	Doncaster	5
Halifax	19	Dewsbury	0
Hull	24	Widnes	0
Hunslet	20	Salford	5
Keighley	12	Barrow	11
Latchford Albion	20	Wigan	40
Leeds	13	Batley	20
Leigh	13	Swinton	4
Liverpool C	5	Oldham	15
Rochdale H	9	Bradford N	9
St Helens	26	Featherstone R	7
Wakefield T	24	Whitehaven	13
Wheldale Colliery	6	Workington T	32
York	18	Hull KR	0

The Latchford Albion game was played at Warrington. The Wheldale Colliery game was played at Castleford.

First Round, Second Leg

Huddersfield	31	Belle Vue R	6
Warrington	17	Bramley	0
Doncaster	7	Castleford	2
Dewsbury	9	Halifax	15
Widnes	2	Hull	5
Salford	3	Hunslet	18
Barrow	6	Keighley	10
Wigan	41	Latchford Albion	2
Batley	6	Leeds	23
Swinton	2	Leigh	17
Oldham	18	Liverpool C	11
Bradford N	11	Rochdale H	2
Featherstone R	16	St Helens	27
Whitehaven	15	Wakefield T	3
Workington T	50	Wheldale Colliery	2
Hull KR	0	York	0

Second Round

Halifax	24	Keighley	5
Huddersfield	12	St Helens	5
Hull	5	Workington	5
Hunslet	10	Whitehaven	2
Leeds	12	Leigh	3
Oldham	4	Warrington	7
Wigan	15	Bradford N	10
York	11	Doncaster	2

Second Round Replay

Workington T	17	Hull	14

Third Round

Hunslet	16	Huddersfield	7
Leeds	31	Workington T	11
Warrington	26	York	5
Wigan	0	Halifax	2

Semi-finals

Halifax	18	Hunslet	3

At Odsal Stadium, Bradford
Attendance: 46,961   *Receipts: £8,262*

Warrington	8	Leeds	4

At Station Road, Swinton
Attendance: 37,249   *Receipts: £7,596*

Final

Saturday, 24 April at Wembley Stadium, London

	T	G	P		T	G	P
Warrington	0	2	4	**Halifax**	0	2	4
E.Frodsham				T.Griffiths		2G	
B.Bevan				A.H.Daniels			
J.Challinor				T.W.Lynch			
A.Stevens				P.Todd			
S.McCormick				D.R.Bevan			
H.R.Price				K.Dean			
G.J.Helme				S.Kielty			
D.Naughton				G.M.J.Thorley			
F.Wright				A.Ackerley			
G.Lowe				J.Wilkinson			
A.H.Bath		2G		A.Fearnley			
A.Heathwood				D.Schofield			
R.Ryan				D.Clarkson			

Referee: R.Gelder (Wakefield)   *Half-time: 0-4*
Attendance: 81,777   *Receipts: £29,706*

Final Replay

Wednesday, 5 May at Odsal Stadium, Bradford

	T	G	P		T	G	P
Warrington	2	1	8	**Halifax**	0	2	4
E.Frodsham				T.Griffiths		2G	
B.Bevan				A.H.Daniels			
J.Challinor	T			T.W.Lynch			
R.Ryder				W.Mather			
S.McCormick				D.R.Bevan			
H.R.Price				K.Dean			
G.J.Helme	T			S.Kielty			
D.Naughton				G.M.J.Thorley			
F.Wright				A.Ackerley			
G.Lowe				J.Wilkinson			
A.H.Bath		G		A.Fearnley			
A.Heathwood				D.Schofield			
R.Ryan				D.Clarkson			

Lance Todd Trophy: G.J.Helme
Referee: R.Gelder (Wakefield)   *Half-time: 3-2*
Attendance: 102,569   *Receipts: £18,623*

Cup presented by Mr C.W.Robinson, Chairman of the Council.

The boys from Barrow hoist their captain Willie Horne shoulder-high to show the Cup to their ecstatic followers in 1955.

BARROW won the Challenge Cup for the first time in a contest that can only be described as the proverbial game of two halves. The first half was abysmal and prompted one reporter to record: '*In the first half one gave up recording the number of dropped passes, knocks-on, interception of poor and ill-directed passes and examples of bad alignment in, both defence and attack. After the interval, however, we had some of the finest Rugby League ever played here.*'

Barrow's forwards were a sensation, their speed and mobility, stout tackling and fine backing-up a constant threat and worry to Workington. Behind such a successful six was their player-coach Willie Horne, who was as shrewd and skilful as ever, always probing and prompting with either well-timed defence-splitting passes or length-of-field touch-finding kicks.

The first half ended 2-2 with Paskins and Horne kicking penalty goals. Horne landed a penalty seven minutes into the second half and then dropped a goal a minute later. An injury to Workington's John Roper led to a rearrangement in the Town ranks, Ike Southward moving to scrum-half and

Brian Edgar to right wing. While Roper was off the field, a splendid pass from Paskins sent Faulder clear on his own '25'. He kicked ahead and beat three Barrow defenders to the touch down, only to be called back when the touch judge ruled that the ball had rolled into touch when he kicked ahead.

Almost on the hour, Barrow finally scored their first try in three visits to Wembley. Jack Grundy burst from some loose play and flicked a quick pass inside to McKeating who scored. Workington protested that the pass was forward but referee Gelder gave the try. Horne added the two points. Six minutes later, some tremendous Barrow backing up enabled Jackson, Castle, Belshaw and Jackson again to handle the ball before Goodwin swept on to the final pass to score a try which Home converted.

Workington reacted immediately when Wookey charged down a poor kick and Gibson carried the movement on for Faulder to score a try which Paskins converted. Barrow launched into attack again and Healey made a quick dash through the Town line. Grundy followed on his shoulder

Rugby League Cup Results

First Round

Batley	2	St Helens	15
Bradford N	9	Warrington	4
Bramley	4	Halifax	9
Dewsbury	8	Barrow	11
Featherstone R	39	Belle Vue	6
Hull KR	7	York	6
Hunslet	43	Whitehaven	10
Keighley	17	Blackpool B	8
Leeds	8	Huddersfield	3
Leigh	19	Doncaster	8
Liverpool C	6	Widnes	3
Oldham	5	Wigan	2
Rochdale H	11	Wakefield T	9
Salford	13	Castleford	5
Swinton	8	Hull	16
Workington T	43	Dewsbury C	0

Second Round

Bradford N	2	Featherstone R	7
Hull	4	Halifax	0
Hull KR	2	Hunslet	33
Keighley	2	St Helens	3
Leigh	5	Oldham	3
Rochdale H	13	Liverpool C	5
Salford	0	Barrow	13
Workington T	13	Leeds	7

Third Round

Hull	5	Hunslet	7
Leigh	9	Featherstone R	13
Rochdale H	2	Barrow	15
Workington T	14	St Helens	4

Semi-finals

Barrow	9	Hunslet	6

At Central Park, Wigan
Attendance: 25,493   *Receipts: £4,674*

Workington T	13	Featherstone R	2

At Headingley, Leeds
Attendance: 36,077   *Receipts: £7,330*

Final

Saturday, 30 April at Wembley Stadium, London

	T	G	P		T	G	P
Barrow	3	6	21	**Workington T**	2	3	12
C.Best				J.Vickers			
J.Lewthwaite				I.Southward			
P.Jackson				A.H.Paskins		3G	
D.Goodwin	T			E.Gibson	T		
F.H.Castle	T			E.Faulder	T		
W.Horne		6G		W.Wookey			
A.E.Toohey				J.Roper			
L.Belshaw				J.A.Hayton			
V.McKeating	T			W.Lymer			
F.Barton				A.Key			
J.J.Grundy				J.R.Mudge			
R.Parker				B.Edgar			
W.Healey				W.H.Ivison			

Lance Todd Trophy: J.J.Grundy

Referee: R.Gelder (Wakefield)   *Half-time: 2-2*
Attendance: 66,513   *Receipts: £27,453*

Cup presented by HRH The Duke of Edinburgh.

---

and, on collecting the pass, ran forward before sending Frank Castle racing down the wing to score a brilliant try. Willie Home landed the extra two points with a brilliant touchline conversion, his sixth goal of the afternoon. Six minutes from time, Workington's Eppie Gibson crowned a superb performance when he completely fooled the Barrow defence into thinking he would pass to Faulder but instead accelerated over the line for a grand and well-deserved try.

Workington's Tony Paskins scored the final points of one of the most thrilling second half performances the stadium had ever seen.

1956 St Helens 13 Halifax 2

ST HELENS fulfilled the clubs's long ambition when they crushed favourites Halifax 13-2 to collect the Challenge Cup for the first time in their history. The Saints thoroughly deserved their victory, playing some superb, clever football in a game which held the vast crowd's interest throughout and compelled their strictest attention in the final 20 minutes.

The leadership of their captain, Alan Prescott, was inspirational and produced an almost perfect display, one newspaper commenting: *'They harassed Halifax so unmercifully in the loose forward play that at the end they had reduced the Yorkshire six to rags and tatters.'*

It was this forward domination combined with McIntyre's success at hooking the ball from the scrums that laid the foundations for the victory. The St Helens backs had a good game, with half-backs Rhodes and Finnan outstanding, although perhaps a shade lucky that the feared Halifax half-back partnership of Dean and Keilty had a rare bad day. Halifax were a strong and very capable side but their defence seemed to be ill-prepared for St Helens' swift and sure changes of direction when attacking. The way in which the Saints handled the ball and threw it about had the Halifax defence almost constantly on the move and at times completely bewildered.

The first half, although scoreless, was far from dull with each side attacking in turn, but with St Helens showing far more enterprise and commitment. Cup Final nerves and the infamous swirling winds of Wembley Stadium combined to prevent both Rhodes and Griffiths kicking relatively easy penalty attempts. St Helens centre Brian Howard did manage to cross the Halifax line in the first half but the play was called back for a forward pass.

Saints started the second half with a tremendous 60-yard break from Alan Prescott but his pass from a tackle was hurried and it missed Carlton and flew straight into touch. Then Vince Karalius carved out an opening but, with Howard and Carlton on his outside, the loose forward held on to the ball a fraction too long and was hauled down by the chasing Halifax defence.

In the 66th minute, McIntyre, Parsons and Rhodes combined to put Howard clear. The centre drew his man and, despite being held in a tackle, tossed the ball to Carlton, who collected it in full flight and easily outpaced Griffiths to score a superb try which Austin Rhodes converted.

Three minutes later Carlton played the ball quickly and it flashed across the line for Llewellyn to score a try which Rhodes once again converted.

Tyssul Griffiths, the Halifax full-back, reduced the Saints' lead with a penalty goal but Halifax were a tired, beaten side.

With the very last movement of the match, St Helens captain, Alan Prescott, collected a pass from Vince Karalius and plunged over the line for a try. Rhodes hit the post with the conversion attempt.

St Helens captain and Lance Todd Trophy winner Alan Prescott is carried from the Wembley pitch in 1956.

Rugby League Cup Results

First Round

Castleford	12	Blackpool B	9
Huddersfield	8	Whitehaven	4
Hull	4	Leeds	9
Hunslet	9	Bradford N	10
Keighley	33	Triangle Valve	8
Leigh	19	Doncaster	10
Liverpool C	13	Hull KR	5
Oldham	31	Dewsbury	2
Rochdale H	55	Stanningley	0
St Helens	15	Warrington	6
Swinton	18	Batley	0
Wakefield T	30	Bramley	10
Widnes	10	Halifax	22
Wigan	24	Featherstone R	11
Workington T	16	Salford	0
York	2	Barrow	26

Second Round

Barrow	47	Liverpool C	5
Halifax	10	Workington T	3
Keighley	3	Wigan	12
Leeds	12	Oldham	7
Leigh	5	Wakefield	11
Rochdale H	2	Bradford N	5
St Helens	48	Castleford	5
Swinton	6	Huddersfield	8

Third Round

Leeds	9	Halifax	14
St Helens	53	Bradford N	6
Wakefield T	10	Barrow	14
Wigan	24	Huddersfield	2

Semi-finals

Halifax 11 Wigan 10
At Odsal Stadium, Bradford
Attendance: 52,273   *Receipts: £9,054*

St Helens 5 Barrow 5
At Station Road, Swinton
Attendance: 38,897   *Receipts: £7,793*

Semi-final Replay

St Helens 10 Barrow 5
At Central Park, Wigan
Attendance: 44,731   *Receipts: £7,768*

Final

Saturday, 28 April at Wembley Stadium, London

	T	G	P		T	G	P
St Helens	3	2	13	**Halifax**	0	1	2
A.G.Moses				T.Griffiths		G	
S.M.Llewellyn	T			A.H.Daniels			
D.Greenall				T.W.Lynch			
B.Howard				J.G.Palmer			
F.Carlton	T			J.Freeman			
W.Finnan				K.Dean			
A.J.Rhodes		2G		S.Kielty			
A.G.Prescott	T			J.Wilkinson			
L.McIntyre				A.Ackerley			
D.Silcock				J.B.Henderson			
G.Parsons				L.Pearce			
R.Robinson				A.Fearnley			
V.P.P.Karalius				K.Traill			

Lance Todd Trophy: A.G.Prescott

Referee: R.Gelder (Wakefield)   *Half-time: 0-0*
Attendance: 79,341   *Receipts: £29,424*

Cup presented by Field Marshal The Earl Alexander of Tunis.

1957 Leeds 9 Barrow 7

'ONE of the most exciting Finals in the Wembley series, one always had the feeling that something was likely to happen because both sides were quick and enterprising in their efforts to beat deadly tackling.' That is how one newspaper described the game that, unlike so many previous Finals, never once stagnated.

Leeds started well and seemed to master any big-match nerves quickly and were by far the more settled side for the majority of the game. In contrast Barrow were a tense and erratic side that made far too many basic handling errors to keep their game flowing.

Leeds opened the scoring in the 23rd minute when Pat Quinn unexpectedly joined the attacking line to collect a clever pass from hooker Bernard Prior. The full-back feigned to pass to Welsh centre Lewis Jones, then accelerated to the line and forced himself over for a well-worked try. Jones, one of the finest kickers in the game, missed the conversion attempt.

Three minutes into the second half, Leeds used a well-worked set-piece to completely bamboozle the first line of the Barrow defence. Using two dummy runners around the base of a scrum, they flicked the ball to the unmarked Jones, who made superb ground before handing to Delmos Hodgkinson on the wing. The 18-year-old hugged the touchline then cut inside the advancing Joe Ball with perfect timing to score a brilliantly-executed try. Once again Jones failed with the goal-kick.

Five minutes later Willie Horne landed a penalty to pull back two precious points. Around ten minutes later, Barrow's Jack Grundy, ten yards from his own line and apparently confused over a call for the ball, passed into the hands of Don Robinson who ambled over the line for a gift try.

Leeds seemed to have the game sown up, but in the 64th minute Barrow finally put together a string of passes and scored a spectacular try when Castle's perfect pass sent Phil Jackson hurtling for the line. The full-back evaded Broughton's grasping tackle and he grounded the ball in the corner for a brilliant try to which Willie Horne added a superb goal. With 16 minutes remaining and only two points behind, Barrow launched themselves at the swarming Leeds defence. With barely a minute of time left, and almost on his own line, Horne created a brief gap for Johnny Rea to race through towards the line. Leeds were in almost complete disarray and with a host of his own players backing him up, the 20-year-old centre punted ahead and sprinted for the loose ball. But in a dramatic last effort, George Broughton, the Leeds wingman, somehow found the energy to race back and collect the ball safely.

Leeds second row forward Don Robinson barges his way through the Barrow defence in the 1957 Final.

Rugby League Cup Results

First Round

Barrow	53	Wakefield Loco	12
Bradford N	20	Dewsbury	7
Doncaster	5	Castleford	15
Halifax	48	Widnes St Mary's	0
Hull	15	Keighley	12
Hull KR	2	Salford	10
Hunslet	14	Batley	7
Leeds	13	Wigan	11
Leigh	17	Featherstone R	11
Liverpool C	2	Widnes	11
Rochdale H	10	Blackpool B	18
Swinton	5	Huddersfield	5
Wakefield T	37	York	15
Warrington	14	Bramley	2
Whitehaven	9	St Helens	8
Workington T	5	Oldham	14

First Round Replay

Huddersfield	5	Swinton	0

Second Round

Bradford N	8	Widnes	10
Castleford	2	Barrow	9
Hull	3	Halifax	9
Leeds	28	Warrington	6
Leigh	5	Oldham	0
Salford	2	Huddersfield	6
Wakefield T	9	Blackpool B	11
Whitehaven	7	Hunslet	0

Third Round

Barrow	10	Huddersfield	0
Blackpool B	13	Leigh	24
Halifax	10	Leeds	16
Whitehaven	2	Widnes	0

Semi-finals

Barrow	2	Leigh	2

At Central Park, Wigan
Attendance: 34,628   *Receipts: £6,322*

Leeds	10	Whitehaven	9

At Odsal Stadium, Bradford
Attendance: 49,094   *Receipts: £8,967*

Semi-final Replay

Barrow	15	Leigh	10

At Station Road, Swinton
Attendance: 28,431   *Receipts: £5,694*

Final

Saturday, 11 May at Wembley Stadium, London

	T	G	P		T	G	P
Leeds	3	0	9	**Barrow**	1	2	7
J.P.Quinn	T			J.Ball			
D.Hodgkinson	T			J.Lewthwaite			
K.McLellan				P.Jackson	T		
B.L.Jones				J.Rea			
G.Broughton				F.Castle			
J.Lendill				W.Horne		2G	
J.M.Stevenson				J.Harris			
J.Anderson				C.Woosey			
B.Prior				M.Redhead			
W.E.Hopper				R.Parker			
B.Poole				J.J.Grundy			
D.Robinson	T			D.Wilson			
H.Street				W.Healey			

Lance Todd Trophy: J.M.Stevenson

Referee: C.F.Appleton (Warrington)

Half-time: 3-0

Attendance: 76,318   *Receipts: £32,617*

Cup presented by The Earl of Derby.

WIGAN fully deserved their four-point victory over Workington and they achieved it in fine style, throwing the ball around in a brilliant exhibition of open play.

The Riversiders blended their strong forward bursts perfectly with the thrust of their clever and forceful backs. At the hub of almost everything Wigan did was Rees Thomas, their Welsh scrum-half whose superb display of sheer hard work rather than brilliant play won him the Lance Todd Trophy for Man of the Match. Rees was the schemer, orchestrating the attack and fusing the forwards with the backs so that they dove-tailed together perfectly.

Workington contributed well to a fine, exciting game, adopting open tactics whenever possible, but their usually resolute defence proved to be off form for the day. They had terrible luck when an injury to Archer, received in a high tackle by Sullivan after ten minutes, affected the little stand-off for the rest of the game, and later hard knocks to Edgar, Key and Roper played a part in disrupting Town's rhythm.

Wigan dominated the initial stages but a mixture of Wembley nerves and poor finishing saw them waste several try-scoring chances. In the 11th minute Workington's Brian Edgar burst clean through Wigan's first line of defence and passed straight to Ike Southward, who swept down the field to score a glorious try which he converted himself. Six minutes later, and with Archer off the field receiving treatment for his injury, Wigan changed the direction of attack with such speed that Billy Boston was able to release a pass to Sullivan that saw the wingman romp over in the corner. Cunliffe kicked the goal from near the touchline.

Workington responded well and with Archer back on the field, albeit still a little groggy, they matched the Riversiders in both attack and defence. Then, with some 12 minutes of the first half to play, Thomas set off on a swerving run that had the Town defence fooled. The stand-off passed to Barton, who scored a fine try near the posts. Cunliffe kicked the conversion and Wigan were 10-5 up.

With five minutes to go to half-time, Southwold gave

Eric Ashton, the Wigan captain, carries the Challenge Cup trophy from the pitch in 1958.

Rugby League Cup Results

First Round

Barrow	36	Liverpool C	2
Batley	6	Warrington	27
Bramley	9	Bradford N	15
Dewsbury	2	Blackpool B	4
Huddersfield	0	Halifax	15
Hull	13	Rochdale H	16
Hunslet	0	St Helens	15
Keighley	12	Salford	6
Leeds	31	Castleford	6
Oldham	23	Hull KR	6
Swinton	6	Featherstone R	9
Wakefield T	29	Doncaster	0
Widnes	51	Orford Tannery	2
Wigan	39	Whitehaven	10
Workington T	3	Leigh	0
York	50	Lock Lane	5

Second Round

Blackpool B	5	Oldham	12
Featherstone R	9	Barrow	5
Halifax	12	Warrington	17
Keighley	4	St Helens	19
Rochdale H	11	Bradford N	8
Wakefield T	5	Wigan	11
Widnes	5	Workington T	8
York	7	Leeds	2

Third Round

Featherstone R	5	St Helens	0
Oldham	0	Wigan	8
Rochdale H	8	York	5
Workington T	11	Warrington	0

Semi-finals

Wigan	5	Rochdale H	3

At Station Road, Swinton
Attendance: 28,597   *Receipts: £6,328*

Workington T	8	Featherstone R	2

At Odsal Stadium, Bradford
Attendance: 31,715   *Receipts: £6,207*

Final

Saturday, 10 May at Wembley Stadium, London

	T	G	P		T	G	P
Wigan	3	2	13	**Workington T**	1	3	9
J.Cunliffe		2G		J.McAvoy			
T.O'Grady				I.Southward	T	3G	
E.Ashton				J.O'Neill			
W.J.Boston				D.Leatherbarrow			
M.Sullivan	T			W.Wookey			
D.R.Bolton				H.Archer			
R.Thomas				J.Roper			
J.T.Barton	T			N.Herbert			
W.Sayer				H.Eden			
B.McTigue	T			A.Key			
N.Cherrington				B.Edgar			
F.Collier				C.T.Thompson			
B.McGurrin				J.B.Eve			

Lance Todd Trophy: R.Thomas

Referee: R.Gelder (Wakefield)   *Half-time: 10-7*
Attendance: 66,109   *Receipts: £33,175*

Cup presented by His Excellency Mr J.H.Whitney, the American Ambassador.

Workington a little hope when he kicked a penalty goal after McTigue had been caught obstructing.

Within ten minutes of the restart, Wigan's Brian McTigue had Town's defence in total disarray as he side-stepped, then dummied his way over for a brilliant try in the corner. The kick was too far out for Cunliffe to convert.

Workington never gave up the fight and Southward landed another penalty goal on the hour. Minutes later, Southwold, always the danger to Wigan, set off on a barnstorming run down the right-hand flank but was caught and tackled by McTigue just as he was diving for the line and Wembley glory.

Wigan celebrate after their six-try victory over Hull in 1959. Back row (left to right): McTigue, Thomas, Barton, Sullivan, Ashton, Bretherton, Sayer, Boston, Evans. In front: Holden, Griffiths, Cherrington, Bolton.

HULL'S first appearance at Wembley and their first Final since 1923 was hardly a memorable one as the supremely confident Wigan simply found the Airlie Birds' shortcomings and then exploited them in a totally ruthless display of attacking football. Some of the Hull flaws were due to an attack of the notorious Wembley nerves but their much-talked about and well-respected set of forwards were far too easily beaten by the Wigan six.

One newspaper commented: *'On reflection perhaps only one thing was surprising – that Wigan gained and held such a dominance as they did forward. This was the result of as fine an example of teamwork as it is possible to imagine.'*

The jewel in the crown of the Wigan pack was Brian McTigue who has an absolutely outstanding game that totally justified him collecting the Lance Todd Trophy for Man of the Match and winning praise from both his own players and those on the Hull side.

Behind the Wigan pack lurked the danger of the shrewd and experienced Rees Thomas, whose wily skills, coupled with the sheer power and pace of Dave Bolton, his half-back partner, were far too much for Hull.

Almost everything went right for Wigan, especially in the first half when a series of movements performed at high speed had the Hull side in complete disorder. Speed, or the lack of it, contributed to Hull's dismal display. Three times in the first half they built overlaps but total lack of pace lost them.

Wigan opened the scoring in the eighth minute when a break by Ashton allowed Holden to side-step the Hull defence and score under the posts. Griffiths landed the goal, and four minutes later Hull's full-back Arthur Keegan kicked a penalty goal. Wigan took control and effectively won the match in a fiery 13-minute spell when they scored three tries. First Mick Sullivan latched on to a well-timed pass from Dave Bolton and sped almost 70 yards for a sensational try. Then Bolton himself ran in a long-range effort, before creating more space for Billy Boston score in the corner. Fred Griffiths, Wigan's South African full-back, kicked all three

Rugby League Cup Results

First Round

Bradford N	2	Huddersfield	11
Bramley	8	Castleford	11
Doncaster	9	Dewsbury	15
Hull	11	Blackpool B	2
Hull KR	3	Widnes	2
Hunslet	55	Kells Rec Centre	9
Leigh	19	Batley	2
Oldham	6	St Helens	7
Rochdale H	9	Halifax	10
Salford	15	Barrow	0
Wakefield T	18	Swinton	2
Warrington	26	Keighley	7
Whitehaven	25	Liverpool C	6
Wigan	12	Leeds	5
Workington T	5	Featherstone R	8
York	54	Astley & Tyldesley Coll	2

Second Round

Hull	4	Wakefield T	4
Hull KR	20	Castleford	0
Leigh	13	Warrington	3
St Helens	35	Dewsbury	8
Salford	15	Huddersfield	2
Whitehaven	2	Halifax	7
Wigan	22	Hunslet	4
York	7	Featherstone R	18

Second Round Replay

Wakefield T	10	Hull	16

Third Round

Featherstone R	20	St Helens	6
Halifax	0	Wigan	26
Hull	23	Hull KR	9
Leigh	6	Salford	6

Third Round Replay

Salford	4	Leigh	6

Semi-finals

Hull	15	Featherstone R	5

At Odsal Stadium, Bradford
Attendance: 52,500   *Receipts: £9,200*

Wigan	5	Leigh	0

At Station Road, Swinton
Attendance: 27,900   *Receipts: £6,068*

Final

Saturday, 9 May at Wembley Stadium, London

	T	G	P		T	G	P
Wigan	6	6	30	**Hull**	1	5	13
W.F.Griffiths		6G		A.Keegan		5G	
W.J.Boston	2T			S.Cowan			
E.Ashton				B.Cooper			
K.Holden	T			B.Saville			
M.Sullivan	T			I.J.Watts			
D.R.Bolton	T			G.A.Matthews			
R.Thomas				T.Finn	T		
W.Bretherton				M.Scott			
W.Sayer				P.T.Harris			
J.T.Barton				G.J.Drake			
N.Cherrington				C.Sykes			
B.McTigue	T			W.D.Drake			
R.Evans				J.W.Whiteley			

Lance Todd Trophy: B.McTigue

Referee: C.F.Appleton (Warrington)

Half-time: 20-4

Attendance: 79,811   *Receipts: £35,718*

Cup presented by HRH The Princess Royal.

---

conversions. Sandwiched between this flurry of activity was a solitary penalty goal from Hull's Arthur Keegan.

The Airlie Birds opened the scoring in the second half when Keegan landed two more penalties, but then McTigue powered over for the Riversiders in the 60th minute. Ten minutes later, Boston scored his second of the match and Griffiths landed two further goals.

With around eight minutes remaining, Jim Drake salvaged some much-needed pride when his strong surge created a small gap in the Wigan defence and scrum-half Finn shot threw the opening to score under the posts. Keegan kicked the goal, the 100th scored in a Challenge Cup Final at Wembley.

1960 Wakefield Trinity 38 Hull 5

The jubilant Wakefield Trinity team carry captain Derek 'Rocky' Turner following their victory over Hull in 1960.

HULL earned the unfortunate distinction of being the first side to lose in successive Wembley Finals when their injury-hit team was trounced by a Wakefield Trinity side that produced a near-perfect display of Rugby League Football.

Hull's injury problems were so severe that the club were without the majority of their regular first-team players and were forced to include 22-year-old Mike Smith, a second-row forward who made his first-team debut in the Final at Wembley. Yet despite their difficulties, the Airlie Birds were by far the better side in the first half and led superbly by their hooker Tom Harris, tore into Trinity's far more experienced side. Wakefield seemed to be overawed by the occasion and although they were inspired by a brilliant individual try from Ken Rollin in the third minute, they were very reluctant to open play out.

Hull hit back and scored their only points of the game when Stan Cowan burst between his own half-backs after a scrum and Broadhurst flicked a clever back pass to him to fool the Wakefield defence and put the centre over for a well-

worked try which Evans converted. The Hull injury curse struck again when it was discovered, after the game, that Cowans had broken a rib in the act of scoring the try.

Two minutes after the Hull try, Fox restored Trinity's lead with a well-struck penalty goal. And ten minutes before the break, Hull suffered another dreadful setback when their captain, Tommy Harris, was injured in a tackle and left the field, suffering from what was later discovered to be severe concussion. Harris returned to the action but finally left the game for good with about 15 minutes remaining. His courage and the major part he played in the game earned him the Lance Todd Trophy.

Five minutes into the second half, Wakefield's backs cut loose in brilliant fashion and Fox crossed for a try. It was the beginning of a series of movements that at first completely baffled and then simply demoralised the injury-ravaged Hull side. Trinity's second-half display prompted this newspaper comment: *'It is doubtful if any side, even at full strength, could have contained them. Had they played such brilliant open*

Rugby League Cup Results

First Round

Barrow	2	Whitehaven	8
Batley	2	Keighley	5
Blackpool B	2	Leigh	10
Castleford	4	Bradford N	8
Dewsbury	4	Swinton	23
Doncaster	0	Rochdale H	15
Hunslet	5	Wigan	9
Leeds	8	Hull KR	5
Liverpool C	3	Bramley	3
Oldham	13	Huddersfield	11
Salford	0	Halifax	5
St Helens	10	Wakefield T	15
Walney Central	10	Lock Lane	5
Widnes	14	Warrington	0
Workington T	0	Featherstone R	15
York	0	Hull	2

First Round Replay

Bramley	39	Liverpool C	0

Second Round

Halifax	10	Featherstone R	16
Keighley	2	Hull	32
Leigh	8	Whitehaven	11
Oldham	55	Walney Central	4
Rochdale H	0	Bramley	4
Swinton	13	Bradford N	9
Widnes	2	Wakefield T	5
Wigan	14	Leeds	11

Third Round

Hull	12	Wigan	8
Oldham	8	Bramley	2
Swinton	7	Featherstone R	11
Whitehaven	10	Wakefield T	21

Semi-finals

Hull	12	Oldham	9

At Station Road, Swinton
Attendance: 27,592   *Receipts: £6,097*

Wakefield T	11	Featherstone R	2

At Odsal Stadium, Bradford
Attendance: 55,800   *Receipts: £10,348*

Final

Saturday, 14 May at Wembley Stadium, London

	T	G	P		T	G	P
Wakefield T	8	7	38	**Hull**	1	1	5
G.V.Round				J.Kershaw			
F.Smith	T			G.R.Harrison			
A.Skene	2T			S.Cowan	T		
N.Fox	2T	7G		N.Halifihi			
J.Etty				D.Johnson			
K.Rollin	T			F.Broadhurst			
K.Holliday	2T			T.Finn			
J.Wilkinson				M.Scott			
G.Oakes				P.T.Harris			
D.G.Vines				S.Evans		G	
L.Chamberlain				T.Sutton			
A.Firth				M.Smith			
D.Turner				J.W.Whiteley			

Lance Todd Trophy: P.T.Harris

Referee: E.Clay (Rothwell)   *Half-time: 7-5*
Attendance: 79,773   *Receipts: £35,754*

Cup presented by HM The Queen.

---

football throughout, imagination boggles at what the score might have been.'

Trinity's South African centre, Alan Skene, crossed in the 49th minute, a try which Fox failed to convert, and then scored another try a quarter of an hour later. Sandwiched between these scores was a try from Keith Holliday and a conversion from Neil Fox. In the final eight minutes, Trinity rattled up 15 points when Holliday, Smith and Fox scored tries and Fox landed three more goals to bring his own points tally up to 20.

1961 St Helens 12 Wigan 6

Vince Karalius (with Cup) and the St Helens side celebrate their 1961 victory over rivals Wigan.

WIGAN made a record seventh appearance at Wembley and a huge crowd of just under 95,000 packed the Empire Stadium to witness the all Lancashire encounter with deadly rivals St Helens.

Brilliant sunshine and searing heat, coupled with the strength of both defences, prevented a fine open game but the match did produce some spasmodic bouts of good football and thrilling movements.

The temperature of around 75 degrees affected both sides, especially the heavier Wigan forwards who were visibly wilting towards the end of the game.

Wigan opened the scoring in the fourth minute when Griffiths kicked a penalty goal when Alex Murphy had been caught offside. After half an hour's play, Karalius burst through the Wigan defensive line and passed to Dick Huddart, who, as always, was by his side. Huddart beat two

men then transferred to Murphy who sprinted through the huge gap created to score a well-worked try. Full-back Rhodes missed the conversion but landed a long-range penalty just before the half-time break.

Trailing by three points at half-time, Wigan stormed into attack from the start of the second half like, as one newspaper commented, *'An enraged bull determined to get the better of the tormenting matador.'*

Wingman Canton raced over the line for a 'try' but was called back because an earlier pass from Bolton to Bootle was adjudged forward. The pressure paid off when Griffiths kicked a penalty goal to leave the Riversiders only one point adrift. Within minutes the ball was worked across to Billy Boston who, head down and in full flight, hurtled towards the line, leaving a trail of bruised and battered defenders behind. A last desperate attempted tackle caught Boston and

Rugby League Cup Results

First Round

Batley	9	Bradford N	0
Bramley	5	Rochdale H	6
Dewsbury Celtic	0	Castleford	32
Doncaster	0	Warrington	39
Huddersfield	8	Liverpool C	2
Hull	4	Oldham	2
Hull KR	56	Pilkington Rec	8
Hunslet	0	Halifax	8
Keighley	5	Featherstone R	11
Leeds	5	Wigan	5
Leigh	6	Swinton	8
St Helens	5	Widnes	5
Salford	22	Dewsbury	8
Wakefield T	11	York	3
Whitehaven	8	Blackpool B	3
Workington T	9	Barrow	5

The Dewsbury Celtic game was played at Dewsbury.

First Round Replays

Widnes	10	St Helens	29
Wigan	32	Leeds	7

Second Round

Castleford	10	St Helens	18
Hull	16	Hull KR	3
Rochdale H	9	Whitehaven	2
Salford	13	Huddersfield	5
Swinton	11	Batley	2
Wakefield T	0	Wigan	2
Warrington	10	Featherstone R	13
Workington T	0	Halifax	4

Third Round

Halifax	18	Rochdale H	5
Hull	10	Featherstone R	9
St Helens	17	Swinton	9
Wigan	22	Salford	5

Semi-finals

St Helens	26	Hull	9

At Odsal Stadium, Bradford
Attendance: 42,074   *Receipts: £9,230*

Wigan	19	Halifax	10

At Station Road, Swinton
Attendance: 35,398   *Receipts: £7,557*

Final

Saturday, 13 May at Wembley Stadium, London

	T	G	P		T	G	P
St Helens	2	3	12	**Wigan**	0	3	6
A.J.Rhodes		3G		F.Griffiths		3G	
K.T.Van Vollenhoven	T			W.J.Boston			
K.Large				E.Ashton			
J.B.McGinn				C.Bootle			
M.Sullivan				F.Carlton			
A.J.Murphy	T			D.R.Bolton			
W.Smith				T.W.Entwistle			
A.E.Terry				J.T.Barton			
R.Dagnall				W.Sayer			
C.H.Watson				B.McTigue			
D.G.Vines				F.Collier			
R.Huddart				G.Lyon			
V.P.P.Karalius				R.Evans			

Lance Todd Trophy: R.Huddart

Referee: T.W.Watkinson (Swinton)   *Half-time: 5-2*
Attendance: 94,672   *Receipts: £38,479*

Cup presented by Lord Derby.

---

just as he was about to touch down and he stumbled and staggered into the corner flag. It was to be Wigan's last serious assault on the Saints' line.

In the 63rd minute Sayer spilled the ball almost on the Saints' line and involuntary set up one of Wembley's classic tries. The loose ball was snapped up and whipped out to Tom Van Vollenhoven, the South African speedster, who was waiting on the wing. Vollenhoven's initial acceleration took him past Collier and he sped 30 yards upfield to face the advancing Griffiths. A quick inside pass to his supporting centre, Ken Large, took the pair past the danger and hurtling, side by side, deeper into the Wigan half. Boston and Ashton raced across to cover but as Ashton tackled Large, the centre flicked the ball back to Vollenhoven who swept over the line and grounded it behind the posts for Rhodes to add the two points to a memorable try.

The try, in effect, ended the contest, Rhodes and Griffiths each kicked a penalty to make the final score 12-6 to St Helens.

Wakefield Trinity's Geoff Oakes attempts to break free of three Huddersfield defenders during the 1962 Final.

WAKEFIELD made it a hat-trick of Wembley victories in a hard but not particularly good Final. Trinity were by far the better side and although beaten for possession from the scrums, they showed far more method in their play and were the quicker and more forceful side. They also had the brilliant skills of Neil Fox, the 22-year-old international who was outstanding, but irregular, with his goal-kicking. The Lance Todd Trophy winner missed all place-kicks attempted but landed three drop-goals. One newspaper wrote of the centre's performance: *'Fox not only was, considering the place and the occasion, remarkably calm when making his drops at goal but had the thrust and a strong hand off which helped considerably towards making the first inroads into Huddersfield's tightly knit defence.'*

In the forwards Briggs had a great game, his clever little forays forward created havoc in the heart of the Huddersfield defence and tremendous openings for his backs. Huddersfield were never very convincing but were far from disgraced. The

Fartowners were beaten everywhere for pace but squandered much of their hard-won possession by playing down the middle of the field, constantly turning the ball inside, more often than not to a forward. Frank Dyson, the Huddersfield full-back, had a nightmare afternoon with his usually reliable goal-kicking, missing everything he attempted.

Fox opened the scoring with a clever drop-kick after 17 minutes and three minutes later, following some ingenious inter-passing with Kenny Hirst, he scored Wakefield's first try. Both scores were made with captain Derek Turner off the field receiving treatment for concussion. Turner returned to the game after ten minutes but was never his usual commanding self.

Huddersfield kept plugging away at Wakefield's defence and, aided by the majority of the possession, never gave in. Their persistence finally paid off when some quick passing gave the ball to Smales who rounded full-back Gerry Round with ease to score a try. Dyson failed with the conversion

Rugby League Cup Results

First Round

Barrow	14	Whitehaven	3
Blackpool B	18	Liverpool C	2
Brookhouse	4	Doncaster	7
Castleford	12	Bradford N	0
Dewsbury	5	Halifax	3
Featherstone R	21	Batley	14
Hunslet	53	St Annes	10
Keighley	3	Wigan	25
Leeds	34	Bramley	6
Oldham	32	Hull	16
Salford	2	St Helens	15
Swinton	0	Hull KR	2
Wakefield T	40	Warrington	18
Widnes	3	Leigh	13
Workington T	14	Rochdale H	2
York	7	Huddersfield	8

Second Round

Blackpool B	4	Wakefield T	16
Castleford	27	Hunslet	14
Featherstone R	14	Doncaster	2
Hull KR	14	Barrow	5
Leigh	7	Leeds	7
Oldham	0	Workington T	5
St Helens	2	Huddersfield	13
Wigan	50	Dewsbury	2

Second Round Replay

Leeds	16	Leigh	17

Third Round

Castleford	4	Huddersfield	4
Featherstone R	23	Leigh	9
Wakefield T	5	Wigan	4
Workington T	3	Hull KR	15

Third Round Replay

Huddersfield	10	Castleford	4

Semi-finals

Huddersfield	6	Hull KR	0

At Odsal Stadium, Bradford
Attendance: 31,153   Receipts: £6,681

Wakefield T	9	Featherstone R	0

At Odsal Stadium, Bradford
Attendance: 43,627   Receipts: £8,023

Final

Saturday, 12 May at Wembley Stadium, London

	T	G	P		T	G	P
Wakefield T	2	3	12	**Huddersfield**	2	0	6
G.Round				F.Dyson			
F.Smith				A.M.Breen			
A.Skene				L.Booth			
N.Fox	T	3G		R.Haywood			
K.Hirst	T			M.W.Wicks			
H.Poynton				H.Deighton			
K.Holliday				T.Smales	T		
J.Wilkinson				E.Slevin			
G.Oakes				D.Close			
A.Firth				K.Noble			
B.Briggs				M.Clark			
D.Williamson				K.D.Bowman			
D.Turner				P.Ramsden	T		

Lance Todd Trophy: N.Fox

Referee: D.T.H.Davies (Manchester)

Half-time: 5-3

Attendance: 81,263   *Receipts: £33,390*

Cup presented by Earl Alexander of Tunis.

---

attempt and minutes later missed what should have been, for him, an easy kick at goal from a penalty.

In the 63rd minute Fox extended Trinity's lead with a superb drop-goal after taking a well-timed pass from Turner. A minute later Kenny Hirst completely wrong-footed Dyson with a clever side-step to score Wakefield's second try. Fox missed the goal-kick and later hit the post with a penalty attempt.

Still Huddersfield refused to concede defeat and, with Hirst off the field receiving treatment to an injured leg, they scored a try when Smales passed to Ramsden. But it was far too late for gallant Huddersfield and with a minute remaining, Turner passed to Fox who dropped his third goal to give Wakefield a 12-6 victory.

WAKEFIELD were making their third Wembley appearance in four years but it was Wigan who were installed as favourites to take the trophy, the critics pointing to their full strength side and excellent team spirit.

Wakefield simply ignored the pre-match predictions and played a brilliant game founded on superb team work. They weathered the Riversiders' fierce attacks in the first half with some solid defensive work, then composed themselves for their own assaults on the Wigan line. When they did launch their offensive, Wigan found it impossible to cope with the precision passing and high-speed movements of the Trinity backs and with Harold Poynton playing a tremendous game alongside his half-back partner Keith Holliday, the Riversiders looked a tired and lethargic side. Poynton's display of skill, craft and solid tackling earned him the Lance Todd Trophy for Man of the Match.

Trinity opened the scoring in the 38th minute when prop forward Dave Sampson crossed the line for a try which Neil Fox converted. Within seconds of the score, Wigan were dealt a terrible blow when Dave Bolton, the full-back, was badly concussed and had to carried from the field. Bolton's injuries were so severe that he failed to return for the start of the second half, eventually coming on almost 20 minutes into the game. During his absence Wigan hit back with a tremendous try from scrum-half Frank Pitchford in the very first minute of the second period.

The 1963 kings of Wembley, Wakefield Trinity, and their captain Derek Turner celebrate their third Challenge Cup Final win in four years.

Rugby League Cup Results

First Round

Barrow	7	Workington T	16
Blackpool B	12	Dewsbury	0
Castleford	8	Leeds	10
Featherstone R	32	Batley	2
Halifax	9	St Helens	2
Huddersfield	10	Whitehaven	11
Hull	0	Wigan	7
Hull KR	6	Keighley	5
Leigh	10	Oldham	18
Liverpool C	11	Roose	0
Rochdale H	3	Hunslet	16
Salford	11	York	29
Swinton	6	Widnes	6
Wakefield T	15	Bradford N	3
Warrington	15	Doncaster	2
York Imperial	4	Bramley	15

First Round Replay

Widnes	3	Swinton	3

First Round Second Replay

Widnes	6	Swinton	4
At Hilton Park, Leigh			

Second Round

Blackpool B	12	York	16
Bramley	9	Warrington	17
Halifax	3	Hunslet	16
Hull KR	12	Featherstone R	2
Wakefield T	14	Liverpool C	12
Widnes	5	Whitehaven	0
Wigan	20	Leeds	11
Workington T	0	Oldham	13

Third Round

Oldham	0	Wigan	18
Warrington	7	Hunslet	5
Widnes	7	Hull KR	10
York	9	Wakefield T	9

Third Round Replay

Wakefield T	25	York	11

Semi-finals

Wakefield T	5	Warrington	2
At Station Road, Swinton			
Attendance: 15,566		*Receipts: £3,530*	
Wigan	18	Hull KR	4
At Headingley, Leeds			
Attendance: 21,479		*Receipts: £6,024*	

Final

Saturday, 11 May at Wembley Stadium, London

	T	G	P		T	G	P
Wakefield T	5	5	25	**Wigan**	2	2	10
G.V.Round				D.R.Bolton			
C.Greenwood				W.J.Boston			
I.Brooke	T			E.Ashton		2G	
N.Fox		5G		A.Davies			
G.Coetzer	2T			F.Carlton	T		
H.Poynton	T			S.McLeod			
K.Holliday				F.Pitchford	T		
J.Wilkinson				J.T.Barton			
M.Kosanovic				W.Sayer			
M.Sampson	T			B.McTigue			
D.G.Vines				F.Collier			
D.Turner				C.Lyon			
R.Pearman				R.Evans			

Lance Todd Trophy: H.Poynton

Referee: D.T.H.Davies (Manchester)

Half-time: 5-0

Attendance: 84,492   *Receipts: £44,521*

Cup presented by Field-Marshal the Rt Hon Viscount Montgomery of Alamein.

From then on Wigan visibly wilted, gone was the almost telepathic understanding of their forwards and with it their enthusiasm in loose play. Wakefield's forwards, led admirably by Turner, Wilkinson and Vines, punched some remarkable holes in the Riversiders' first line of defence and behind them Poynton and Holliday began to take control.

In the 50th minute Gert 'Oupa' Coetzer, Trinity's South African wingman, sped half the length of the field for a glorious try in the corner which the ever-reliable Fox converted to extend Wakefield's lead to seven points.

Eric Ashton pulled back two points with a penalty-goal but two minutes later the boot of Fox cancelled it out when he landed a penalty. Ashton reduced the lead again with another penalty in the 65th minute. Three minutes later, however, the ubiquitous Poynton delivered the killer blow. A still groggy Bolton made a half-break on the right-hand side and passed inside to Ashton, but the ever-attentive Poynton snatched the ball in mid-air and sprinted over the line completely unopposed.

Wigan hit back with a brave try from wingman Frank Collier but in reality the match as a contest was over. Wakefield scored eight points in the final three minutes when first Coetzer, then 20-year-old Ian Brooke scored tries and Neil Fox landed his fifth goal of the match.

Widnes, pictured with the Cup in 1964, back at their Naughton Park home.

WEMBLEY debutants and pre-match favourites, Hull Kingston Rovers were beaten by a Widnes side that was both tactically and technically superior. Widnes looked confident and relaxed, but Hull KR seemed to be tense and their play often vague and lacking direction. The Chemics pack laid the foundations for the victory, winning a commanding amount of possession in the scrums and, eventually, gaining the upper hand in the loose play.

Frank Collier, who had played at Wembley the previous season for Wigan, was the pick of the Widnes six, his strong surges into the Rovers pack earning the prop forward the Lance Todd Trophy.

Loose forward and captain Vince Karalius was also at his awesome best, his ability to entice men into a tackle and then release the ball to a supporting colleague one of the many tactics that proved crucial to the Widnes victory. At half-back Owen and Lowe were outstanding, linking the force up front to the pace of centres Myler and Briers with a clever blend of speed and constant changes of direction.

Inability to win enough of the ball was a huge handicap to Hull Kingston, whose forwards appeared to lose heart towards the end of the game while the backs had not enough chances to set in motion their variety of set-piece movements. However, when the backs did have the ball, they were too cumbersome, passing across the line far too slowly

and without the drive needed to beat the Chemics' resolute defence. Rovers were far from their best and towards the end they played as if they knew it.

From the kick-off Widnes searched hard and often for any gaps in the Rovers' defence, but just as they had done in the earlier rounds they were content to bide their time until they thought the opportunities were there. The softening-up process continued for the whole of the 40 minutes, the only score being a penalty goal from Bob Randall when Hull Kingston were penalised for 'foot up' in a scrum after 35 minutes.

In the seventh minute of the second half, Widnes finally broke through when Measures created enough space to pass to Owen and send him careering through a gap, only to be hauled down on the line by Palmer. Rovers made a mess of clearing their line and Karalius whipped a clever pass to Briers who crashed through two men and side-stepped Palmer to score. Randall converted the try.

Five minutes later they struck again when Hurstfield and Hughes interpassed well and Myler surged through a huge hole in the defence to score a fine try which Randall converted. Hull Kingston scored a good consolation try when Burwell raced clear from a scrum but Widnes had the last word when Collier burst over from a play the ball with two minutes remaining.

Rugby League Cup Results

First Round

Barrow	11	Dewsbury	6
Blackpool B	25	Doncaster	2
Featherstone R	60	Stanningley	4
Halifax	0	Batley	3
Hull KR	12	Rochdale H	12
Hunslet	4	Wakefield T	4
Keighley	4	Oldham	11
Leigh	2	Widnes	2
Liverpool C	3	Huddersfield	0
St Helens	6	Castleford	13
Salford	10	Leeds	6
Whitehaven	7	Hull	4
Wigan	15	Swinton	15
Workington T	21	Warrington	3
York	5	Bramley	2

Bye: Thames Board Mills.

First Round Replays

Rochdale H	7	Hull KR	22
Wakefield T	7	Hunslet	14
Widnes	11	Leigh	11
Swinton	13	Wigan	8

First Round Second Replay

Widnes	14	Leigh	2

At Knowsley Road, St Helens.

Second Round

Batley	6	Hunslet	14
Blackpool B	48	Thames Board Mills	8
Oldham	9	Featherstone R	7
Salford	4	Barrow	10
Whitehaven	5	Castleford	29
Widnes	16	Liverpool C	6
Workington T	3	Swinton	11
York	7	Hull KR	23

Third Round

Blackpool B	4	Castleford	25
Hull KR	38	Barrow	4
Hunslet	5	Oldham	7
Widnes	5	Swinton	5

Third Round Replay

Swinton	0	Widnes	0

Third Round Second Replay

Widnes	15	Swinton	3

At Central Park, Wigan

Semi-finals

Hull KR	5	Oldham	5

At Headingley, Leeds
Attendance: 28,556 *Receipts: £7,402*

Widnes	7	Castleford	7

At Station Road, Swinton
Attendance: 25,602 *Receipts: £5,541*

Semi-final Replays

Hull KR	14	Oldham	17

At Station Road, Swinton
Attendance: 27,209 *Receipts: £5,929*
(Abandoned after 12 minutes extra-time)

Widnes	7	Castleford	5

At Belle Vue, Wakefield
Attendance: 28,732 *Receipts: £5,309*

Semi-final Second Replay

Hull KR	12	Oldham	2

At Fartown, Huddersfield
Attendance: 32,757 *Receipts: £6,153*

Final

Saturday, 9 May at Wembley Stadium, London

	T	G	P		T	G	P
Widnes	**3**	**2**	**13**	**Hull Kingston R**	**1**	**1**	**5**
R.J.Randall		2G		C.Kellett		G	
R.Chisnall				G.Paul			
A.Briers	T			T.Major			
F.Myler	T			D.Elliott			
W.Thompson				M.Blackmore			
G.Lowe				A.Burwell	T		
R.Owen				A.Bunting			
W.Hurstfield				B.Tyson			
G.Kemel				P.J.Flanagan			
F.Collier	T			B.Mennell			
J.Measures				E.Palmer			
A.Hughes				L.Clark			
V.P.P.Karalius				H.Poole			

Lance Todd Trophy: F.Collier

Referee: R.L.Thomas (Oldham) *Half-time: 2-0*
Attendance: 84,488 *Receipts: £44,840*

Cup presented by the Earl of Derby.

Wigan centre, Keith Holden, dives past Gabbitas and Lee for the opening try of the 1965 Final.

'EIGHTY minutes of excellent, fast, open football with only four points between the sides at the end of them. Such was the outcome of the best Rugby League Challenge Cup Final seen at Wembley for many years.'

That is how one contemporary match report described the game that is still regarded as one of the greatest-ever Wembley Finals.

In the days leading up to the match, the general belief was the pace, power and class of Wigan, coupled with the fact that the open spaces of the Empire Stadium would be just too much for Hunslet to cope with. The south Leeds club and its home-grown players did have one ally. Ramon Joyce, writing in *The Rugby Leaguer*, observed: *'I believe the Parksiders are a far better footballing side than they give themselves credit for and if given a chance to show their attacking skill Wigan and the spectators could be in for a thrilling surprise.'*

At Wembley the high drama and pulsating action began after only 33 seconds when Wigan's Laurie Gilfedder landed a penalty-kick from the half-way line following Marchant's kick-off straight into touch. Two minutes later, Hunslet equalised with a 45-yard penalty from full-back Billy Langton.

Hunslet's Welsh wingman Griffiths had a try disallowed when he put a foot into touch, and then Wigan struck with a superb try from Keith Holden after Gilfedder and Ray Ashby

had prised open a gap. The conversion attempt was missed, and then Langton clawed back the score to 5-4 with another well-struck penalty.

Gilfedder landed a further penalty and, moments later, the Riversiders backs combined as they had threatened to do, and Trevor Lake swept in at the corner. Wigan seemed to be cruising to an easy victory when a superb Brian Gabbitas pass sent Shelton crashing through two would-be tacklers and over the line for a great try. Langton kicked the goal and Hunslet were back in the game.

Wigan began the second half in storming fashion, anxious to wrap the game up as soon as possible. First Gilfedder raced 45 yards for a try which Ashby converted, then Ashby himself scooped up a ball, sped half the length of the pitch before passing to Lake who, despite a last-gasp effort from Griffiths, swallow-dived in at the corner for a spectacular try.

Twenty points to nine with 20 minutes remaining, Wigan were almost there. But, Hunslet were still not beaten and Denis Hartley fed Griffiths a quick, short ball and the winger cut inside and through Ashby's tackle to score a well-worked try. Langton kicked the conversion and then, with four minutes to go, landed a penalty to put Hunslet only four points behind. But Wigan held on and were themselves pressing the Hunslet line when the final whistle blew.

Rugby League Cup Results

First Round

Blackpool B	27	Crosfield	4
Dewsbury	2	Wakefield T	11
Doncaster	4	Whitehaven	5
Featherstone R	24	York	7
Halifax	17	Rochdale H	12
Huddersfield	5	Bramley	20
Hull KR	5	Batley	7
Hunslet	12	Oldham	4
Keighley	8	Salford	11
Leeds	19	Liverpool C	6
Leigh	6	Bradford N	7
St Helens	22	Castleford	9
Swinton	48	Dewsbury Celtic	5
Warrington	7	Hull	4
Widnes	2	Workington T	2
Wigan	16	Barrow	0

Crosfield gave up ground advantage.

First Round Replay

Workington T	2	Widnes	0

Second Round

Blackpool B	5	Whitehaven	2
Bradford N	7	Wakefield T	10
Featherstone R	2	Swinton	9
Hunslet	24	Batley	4
Leeds	13	Bramley	9
Warrington	16	Salford	2
Wigan	7	St Helens	2
Workington T	18	Halifax	5

Third Round

Hunslet	7	Leeds	5
Wakefield T	4	Blackpool B	0
Warrington	10	Swinton	11
Workington T	4	Wigan	10

Semi-finals

Hunslet	8	Wakefield T	0

At Headingley, Leeds
Attendance: 21,262   *Receipts: £6,208*

Wigan	25	Swinton	10

At Knowsley Road, St Helens
Attendance: 26,658   *Receipts: £6,384*

Final

Saturday, 8 May at Wembley Stadium, London

	T	G	P		T	G	P
Wigan	4	4	20	**Hunslet**	2	5	16
R.Ashby				H.W.Langton		5G	
W.J.Boston				J.Griffiths	T		
E.Ashton		G		G.Shelton	T		
K.Holden	T			A.Preece			
T.Lake	2T			B.Lee			
C.J.Hill				B.L.Gabbitas			
F.Parr				A.Marchant			
R.B.Gardiner				K.Eyre			
C.Clarke				B.Prior			
B.McTigue				D.Hartley			
A.Stephens				G.Gunney			
R.Evans				W.Ramsey			
L.Gilfedder	T 3G			F.Ward			

Lance Todd Trophy: Shared by R.Ashby and B.L.Gabbitas

Referee: J.Manley (Warrington)   Half-time: 12-9
Attendance: 89,016   Receipts: £48,080

Cup presented by HRH Princess Alexandra.

THE meeting of the two great Lancashire rivals on Wembley's hallowed turf was a mouth-watering prospect and it was expected that the game would produce a rousing struggle and one of the classic Finals. Alas as a spectacle the match was a great disappointment, prompting *The Guardian* to comment: *'The game was not a fine struggle, it was so poor it might even have been declared "no contest" by a boxing referee. Indeed, though it was never quite like watching the tortoise and the hare, the comparison in the circumstances is not too exaggerated.'*

Wigan were without regular hooker Colin Clarke, who was suspended, and had drafted utility forward Tom Woosey into the specialist position, a fact noticed by Alex Murphy and Tommy Bishop, the Saints' clever tacticians. Both players knew that every time a penalty was kicked into touch, a scrum would be formed and without an expert hooker Wigan would struggle to win precious possession of the ball.

In the first half the two persistently strayed offside at set-piece play-the-balls, much to the annoyance of Wigan and the majority of the huge crowd. Their ploy worked well, for the St Helens hooker, Bill Sayer, shovelled the ball out of two-thirds of the scrums, giving his side a clear advantage. With the possession Sayer gained, Saints created problems galore for the Wigan defence. Ray French, in the second row, ran with strength and purpose throughout and props

Halsall and Watson punched huge holes in the Riversiders' defences.

Wigan were dreadfully disappointing. Their attack had little spirit or determination and their defence was feeble with little co-ordination. Trevor Lake tried well throughout the game and Ashby and Parr did well in parts, but it was a display which on Wigan's normal standards was hard to believe.

Len Killeen opened the scoring with a penalty in the fourth minute and then six minutes later he kicked another from five yards inside his own half and ten yards from touch. In the 17th minute Saints loose forward John Mantle crashed over the line after he had brushed aside some flimsy attempted tackles by Lake and Ashby. Killeen landed the extra two points and then Gilfedder kicked a penalty to give Wigan their only points of the game.

St Helens returned for the second half brimming with confidence and soon increased their lead when Killeen kicked a penalty with only four minutes played. The South African winger, who collected the Lance Todd Trophy, was on the score sheet again when he crossed for a try, but missed the conversion. With around ten minutes to go, Bishop jinked over for a try, which Killeen converted and then with two minutes remaining Alex Murphy had the final say when he dropped a clever goal.

St Helens with the Cup at Knowsley Road. Back row (left to right): Coslett, Sayer, Dagnall, Watson, Warlow, Mantle, Barrow, Hitchen. In front: Halsall, Benyon, Bishop, Barrow, Van Vollenhoven, French, Harvey, Prosser, Killeen.

Rugby League Cup Results

First Round

Barrow	11	Crosfield Recreation	2
Batley	4	Huddersfield	4
Blackpool B	2	Workington T	16
Bradford N	23	Doncaster	2
Bramley	5	Hull KR	5
Featherstone R	22	Rochdale H	6
Hull	11	Salford	2
Hunslet	7	Whitehaven	9
Keighley	4	Dewsbury	5
Leeds	17	York	4
Leigh	15	Liverpool C	6
Swinton	18	Oldham	5
Wakefield T	0	St Helens	10
Warrington	15	Castleford	7
Widnes	23	Brookhouse	5
Wigan	8	Halifax	4

First Round Replays

Huddersfield	23	Batley	5
Hull KR	7	Bramley	2

Second Round

Dewsbury	23	Barrow	15
Featherstone R	14	Warrington	15
Huddersfield	8	Leigh	0
Leeds	22	Hull	12
St Helens	16	Swinton	4
Widnes	6	Bradford N	7
Wigan	40	Whitehaven	6
Workington T	5	Hull KR	7

Third Round

Bradford N	6	Wigan	15
Dewsbury	8	Huddersfield	2
St Helens	12	Hull KR	10
Warrington	2	Leeds	2

Third Round Replay

Leeds	8	Warrington	0

Semi-finals

St Helens 12 Dewsbury
At Station Road, Swinton
Attendance: 13,046 *Receipts: £3,102*

Wigan 7 Leeds 2
At Fartown, Huddersfield
Attendance: 22,758 *Receipts: £5,971*

Final

Saturday, 21 May at Wembley Stadium, London

	T	G	P		T	G	P
St Helens	3	6	21	**Wigan**	0	1	2
F.Barrow				R.Ashby			
T.K.Van Vollenhoven				W.J.Boston			
A.J.Murphy		G		D.Stephens			
W.Benyon				E.Ashton			
L.M.A.Killeen	T	5G		T.Lake			
P.Harvey				C.Hill			
T.Bishop	T			F.Parr			
A.Halsall				R.B.Gardiner			
W.Sayer				T.Woosey			
C.H.Watson				B.McTigue			
R.French				A.Stephens			
D.J.Warlow				L.Gilfedder		G	
J.Mantle	T			H.Major			

Lance Todd Trophy: L.M.A.Killeen

Referee: H.G.Hunt (Prestbury) *Half-time: 9-2*
Attendance: 98,536 *Receipts: £50,409*

Cup presented by the Prime Minister, The Rt Hon Harold Wilson OBE MP.

1967 Featherstone Rovers 17 Barrow 12

Featherstone Rovers with the Cup at Post Office Road in 1967.

FEATHERSTONE Rovers won the Cup for the first time in their history in a fast, fluid game which had plenty of variety and excitement. Barrow were favourites to take the trophy after finishing five places above Featherstone in the League with a clear nine points between the sides.

Rovers started nervously and it seemed the vast stadium and sheer occasion would prove to be too much for them. They controlled their nerves well, however, and after a shaky 20 minutes they began to take command of the game.

Featherstone's tactics were simple: they had to ensure that Brophy, the Barrow scrum-half and former English Rugby Union international, had little room to manoeuvre and control the Shipbuilders' attack. The other danger to Featherstone was the pace of Burgess and Murray, the two Barrow wingmen.

Despite looking decidedly nervous from the kick-off, Rovers took the lead as early as the second minute when Tommy Smales landed a 45-yard penalty-kick. Nine minutes later Barrow drew level when Delooze kicked a penalty-goal. After a quarter of an hour's play, Tom Brophy showed his class and accelerated around the Featherstone cover to score a fine try which Delooze converted to give the Shipbuilders a 7-2 lead.

The try against them spurred Rovers on and on the half-hour Arnold Morgan powered his vast 18st frame over the line for a try which Smales converted to bring Featherstone back on level points. A minute later Carl Dooler dropped a spectacular goal from 40 yards to put Rovers in a 9-7 lead.

Early in the second half Barrow were storming towards the Rovers line when scrum-half Ged Smith threw a poor pass in the general direction of Murray. The ball fell short and the Barrow wingman hesitated just long enough for Vaughan Thomas to react first, scoop up the loose ball and sprint almost the length of the pitch to score a fine try. Smales landed the conversion in front of the posts with ease and Featherstone were 14-7 in front.

In the 64th minute Carl Dooler exploded through a huge gap left after Burgess, the Barrow wing, had been caught hopelessly out of position on the opposite flank. The Featherstone scrum-half made just enough ground before transferring the ball to Smales, who darted over for a try. Smales failed to convert his own try but Rovers were almost home and dry with a 17-7 lead.

In the last minute, Barrow's loose forward Mike Watson plunged over for a consolation try which Eddie Tees converted.

Featherstone's surprising victory was a triumph of teamwork and meticulous planning and although no individual player stood out, Carl Dooler, the Rovers scrum-half, was voted the Man of the Match for his outstanding contribution to the victory.

Rugby League Cup Results

First Round

Batley	10	Keighley	6
Blackbrook	12	York	23
Bradford N	8	Featherstone R	15
BOCM	9	Liverpool C	20
Dewsbury	9	Workington T	5
Doncaster	14	Bramley	11
Huddersfield	7	Oldham	12
Hull	24	Halifax	11
Hull KR	18	Rochdale H	2
Hunslet	2	Wakefield T	28
Leeds	15	Blackpool B	3
Leigh	8	Castleford	10
Salford	5	St Helens	5
Swinton	16	Widnes	7
Warrington	19	Wigan	19
Whitehaven	2	Barrow	8

First Round Replays

St Helens	3	Salford	8
Wigan	20	Warrington	3

Second Round

Barrow	8	Liverpool C	4
Batley	0	Swinton	22
Doncaster	4	Dewsbury	10
Featherstone R	11	Wakefield T	7
Hull KR	9	Castleford	9
Oldham	4	Leeds	13
Wigan	6	Salford	18
York	10	Hull	15

Second Round Replay

Castleford	13	Hull KR	6

Third Round

Dewsbury	9	Salford	7
Featherstone R	8	Castleford	7
Hull	5	Barrow	6
Leeds	17	Swinton	15

Semi-finals

Barrow	14	Dewsbury	9

At Station Road, Swinton
Attendance: 13,744   *Receipts: £4,560*

Featherstone R	16	Leeds	8

At Fartown, Huddersfield
Attendance: 20,052   *Receipts: £6,276*

Final

Saturday, 13 May at Wembley Stadium, London

	T	G	P		T	G	P
Featherstone R	3	4	17	**Barrow**	2	3	12
B.Wrigglesworth				E.Tees		G	
V.Thomas	T			W.Burgess			
K.Cotton				J.Challinor			
G.Jordan				H.Hughes			
K.Greatorex				M.Murray			
M.J.Smith				T.Brophy	T		
C.Dooler		G		G.Smith			
L.Tonks				I.Kelland			
G.Harris				M.Redhead			
M.Dixon				R.Hopwood			
A.Morgan	T			M.Sanderson			
J.Thompson				H.Delooze		2G	
T.Smales	T	3G		M.Watson	T		

Lance Todd Trophy: C.Dooler

Referee: E.Clay (Rothwell)   *Half-time: 9-7*
Attendance: 76,290   *Receipts: £53,465*

Cup presented by HM The Queen.

1968 Leeds 11 Wakefield Trinity 10

Saturated but victorious, Leeds hoist their captain Mick Clarke shoulder high after the most eventful ever Wembley Final, in 1968.

LEEDS collected the trophy for the seventh time in a game that was reduced to pure farce by some of the most bizarre conditions that the Final has ever witnessed.

A heavy rainstorm drenched the famous Wembley turf an hour before the kick-off and despite the attentions of a small army of men armed with garden forks, the pools of water remained as the teams took to the pitch.

It soon became obvious to the players and the vast crowd that the pitch had been reduced to a rain-soddened mess which made it difficult for players to simply stand let alone run or turn.

Unbelievably the sides managed to produce a game that throbbed with excitement and thrills, but hardly ever resembled Rugby League football.

Leeds opened the scoring when full-back Bev Risman kicked a third-minute penalty-goal. Three minutes later Don Fox levelled the scores with a well-struck penalty-goal, and then Risman kicked a further penalty to regain the lead for Leeds.

A few minutes later still, Don Fox hoisted a kick deep into the Loiners' half, John Atkinson moved to collect the ball but slipped and skimmed across the wet surface into touch. Wakefield's Ken Hirst, who had followed the kick upfield, kept his head and balance and dribbled the ball over the line for a try which Fox converted.

Then the heavens opened up and Wembley was lashed with a mixture of torrential rain and hailstones, the whole scene illuminated with sporadic bouts of thunder and lightning. Despite the horrendous conditions, referee Hebblethwaite stuck to his earlier decision and the game continued, scoreless, to half-time.

Play resumed in the same fashion and with ten minutes to go Leeds wingman John Atkinson kicked the ball up over the Wakefield line of defence and set off in pursuit. In the mayhem that followed Atkinson lost his footing and was impeded by several Wakefield players who were trying vainly to keep their feet. Referee Hebblethwaite deemed the actions of the Trinity men illegal and awarded Leeds a penalty try which Risman converted. Two minutes from time Risman landed his fourth goal and seemed as though Leeds were home if not dry.

Rugby League Cup Results

First Round

Barrow	4	Wakefield T	8
Castleford	39	BOCM	6
Dewsbury	2	Bradford N	12
Doncaster	9	Widnes	10
Halifax	24	Leigh Miners Welfare	7
Hull	3	Wigan	10
Hull KR	0	Featherstone R	9
Hunslet	4	Oldham	9
Keighley	7	Batley	2
Leeds	23	Liverpool C	12
Leigh	11	Warrington	5
St Helens	0	Huddersfield	5
Salford	16	Blackpool B	5
Swinton	5	Bramley	13
Workington T	5	Whitehaven	2
York	24	Rochdale H	2

BOCM (Hull) and Leigh Miners Welfare gave up ground advantage.

Second Round

Bradford N	7	Oldham	7
Featherstone R	12	York	0
Halifax	5	Huddersfield	23
Leeds	29	Bramley	0
Leigh	2	Wigan	20
Salford	4	Wakefield T	8
Widnes	5	Keighley	15
Workington T	2	Castleford	7

Second Round Replay

Oldham	12	Bradford N	2

Third Round

Huddersfield	9	Featherstone R	7
Keighley	2	Wigan	11
Oldham	0	Leeds	13
Wakefield T	18	Castleford	5

Semi-finals

Huddersfield	0	Wakefield T	0

At Odsal Stadium, Bradford
Attendance: 21, 569 *Receipts: £6,195*

Leeds	25	Wigan	4

At Station Road, Swinton
Attendance: 30,058 *Receipts: £9,845*

Semi-final Replay

Wakefield T	15	Huddersfield	10

At Headingley, Leeds
Attendance: 20,983 *Receipts: £6,425*

Final

Saturday, 11 May at Wembley Stadium, London

	T	G	P		T	G	P
Leeds	1	4	11	**Wakefield T**	2	2	10
A.B.W.Risman		4G		G.Cooper			
M.A.Smith				K.Hirst	2T		
S.Hynes				I.Brooke			
B.Watson				G.Coetzer			
J.B.Atkinson	T			K.Batty			
M.D.Shoebottom				H.Poynton			
B.Seabourne				R.Owen			
M.Clark				H.D.Jeanes			
A.Crosby				G.Shepherd			
K.Eyre				D.Fox		2G	
W.Ramsey				R.Haigh			
A.Eyre				M.McLeod			
R.Batten				D.Hawley			

Lance Todd Trophy: D Fox

Referee: J.P.Hebblethwaite (York)   *Half-time: 4-7*
Attendance: 87,100   *Receipts: £56,171*

Cup presented by His Royal Highness the Duke of Kent.

The drama, however, continued to the end. From the kick-off, the ball bounced off a Leeds player's foot and the ever-resourceful Hirst was there again, booting the ball over the line and sliding on to it for a last-minute try.

Up stepped Don Fox, who had already been announced as Man of the Match, to finish the job off and take the Cup back to Wakefield. As he shaped to kick, he slipped and the ball bounced harmlessly off his foot.

The words of the BBC commentator, Eddie Waring best sums up the moment: *'He's missed it… poor lad.'*

1969 Castleford 11 Salford 6

AS WAS generally expected, Castleford won the 1969 Challenge Cup with ease, scoring three tries to nil. Salford did well, but their efforts were best summed up by their captain Watkins who said after the game: *"Castleford came at us from the start, knocked us off our game, and then regained their own game quickly, whereas we never did."*

Salford created several chances in the first half and took the lead in the third minute when Hill kicked a penalty after Castleford had been caught stealing the ball in tackle. Minutes later Whitehead took the wrong option when he showed more force than finesse and charged at the Castleford defence instead of passing to the perfectly placed Burgess to his left. He repeated his misguided tactics later, when he once again took the defence on with Brennan, completely unmarked, only 15 yards from the line.

After just over 30 minutes' play, Castleford took the lead when a brilliant break by Malcolm Reilly created an overlap and Keith Howe skipped over the line for a fine try which Redfern failed to convert. Three minutes later, the Red Devils regained the lead when Castleford were penalised for a loose arm in the scrum and Ron Hill kicked the resultant penalty. Then, with three minutes to the interval, Salford's Chris Hesketh grounded the ball over line but had the try disallowed for a double movement.

It was Salford's last real chance of the game. Castleford gradually began to dominate the second half and with a massive sway in the scrums, their forwards soon controlled events. Thirteen minutes into the second half, Malcolm Reilly gathered a wild clearance kick and burst up the field. His surging run took him past several Salford defenders before he passed to Hardisty, who scored under the posts. Redfern kicked the goal and Castleford were four points in the lead.

Six minutes later, Clive Dickinson, the Castleford hooker, was once again caught with his arm loose in a scrum and once again Hill kicked the penalty to give the Reds fresh hope. In the final ten minutes of the game, Castleford pounded at the Salford line until, two minutes from time, Johnny Ward beat three men and, although held, managed to flick a pass to Hepworth who crossed the line for a try.

The victory had a been an all-round team effort based on persistence and fast backing-up, either on attack or defence, of the man with the ball. Malcolm Reilly, the 21-year-old loose forward, won the Man of the Match award for a tremendous display of power play. One reporter commenting: *'Reilly, the Lance Todd winner, really was superb, his burst through broken fields, his determination to fend off tackles and, having done so, his cleverness in getting the ball away contributed to Salford's downfall.'*

Castleford with the Cup at Wheldon Road in 1969.

Rugby League Cup Results

First Round

Blackpool B	10	Bramley	17
Dewsbury	7	Bradford N	21
Doncaster	3	Featherstone R	4
Halifax	12	Leeds	17
Huddersfield	13	Barrow	5
Hull	3	St Helens	13
Hunslet	7	Castleford	19
Keighley	23	Whitehaven	2
Leigh	4	Rochdale H	13
Oldham	12	Hull KR	10
Salford	17	Batley	2
Wakefield T	50	Ackworth	7
Warrington	5	Huyton	2
Widnes	23	York	8
Wigan	61	Leigh Miners	0
Workington T	5	Swinton	2

Huyton gave up ground advantage.

Second Roumd

Bradford N	7	Wakefield T	7
Castleford	12	Wigan	8
Featherstone R	7	Widnes	9
Keighley	2	Leeds	17
Oldham	6	St Helens	15
Rochdale H	7	Bramley	7
Salford	12	Workington T	5
Warrington	19	Huddersfield	8

The Bradford v Wakefield game was played at Leeds.

Second Round Replays

Bramley	4	Rochdale H	7
Wakefield T	10	Bradford N	0

Third Round

Castleford	9	Leeds	5
Salford	20	Widnes	7
Wakefield T	10	Rochdale H	10
Warrington	4	St Helens	2

Third Round Replay

Rochdale H	2	Wakefield T	15

Semi-finals

Castleford	16	Wakefield T	10

At Headingley, Leeds
Attendance: 21,497   Receipts: £8,477

Salford	15	Warrington	8

At Central Park, Wigan
Attendance: 20,600   Receipts: £7,737

Final

Saturday, 17 May at Wembley Stadium, London

	T	G	P		T	G	P
Castleford	3	1	11	**Salford**	0	3	6
D.Edwards				K.W.Gwillian			
T.Briggs				W.Burgess			
K.Howe	T			S.Whitehead			
A.W.Thomas				C.Hesketh			
A.Lowndes				P.Jackson			
A.Hardisty	T			D.Watkins			
K.Hepworth	T			J.Brennan			
D.Hartley				T.Ogden			
C.Dickinson				M.Dickens			
J.Ward				C.H.Bott			
M.Redfearn		G		M.Coulman			
B.Lockwood				C.J.Dixon			
M.J.Reilly				R.S.Hill		3G	

Lance Todd Trophy: M.J.Reilly

Referee: D.S.Brown (Preston)   Half-time: 3-4
Attendance: 97,939   Receipts: £58,848

Cup presented by Sir Denis Blundell KBE, High Commissioner for New Zealand.

1970 Castleford 7 Wigan 2

THIS Final was Wigan's 11th appearance at Wembley, the Riversiders setting a new record. Castleford, meanwhile, returned to Wembley for the third time but the manner of their victory won them precious few friends outside their own town.

Wigan took the lead in the very first minute, when Colin Tyrer landed a penalty-goal, and six minutes later Castleford equalised when Redfern also kicked a penalty-goal.

In the tenth minute Alan Lowndes crossed in the corner for a try created when Castleford swung the ball swiftly to the left of the field following a fast play-the-ball from Hepworth and Reilly.

Then, in the 18th minute, the incident which many people believe changed the whole course of the game, took place. Tyrer fielded a kick in his own half and passed to winger Kevin O'Loughlin in support. A split-second after the ball had gone, Castleford's Keith Hepworth came in high and late. Tyrer crashed to the floor, blood pouring from a facial injury, and after receiving treatment on the field was carried off to the dressing-room. A later X-ray revealed no break but Tyrer had to undergo extensive dental work. Hepworth, never regarded as a dirty player, later claimed that he thought Tyrer was about to kick the ball and that is why he went in with a high tackle. Cliff Hill took the injured Tyrer's place to become the first-ever substitute in a Challenge Cup Final.

It was a cruel blow to Wigan. The full-back was highly regarded as one of the finest players in the game and he was a deadly accurate goal-kicker with the ability to win games on his own. Two minutes after he had left the field, Francis missed what was regarded as an easy kick, and on three other occasions, when Castleford were penalised in positions from which Wigan kicked for touch, Tyrer would have almost certainly have gone for goal, and with a good chance of success.

Castleford won the scrums 16-10 and their forwards utilised the possession gained well, especially Bill Kirkbride whose contribution to the game earned him the Man of the Match award. The Castleford backs played superb in defence and were the far livelier and more business-like when mounting attacks. Hepworth led his backs well and had far more work to do than expected, due mainly to a kidney injury his partner received in the first half. Wigan worked hard and well and although the spirit was certainly there, the skill was sometimes lacking. Ashurst and Ashcroft did well in the forwards but were overshadowed by the Castleford duo of Lockwood and Hartley who made several surging runs.

The final score in the game which was marred and in many ways overshadowed by the Tyrer incident, was when Redfern landed a penalty in the 67th minute to give Castleford a 7-2 victory.

Flashpoint: Wigan's badly injured Colin Tyrer is carried from the field following the 18th-minute incident with Castleford's Keith Hepworth in 1970.

Rugby League Cup Results

First Round

Castleford	15	Hull	0
Dewsbury	6	Wigan	11
Doncaster	22	Glasson Rangers	4
Featherstone R	2	Salford	7
Halifax	9	Swinton	16
Huddersfield	15	Lock Lane	10
Huyton	10	Hunslet	8
Keighley	0	Bramley	7
Leeds	17	Batley	5
Oldham	5	Blackpool B	0
Rochdale H	2	York	0
St Helens	16	Bradford N	3
Wakefield T	9	Hull KR	16
Whitehaven	4	Warrington	20
Widnes	4	Barrow	11
Workington T	6	Leigh	17

Second Round

Barrow	4	Castleford	12
Doncaster	5	Rochdale H	5
Huddersfield	0	Salford	0
Hull KR	7	Swinton	2
Huyton	8	Leigh	8
Oldham	4	Wigan	17
St Helens	17	Bramley	2
Warrington	5	Leeds	11

Second Round Replays

Leigh	2	Huyton	0
Rochdale H	3	Doncaster	4
Salford	11	Huddersfield	5

Third Round

Castleford	15	Salford	0
Doncaster	4	St Helens	4
Hull KR	7	Leeds	2
Leigh	4	Wigan	6

Third Round Replay

St Helens	36	Doncaster	0

Semi-finals

Castleford	6	St Helens	3

At Station Road, Swinton
Attendance: 18,913   *Receipts: £7,170*

Wigan	19	Hull KR	8

At Headingley, Leeds
Attendance: 18,495   *Receipts: £7,861*

Final

Saturday, 9 May at Wembley Stadium, London

	T	G	P		T	G	P
Castleford	1	2	7	**Wigan**	0	1	2
D.Edwards				C.Tyrer		G	
T.Briggs				K.Jones			
A.W.Thomas				W.F.Francis			
I.P.Stenton				P.H.Rowe			
A.Lowndes	T			Kevin O'Loughlin			
A.Hardisty				D.W.Hill			
K.Hepworth				F.Parr			
D.Hartley				K.Ashcroft			
C.Dickinson				R.B.Birdell			
M.Redfearn		2G		B.Hogan			
W.Kirkbride				W.F.Ashurst			
B.Lockwood				D.Robinson			
M.Reilly				C.D.Laughton			
Substitutes:							
D.Hargrave (for Hardisty)				C.J.Hill (for Tyrer)			

Lance Todd Trophy: W.Kirkbride

Referee: C.F.Lindop (Wakefield)   *Half-time: 5-2*
Attendance: 95,255   *Receipts: £89,262*

Cup presented by the Rt Hon The Earl of Derby MC.

1971 Leigh 24 Leeds 7

The mercurial Alex Murphy with the Challenge Cup in 1971.

LEEDS were such firm favourites to win the Cup that many pundits were suggesting that they should merely take to the field and collect the trophy. Most of the media had overlooked Alex Murphy, the Leigh player-coach whose leadership and inspirational skills were renowned. And the difference on the day was simple: Leigh were brimming over with enthusiasm, team spirit and determination to win; Leeds were listless and made more basic errors in 80 minutes than they had probably made all season.

Leigh took the lead in the fifth minute when Fiddler dropped a goal, Ferguson doubled the score in the 11th minute with a well-taken penalty. The Leigh forwards gradually took a firm grip on the game and, led by Peter Smethurst, they tackled everything Leeds could throw at them.

Twenty-six minutes into the game Murphy fed Dorrington with a perfect pass and the centre strode over the line. Ferguson converted and Leigh were 9-0 in front. A Murphy drop-goal and a Ferguson penalty just before the break gave Leigh a 13-0 lead.

Leeds opened their account in the 48th minute when John Holmes kicked a penalty-goal, but minutes later Murphy cancelled the points with another well-struck drop-goal. Ferguson kicked his fourth goal and Leigh were 15 points in front and in almost total control.

Rugby League Cup Results

First Round

Barrow	11	Widnes	15
Batley	4	Wigan	13
Blackpool B	7	Huddersfield	8
Bramley	6	Doncaster	5
Dewsbury	25	BOCM (Hull)	3
Halifax	13	Featherstone R	18
Hunslet	49	Thames Board Mills	5
Keighley	9	Hull KR	9
Leeds	49	Oldham	2
Leigh	9	Bradford N	2
Salford	6	Wakefield T	6
Swinton	13	Huyton	2
Warrington	13	Rochdale H	7
Whitehaven	0	Castleford	15
Workington T	6	St Helens	8
York	0	Hull	2

BOCM (Hull) and Thames Board Mills gave up ground advantage.

First Round Replays

Hull KR	11	Keighley	18
Wakefield T	8	Salford	15

Second Round

Castleford	9	Keighley	6
Dewsbury	13	Bramley	17
Featherstone R	7	Hull	7
Hunslet	0	Huddersfield	16
Leeds	4	St Helens	0
Salford	20	Warrington	9
Swinton	8	Wigan	2
Widnes	11	Leigh	14

Second Round Replay

Hull	12	Featherstone R	8

Third Round

Bramley	0	Leeds	14
Castleford	9	Salford	8
Huddersfield	11	Swinton	8
Leigh	8	Hull	4

Semi-finals

Leeds	19	Castleford	8

At Odsal Stadium, Bradford
Attendance: 24,464   *Receipts: £9,120*

Leigh	10	Huddersfield	4

At Central Park, Wigan
Attendance: 14,875   *Receipts: £5,670*

Final

Saturday, 15 May at Wembley Stadium, London

	T	G	P		T	G	P
Leigh	2	9	24	**Leeds**	1	2	7
D.Eckersley	T	G		J.S.Holmes		2G	
S.Ferguson		5G		J.Langley			
S.Dorrington	T			S.Hynes			
M.Collins				R.C.Cowan			
J.Walsh				J.B.Atkinson			
A.Barrow				A.Wainwright	T		
A.J.Murphy		2G		B.Seabourne			
D.Watts				J.Burke			
K.Ashcroft				A.Fisher			
J.Fiddler		G		E.G.Barnard			
P.Grimes				D.A.Hick			
G.Clarkson				R.Haigh			
P.Smethurst				W.Ramsey			

Substitutes:
L.Chisnall (for Murphy)   L.Dyl (for Cowan)

Lance Todd Trophy: A.J.Murphy

Referee: W.H.Thompson (Huddersfield)
                                         Half-time: 13-0
Attendance: 84,641   *Receipts: £84,402*

Cup presented by The Rt Hon R.Maudling MP, Home Secretary.

Then came the flashpoint of the game. Syd Hynes and Alex Murphy seemed to clash in midfield and the Leigh captain was left motionless on the ground. After discussions with his touch judge, referee Thompson raised his arm and the Leeds captain became the first man sent off in a Wembley Final, for allegedly butting Murphy.

The prostrate Murphy was stretched to the dressing-room for treatment by the Leigh and Wembley Stadium doctors but minutes later returned, apparently fully recovered.

In his absence Dave Eckersley had dropped a goal from 45 yards and then casually brushed aside a posse of would-be tacklers and scored a superb try. Ferguson goaled and Leigh were 24-2 in the lead.

In the final minutes, Ferguson obstructed teenager Tony Wainwright near the line, referee Thompson awarded the try and Holmes kicked the consolation goal. Leigh's famous victory was an all-round team effort but Alex Murphy's contribution to their cause was immeasurable, his display earning him the Lance Todd Trophy and the following comment: *'Gifted with that inestimable quality of bringing the best out in others by example, he was the scourge of Leeds in this game. Apart from having one pass intercepted everything he did furthered his side's cause – whether it was his kicking, through or high, the spotting and running through gaps, the feeding of others better placed than himself, or the successful dropping at goal.'*

1972 St Helens 16 Leeds 13

Jubilant Saints following their victory over Leeds in the 1972 Final.

LEEDS returned to the twin towers for a second successive year and even though they had played so badly the previous season, the bookmakers installed them as 2/1 on favourites. The Loiners had little injury worries in the days leading up to the Final, the only doubt being John Holmes who was eventually declared fit to play.

St Helens, however, had major problems with injuries and bad luck. Both hooker Tony Karalius and forward Eric Prescott were injured in a League fixture the week before the Final and John Mantle was involved in a car accident. The big Welsh second row forward had several stitches in a head wound but still played on, preferring the use of a skull cap to missing a Wembley Final.

Straight from the kick-off the Saints tackled well and held the Loiners firmly down in their own half of the field. After around 30 seconds of play, Leeds hooker Tony Fisher collected the ball at acting half-back and whipped a pass back for a clearance kick. Confusion gripped the Leeds ranks and both Cookson and Clawson shouted for the ball, only to watch helplessly as it rolled loose, Keith Hepworth was the

first to react and he lunged at the ball to attempt to kick the danger away. Quick-thinking St Helens prop Graham Rees darted forward just as Hepworth kicked and he succeeded in charging the kick down and collecting the ball to score one of the swiftest-ever Wembley tries. Welsh captain Kel Coslett converted and St Helens were 5-0 up in an almost fairytale start.

Terry Clawson landed a 12th-minute penalty to pull two points back for the favourites, having earlier hit the upright.

On a quarter of an hour, Mantle and Chisnall combined well to breach the Leeds defence and their excellent play provided a neat overlap for Les Jones to scorch down the wing for a try. Coslett failed with the conversion but seven minutes later kicked a brilliant penalty from inside his own half. The teams turned round at half-time with St Helens leading 12-6, Coslett having kicked two further penalties and Clawson adding one for the Loiners.

In the very first minute of the second half, Welsh hooker Tony Fisher linked up with fellow pack man Ray Batten and the two created the time and space for Phil Cookson to

Rugby League Cup Results

First Round

Barrow	24	Hunslet	6		
Bradford N	17	Keighley	2		
Bramley	19	Pilkington Rec	5		
Dewsbury	4	Huddersfield	17		
Dewsbury Celtic	2	Featherstone R	34		
Doncaster	3	Wakefield T	5		
Hull	7	Hull KR	5		
Huyton	4	Halifax	7		
Leeds	17	Widnes	8		
Leigh	19	Workington T	4		
Oldham	6	St Helens	8		
Salford	12	Wigan	16		
Swinton	33	Blackpool B	12		
Warrington	30	Batley	7		
Whitehaven	0	Castleford	17		
York	13	Rochdale H	5		

Second Round

Barrow	9	York	9
Bramley	8	Bradford N	5
Castleford	8	Warrington	8
Halifax	11	Featherstone R	5
Hull	5	Leeds	16
Leigh	3	Swinton	4
St Helens	32	Huddersfield	9
Wakefield T	6	Wigan	5

Second Round Replays

Warrington	11	Castleford	5
York	15	Barrow	3

Third Round

Bramley	7	Warrington	14
Halifax	9	Swinton	8
Leeds	11	Wakefield T	5
York	5	St Helens	32

Semi-finals

Leeds	16	Halifax	3

At Odsal Stadium, Bradford
Attendance: 17,008   *Receipts: £6,854*

St Helens	10	Warrington	10

At Central Park, Wigan
Attendance: 19,300   *Receipts: £8,250*

Semi-final Replay

St Helens	10	Warrington	6

At Central Park, Wigan
Attendance: 32,180   *Receipts: £12,554*

Final

Saturday, 13 May at Wembley Stadium, London

St Helens	T	G	P	Leeds	T	G	P
	2	5	16		1	5	13
G.W.Pimblett				J.S.Holmes			
L.Jones	T			M.A.Smith			
W.Benyon				S.Hynes			
J.Walsh				L.Dyl			
F.H.Wilson				J.B.Atkinson			
K.Kelly				A.Hardisty			
J.Heaton				K.Hepworth			
G.T.Rees	T			T.Clawson		5G	
L.Greenall				A.Fisher			
J.R.Stephens				W.Ramsey	T		
J.Mantle				P.Cookson			
E.Chisnall				R.Haigh			
T.K.Coslett		5G		R.Batten			
				Substitute:			
				J.Langley (for Hynes)			

Lance Todd Trophy: T.K.Coslett

Referee: E.Lawrinson (Warrington)   *Half-time: 12-6*
Attendance: 89,495   *Receipts: £86,361*

Cup presented by The American Ambassador, The Hon W.Annenberg.

---

charge through the Saints defence for a well-worked try under the posts. Terry Clawson added to his side's misery when he missed the conversion from right in front of the posts.

Six minutes later, St Helens edged further in front when Coslett kicked a penalty, then on the hour he dropped a goal to make it 16-9.

Clawson finally found his kicking form when he landed two late penalty-goals but it was not enough for Leeds to narrow the gap.

Rovers captain John Newlove celebrates with his victorious teammates in 1973.

AS A contest the 1973 Final was in reality over after the first 19 minutes of play, by which time Featherstone Rovers were 17-0 in the lead and in almost complete control.

Rovers took the lead in the third minute when veteran full-back Cyril Kellett kicked a penalty-goal. Seven minutes later the rampant Rovers pack, revelling in the ample possession they were creating, made a huge opening for centre John Newlove to cut through to score a try which Kellett converted.

Northern's pack was in shell-shocked disorder and four minutes later Rovers forward Alan Rhodes took full advantage of the Bradford confusion to burst through the first line of defence. He continued his foray and then passed to Tonks, who had backed up his rush. The huge prop crashed his massive frame through two attempted tackles and then turned like a ballerina to hand the ball to Vince Farrar, who crossed for a try which Kellett goaled. Northern were still attempting to organise themselves six minutes later when Featherstone captain John Newlove crossed for his second try.

Bradford coach Ian Brooke tried to stem the damage from the bench and replaced Earl with the experienced Arnie Long in an attempt to shore up the crumbling pack. It was a good move and certainly slowed things down, but by now the game was over as a contest. The boot of Eddie Tees brought six points for Northern in the ten minutes before half-time, so the teams changed ends at 17-6 to Featherstone.

The second half began with a penalty-goal from Cyril Kellett in the 50th minute and then, eight minutes later, Dave Redfearn crossed the line for Northern's first try.

Four minutes after that Mick Smith crossed for a try which Kellett goaled and Rovers pulled away to a 17-point lead. Stan Fearnley and Eddie Tees added a further five points to the Northern total but within a minute Feather-stone were on the scoreboard again, this time with a clever drop-goal from scrum-half Steve Nash.

Nash played a brilliant game for Featherstone and his display earned him the Lance Todd Trophy for Man of the Match. The diminutive half-back contributed greatly to his side's success, his clever prompting, his bursts of speed when initiating attacks and his ability to beat at least one man then draw another before releasing the ball, all caused constant problems to the already bewildered Northern defence.

Five minutes from time substitute David Hartley scored a fine try which Kellett converted and then in the final minute Kellett landed a penalty, his eighth goal from eight attempts bringing the 34-year-old a well-earned goal-kicking record for a Wembley Final.

Rugby League Cup Results

First Round

Bradford N	17	Whitehaven	4
Bramley	8	Dewsbury	11
Castleford	13	Swinton	9
Featherstone R	18	Salford	11
Halifax	4	Warrington	7
Huddersfield	6	Hull KR	19
Hull	11	Batley	6
Huyton	6	Wakefield T	18
Keighley	8	Rochdale H	44
Leeds	11	Wigan	25
Leigh	27	Dewsbury Celtic	4
Millom	5	Hunslet	18
Oldham	24	Barrow	7
St Helens	41	Doncaster	0
Widnes	53	Blackpool B	3
York	19	Workington T	24

Second Round

Bradford N	13	Hull KR	8
Featherstone R	30	Rochdale H	19
Hull	2	Oldham	24
Hunslet	0	Castleford	39
Leigh	0	Wakefield T	5
Warrington	20	Widnes	8
Wigan	15	St Helens	2
Workington T	8	Dewsbury	10

Third Round

Bradford N	11	Wigan	7
Castleford	25	Oldham	11
Dewsbury	16	Wakefield T	4
Warrington	14	Featherstone R	18

Semi-finals

Bradford N — 23 — Dewsbury — 7
At Headingley, Leeds
Attendance: 14,028   *Receipts: £9,221*

Featherstone R — 17 — Castleford — 3
At Headingley, Leeds
Attendance: 15,369   *Receipts: £9,454*

Final

Saturday, 12 May at Wembley Stadium, London

	T	G	P		T	G	P
Featherstone R	5	9	33	**Bradford N**	2	4	14
C.Kellett		8G		E.Tees		4G	
P.P.Coventry				N.Lamb			
M.J.Smith	T			D.Stockwell			
J.Newlove	2T			B.Watson			
K.Kellett				D.Redfearn	T		
N.Mason				N.Blacker			
S.Nash		G		B.Seabourne			
L.Tonks				B.Hogan			
J.H.Bridges				P.Dunn			
V.Farrar	T			K.Earl			
A.Rhodes				C.Joyce			
J.Thompson				W.Pattinson			
R.Stone				S.Fearnley	T		

Substitutes:

D.Hartley (for Smith)	T		D.Treasure (for Blacker)		
B.Hollis (for Rhodes)			A.Long (for Earl)		

Lance Todd Trophy: S.Nash

Referee: M.J.Naughton (Widnes)   *Half-time: 17-6*
Attendance: 72,395   *Receipts: £125,826*

Cup presented by Earl Mountbatten of Burma.

1974 Warrington 24 Featherstone Rovers 9

FEATHERSTONE Rovers returned to the scene of their triumphant victory the previous season with a much-changed side. Few of the players who won the Cup by beating Bradford Northern remained and although the shrewd Peter Fox was still coach, this time he faced the wily Alex Murphy, player-coach of Warrington.

As early as the third minute Murphy was in the thick of the action – and controversy – when his vigorous tackle on Rovers' centre David Hartley saw referee Sam Shepherd award a penalty to Featherstone. Harold Box landed the kick and Rovers were 2-0 in front, but Murphy's challenge set in motion a bad-tempered first half.

By the 13th minute Warrington were 4-2 in front following two successful penalty-kicks by their full-back Derek Whitehead. Harold Box replied with another penalty in the 16th minute to level the scores at 4-4. The rule-breaking continued and Whitehead landed two more penalties to edge the Wire into an 8-4 lead.

Around ten minutes before the half-time break, disaster struck Warrington when Murphy suffered a rib injury and was substituted. With the inspirational coach receiving treat-

ment in the dressing-room, Featherstone took their chance right on the stroke of half-time. Rovers scrum-half, Steve Nash elected to run a penalty and from the tap, Jimmy Thompson detected a slight chink in the Warrington armour. His inch-perfect pass gave John Newlove the chance to burst through the gap and, despite the attentions of three would-be tacklers, Newlove scored at the side of the posts. Harold Box kicked the goal and Rovers were one point in the lead.

The joy of the Rovers followers was to be short-lived, however for the mercurial Murphy, complete with five pain-killing injections, was back on the pitch for the second half. He made his presence felt within four minutes when his inventive pass sent Noonan racing 20 yards before passing to Ashcroft who dived over the line for a try. Whitehead converted and then added two further penalties to put Warrington into a commanding 17-9 lead.

Exactly on the hour Murphy, sensing Rovers were starting to tire and lose heart, dropped a brilliant goal to strengthen his side's lead. With around eight minutes remaining, and with the contest all but over, the Wire coach dropped another goal to bring the score to 24-9.

Warrington players Brian Brady, Derek Whitehead, Billy Pickup, Bob Wanbon and David Wright celebrate with a traditional lap of honour round the Wembley pitch in 1974.

Rugby League Cup Results

First Round

Barrow	3	Featherstone R	11
Batley	7	Leeds	18
Castleford	4	Bradford N	15
Dewsbury	13	New Hunslet	5
Hull	2	Hull KR	13
Huyton	16	Doncaster	2
Leigh	63	Kippax White Swan	7
Rochdale H	13	Halifax	6
St Helens	27	Keighley	5
Salford	26	Oldham	12
Swinton	19	Blackpool B	8
Warrington	34	Huddersfield	4
Whitehaven	5	Bramley	8
Widnes	27	Wakefield T	7
Wigan	37	Lock Lane	9
Workington T	14	York	4

Lock Lane gave up ground advantage.

Second Round

Hull KR	9	Featherstone R	12
Leeds	10	Salford	6
Leigh	11	Widnes	7
Rochdale H	8	Wigan	25
St Helens	10	Bramley	5
Swinton	10	Bradford N	19
Warrington	21	Huyton	6
Workington T	4	Dewsbury	14

Third Round

Bradford N	0	Featherstone R	5
Dewsbury	9	Leeds	2
Leigh	11	St Helens	5
Wigan	6	Warrington	10

Semi-finals

Featherstone R	21	Leigh	14

At Headingley, Leeds
Attendance: 7,971   *Receipts: £4,461*

Warrington	17	Dewsbury	7

At Central Park, Wigan
Attendance: 11,789   *Receipts: £6,821*

Final

Saturday, 11 May at Wembley Stadium, London

	T	G	P		T	G	P
Warrington	2	9	24	**Featherstone R**	1	3	9
D.Whitehead		7G		H.Box		3G	
M.Philbin				D.Dyas			
D.Noonan				M.J.Smith			
A.Whittle				D.Hartley			
J.Bevan				G.Bray			
A.J.Murphy		2G		J.Newlove	T		
P.Gordon				S.Nash			
D.Chisnall				L.Tonks			
K.Ashcroft	T			J.H.Bridges			
B.Brady				W.Harris			
D.Wright				A.Rhodes			
M.Nicholas	T			J.Thompson			
B.Philbin				K.Bell			

Substitutes:

W.Pickup (for Murphy)   D.Busfield (for Rhodes)
R.Wanbon (for Brady)   R.Stone (for Thompson)

Lance Todd Trophy: D.Whitehead

Referee: S.Shepherd (Oldham)   *Half-time: 8-9*
Attendance: 76,411   *Receipts: £132,021*

Cup presented by the Hon John Armstrong, the Australian High Commissioner.

Five minutes from time, Wire's Welsh second-row forward, Mike Nicholas, strode past four shattered Featherstone defenders to score the final try of the game. From a relatively easy position the ever-reliable Whitehead missed the conversion attempt and failed to equal Cyril Kellett's record eight Wembley goals set the previous year. The former Oldham full-back's goal-kicking prowess in the game did, however, earn him the Lance Todd Trophy for Man of the Match.

1975 Widnes 14 Warrington 7

CUP holders Warrington were firm favourites to keep possession of the Challenge Cup and looked certain to do so after only five minutes play. Wire hooker Kevin Ashcroft dabbed a grass high-kick through a maze of players and the ball bounced towards former RU British Lion John Bevan, who scooped it up and crossed the line for a try. Whitehead landed the conversion.

The early points gave Warrington added determination and they swept towards the Widnes line. The Chemics were more than ready, however, and they easily soaked up the pressure before launching their own forays into the Warrington half. Led superbly by their forwards, Widnes gradually took command of the game with their own particular brand of controlled and methodical football.

The subtle scheming and clever ball distribution of Doug Laughton soon began to tell and the seemingly fitter Widnes forwards soon began to dominate the loose play. The rampant runs of Adams, Foran and Sheridan, the sheer physical strength of Jim Mills and the determined foraging of hooker Keith Elwell were all major factors in the Chemics' success. The side's backs lacked nothing in comparison to the pack, Dutton and Hughes were fast off the mark and seemed to have an almost endless repertoire of attacking options. Behind them Aspey and George ran straight and with purpose and when the ball went to the wing, Anderson and Prescott used it well.

Widnes gnawed at Warrington's lead and two penalty-goals from Dutton brought them to within a point. Then, in

Jim Mills, the Chemics' giant Welsh prop forward, celebrates with the Challenge Cup on the team's return to Widnes in 1975.

Rugby League Cup Results

First Round

Barrow	5	Workington T	5
Bramley	5	St Helens	30
Castleford	13	Bradford N	13
Dewsbury Celtic	15	Hull KR	31
Featherstone R	7	Salford	17
Huddersfield	18	Rochdale H	21
Hull	20	Batley	0
Leigh	36	Doncaster	3
New Hunslet	9	Mayfield	5
Oldham	12	Blackpool B	3
Swinton	4	Widnes	13
Wakefield T	33	Huyton	5
Warrington	32	Halifax	6
Whitehaven	7	Leeds	16
Wigan	33	Dewsbury	2
York	26	Keighley	9

The Dewsbury Celtic game was played at Batley.

First Round Replays

Bradford N	10	Castleford	7
Workington T	14	Barrow	3

Second Round

Hull	12	Widnes	13
Hull KR	19	Workington T	7
Leigh	5	Bradford N	23
New Hunslet	16	York	9
Rochdale H	10	Oldham	10
Salford	12	Leeds	17
Wakefield T	13	St Helens	9
Wigan	17	Warrington	24

Second Round Replay

Oldham	15	Rochdale H	3

Third Round

Leeds	22	Bradford N	6
New Hunslet	3	Warrington	23
Oldham	4	Widnes	10
Wakefield T	27	Hull KR	10

Semi-finals

Warrington	11	Leeds	4

At Central Park, Wigan
Attendance: 13,168   *Receipts: £9,520*

Widnes	13	Wakefield T	7

At Odsal Stadium, Bradford
Attendance: 9,155   *Receipts: £5,856*

Final

Saturday, 10 May at Wembley Stadium, London

	T	G	P		T	G	P
Widnes	1	6	14	**Warrington**	1	2	7
R.Dutton		5G 1D		D.Whitehead		2G	
A.Prescott				M.Philbin			
D.George				D.Noonan			
M.Aspey				F.Reynolds			
C.Anderson				J.Bevan	T		
E.Hughes				A.Whittle			
R.Bowden				P.Gordon			
J.Mills	T			D.Chisnall			
K.Elwell				K.Ashcroft			
B.Sheridan				W.Wanbon			
J.Foran				T.Conroy			
M.Adams				T.Martyn			
C.D.Laughton				B.Philbin			
				Substitutes:			
				W.Briggs (for Reynolds)			
				M.Nicholas (for Martyn)			

Lance Todd Trophy: R.Dutton

Referee: P.Geraghty (York)   *Half-time: 11-5*
Attendance: 86,363   *Receipts: £140,732*

Cup presented by HRH Princess Alexandra.

---

the 33rd minute, the Chemics scored the try that had eluded them for so long. Aspey made the initial break before the ball was whipped across the field to the ever-ready Eric Hughes. The little half-back turned to find Jim Mills in support and when the pass came, the giant prop took his chance well and scored a fine try. Dutton kicked the conversion and Widnes were four points in the lead. Lance Todd Trophy winner Dutton kicked his fourth goal just before half-time and the sides changed ends with Widnes 11 -5 in the lead.

Three minutes into the second half Warrington's Derek Whitehead pulled two points back with a well-struck penalty-goal. It did little to help his side, however, for they were tiring fast and what little initiative they did show in attack was quickly dealt with by a Widnes defence that looked as fresh as when they had kicked-off.

Dutton added three more points when he first dropped and then kicked a penalty before the final whistle and the little underdogs from Widnes had pulled off a major Wembley upset and done it in great style.

The first-ever Wembley defeat for the mercurial Alex Murphy, the Warrington coach, did little to silence him and he came up with one of his famous quotes: *"Things do go wrong sometimes – the Titanic sank."*

1976 St Helens 20 Widnes 5

CUP holders Widnes were installed as firm favourites to take the trophy against the 'old men' of St Helens, as some sections of the media had christened them. The weather on the day certainly seemed to be more of an advantage for the younger Chemics, as the stadium sweltered on a scorching afternoon when the temperature soared.

Widnes charged into attack from the kick-off but it was the Saints who had the first chance after only four minutes, when a beautifully weighted high kick by Pimblett bounced just out of reach of Heaton who would have almost certainly scored a try had he gained possession. Nine minutes later, sustained Saints pressure culminated when centre Eddie Cunningham raced over the line for the first try which full-back Geoff Pimblett converted. Pimblett tagged on a single point with a drop-goal before Ray Dutton pulled two points back for Widnes with a penalty on the stroke of half-time.

In the second half St Helens established a grip on the game which Widnes, no matter how hard they tried, could not loosen. The Chemics seemed slow and lethargic in the heat and their usually perfect backing-up was nowhere to be seen. On several occasions the man with the ball would break through and then be stranded, looking for support which, by the time it arrived, was far too late. In contrast St Helens were eager for the ball and the forwards in particular played a splendid game with some hard, straight running into the Chemics' defence. The Saints backs had a fine game as well with full-back Pimblett completing the back division with his well-timed incursions into the line that his display won him the Man of the Match award.

Ten minutes into the second half, Keith Elwell dropped a goal to put Widnes just a point adrift and poised for a late rally. Saints struck again, however, Pimblett dropping another one-pointer, and a minute later Jeff Heaton held on to a clever pass by Tony Karalius and slid through a tiny gap to score a try which Pimblett converted.

The score broke the Widnes resistance and six minutes later Jones collected the ball deep inside his own territory and sprinted toward the Chemics' line. Half-stopped by Watkins, he regained his feet and continued his dash for the

Saints' Welsh forward Kel Coslett and his teammates celebrate after their victory over Widnes in 1976, in one of the hottest-ever Wembley Finals.

Rugby League Cup Results

First Round

Bramley	5	Wigan	10
Castleford	3	Salford	25
Doncaster	13	Barrow	9
Featherstone R	23	Wakefield T	9
Halifax	9	Keighley	13
Huddersfield	10	Leeds	34
Hull	3	St Helens	5
Hull KR	21	Whitehaven	12
Huyton	4	Oldham	16
Leigh	37	Pointer Panthers	8
New Hunslet	17	Blackpool B	12
Rochdale H	2	Bradford N	15
Warrington	16	Leigh Miners Welfare	12
Widnes	26	Batley	4
Workington T	10	Swinton	7
York	25	Dewsbury	15

Second Round

Featherstone R	25	Hull KR	10
Keighley	17	Workington T	12
Leeds	30	Bradford N	12
Leigh	29	Doncaster	6
New Hunslet	4	Warrington	17
Oldham	6	York	5
Salford	11	St Helens	17
Widnes	7	Wigan	5

Third Round

Featherstone R	33	Leeds	7
Keighley	13	Leigh	7
St Helens	17	Oldham	9
Warrington	0	Widnes	6

Semi-finals

St Helens	5	Keighley	4

At Fartown, Huddersfield
Attendance: 9,829   *Receipts: £6,112*

Widnes	15	Featherstone R	9

At Station Road, Swinton
Attendance: 13,019   *Receipts: £9,078*

Final

Saturday, 8 May at Wembley Stadium, London

	T	G	P		T	G	P
St Helens	4	5	20	**Widnes**	0	3	5
G.Pimblett		3G	2D	R.Dutton		2G	
L.Jones				A.Prescott			
E.Cunningham	T			E.Hughes			
D.Noonan				M.George			
R.Mathias				D.Jenkins			
W.Benyon				D.Eckersley			
J.Heaton	T			R.Bowden			
J.Mantle				N.Nelson			
A.Karalius				K.Elwell			1D
T.K.Coslett				J.Wood			
C.Nicholls				J.Foran			
E.Chisnall				M.Adams			
D.Hull				C.D.Laughton			

Substitutes:

P.Glynn (for Benyon)	2T	D.O'Neill (for Prescott)	
M.James (for Mantle)		B.Sheridan (for Foran)	

Lance Todd Trophy: G.Pimblett

Referee: R.Moore (Wakefield)   *Half-time: 6-4*
Attendance: 89,982   *Receipts: £190,129*

Cup presented by The Rt Hon Mrs Margaret Thatcher MP.

line, only to be finally caught by O'Neill. The Widnes defence was in chaos and substitute Peter Glynn took full advantage to score a try which Pimblett improved. Despite the heat, St Helens pressed home their advantage and Glynn chipped the ball over the Widnes defence and beat O'Neill to the touch to give the Saints a resounding 20-5 victory.

After the game, veteran prop John Mantle said: *"We are like marathon runners. We may be over 30 but we just keep on going."*

Lance Todd Trophy winner Steve Pitchford launches himself on another surging run which caused havoc for Widnes throughout the 1977 Final.

WIDNES were making their third consecutive appearance at Wembley, equalling Bradford Northern's record set in the late 1940s, and were firm favourites to beat Leeds and regain the trophy they had lost the previous year. Leeds, who had had an erratic League season, were making their 11th Challenge Cup Final appearance and their seventh visit to the twin towers.

Leeds started well and took the first two scrums before they were awarded a third-minute penalty when their young scrum-half, Kevin Dick, was fouled by Bill Ramsey. Dick took the kick himself and put his side into an early and nerve-settling 2-0 lead. Minutes later, Steve Pitchford tore through the Widnes defence, broke through Dutton's attempted tackle and lobbed a pass out to wingman John Atkinson who dived over the line, only to brought back when the pass was ruled to be forward.

Widnes levelled the score after 11 minutes when Ray Dutton kicked a 40-yard penalty, awarded when Leeds were caught offside. Eight minutes later Chemics' scrum-half, Reg

Bowden switched the point of attack and Mal Aspey beat four Leeds defenders to score a brilliant try which Dutton converted.

Almost on the hour, the Leeds stand-off, John Holmes, lofted a cross-kick deep towards the Widnes line. The bounce of the ball completely beat Stuart Wright and John Atkinson swooped on to the ball for a try. Dick failed with the conversion kick.

Widnes pressed hard at the start of the second half and went close to scoring on several occasions. After soaking up the Widnes pressure, the Loiners finally broke into attack and in the 53rd minute they took the lead. From a scrum, Dick passed to Holmes to whose clever reverse pass opened the way for Les Dyl to race through the Chemics' defence and score.

The try seemed to drain the energy from Widnes and Steve Pitchford's charging runs, which had caused the Chemics earlier problems, began to punch holes in the defensive line. On the hour one of his superb surges into the

Rugby League Cup Results

First Round

Beecroft & Wightman	2	Swinton	10
Blackpool B	8	Bradford N	38
Bramley	6	Widnes	11
Castleford	27	New Hunslet	6
Hull	34	Doncaster	11
Hull KR	20	Keighley	10
Huyton	3	Workington T	10
Leeds	40	Batley	6
Oldham	8	Dewsbury	15
Pilkington Recreation	4	Wigan	10
Rochdale H	23	Leigh	8
Salford	25	Huddersfield	2
Wakefield T	12	Halifax	3
Warrington	12	St Helens	13
Whitehaven	5	Featherstone R	6
York	9	Barrow	15

The Beecroft game was played at Hull. The Pilkington game was played at St Helens.

Second Round

Bradford N	12	Featherstone R	7
Dewsbury	3	Wakefield T	0
Hull KR	12	Hull	9
Leeds	21	Barrow	11
Rochdale H	2	Castleford	10
Widnes	36	Swinton	5
Wigan	4	St Helens	9
Workington T	13	Salford	4

Third Round

Castleford	15	Hull KR	25
Dewsbury	8	St Helens	11
Widnes	19	Bradford N	5
Workington T	2	Leeds	8

Semi-finals

Leeds	7	St Helens	2

At Central Park, Wigan
Attendance: 12,974   *Receipts: £11,378*

Widnes	14	Hull KR	5

At Headingley, Leeds
Attendance: 17,053   *Receipts: £16,066*

Final

Saturday, 7 May at Wembley Stadium, London

	T	G	P		T	G	P
Leeds	3	4	16	**Widnes**	1	2	7
B.Murrell				R.Dutton		2G	
M.A.Smith				S.Wright			
N.Hague				M.Aspey	T		
L.Dyl	T			D.Eckersley			
J.B.Atkinson	T			D.O'Neill			
J.S.Holmes				E.Hughes			
K.Dick	T	3G	D	R.Bowden			
M.Harrison				W.Ramsey			
D.Ward				K.Elwell			
S.Pitchford				J.Mills			
G.Eccles				A.Dearden			
P.Cookson				M.Adams			
S.Fearnley				C.D.Laughton			

Substitutes:

D.Smith (for M.A.Smith)   M.George (for Wright)
R.Dickinson (for Fearnley)   J.Foran (for Dearden)

Lance Todd Trophy: S.Pitchford

Referee: J.V.Moss (Manchester)   *Half-time: 5-7*
Attendance: 80,871   *Receipts: £241,487*

Cup presented by The Rt Hon Denis Howell MP.

heart of the Widnes side, which helped him win the Lance Todd Trophy, created a fine platform for a Leeds attack. Cookson, Ward and Fearnley kept the momentum going and Les Dyl, in a great run, was held yards short of the line. The centre hastily regained his feet and immediately played the ball to Kevin Dick, who feigned to pass, then dived over for a brilliant solo try. The 19-year-old landed the conversion attempt and then dropped a clever goal with around three minutes of the game remaining. Right on the whistle for full time, the young Leeds scrum-half crowned a brilliant game with a penalty to give the Loiners a 16-7 victory and himself a personal tally of ten points.

Leeds wingman John Atkinson turns away in despair as Saints' Graham Liptrot celebrates his fourth-minute try in the 1978 Final.

IN a re-run of the 1972 game, both Leeds and St Helens contributed greatly to one of the all-time classic Wembley Finals.

The action began in the fourth minute when Saints loose forward Harry Pinner hoisted one of his spectacular high kicks deep towards the Loiners' try line. The towering kick dropped neatly over the Leeds line and full-back Willie Oulton missed in his attempt to gather. A rebound off John Atkinson saw the ball fall perfectly for Graham Liptrot, the Saints' hooker, to drop on and score a gift try. Geoff Pimblett converted with ease and St Helens were 5-0 up in as many minutes.

Led from the front by Nicholls, James and Chisnall, St Helens poured forward with wave after wave of sweeping attacks. Once again Pinner lifted a high kick towards the Leeds line, but this time Oulton caught and held the ball firm. Minutes later Oulton missed with a penalty attempt and once again the Saints were racing towards the Leeds defences. A brilliantly worked overlap put Jones into the

clear and the wingman swept past Oulton, only to be stopped by a magnificent diving tackle from Sanderson.

The danger was far from over, however. From a scrum moments later, Gwilliam whipped the ball to Bill Francis who sprinted through the cover to score a try which Pimblett converted.

Gradually Leeds regrouped, settled down and at last injected some rhythm and sense of purpose to their play. In the 22nd minute a long and deadly accurate pass from Holmes gave Crane the time and space to beat his man and accelerate away. He passed to Les Dyl who transferred to Atkinson who swept past Pimblett to race 30 yards for a try in the corner. Willie Oulton kicked a towering goal from the touchline and Leeds, five points behind, were back in a the game they had looked to have lost.

One minute into the second half, Loiners captain David Ward dropped a goal to pull another point back. Then around a quarter of an hour later, following a bout of strong Leeds pressure, Holmes passed to Hague who threw a long

Rugby League Cup Results

First Round

Blackpool B	7	Huddersfield	9
Bradford N	21	Barrow	13
Dewsbury	13	New Hunslet	22
Dewsbury Celtic	5	Wigan	15
Hull	9	Hull KR	7
Leeds	25	Halifax	5
Leigh	14	Featherstone R	23
Oldham	21	Doncaster	7
Pilkington Recreation	22	Castleford	23
St Helens	36	Huyton	8
Salford	9	Bramley	7
Swinton	13	Batley	0
Whitehaven	13	Wakefield T	21
Widnes	15	Rochdale H	8
Workington T	16	Keighley	5
York	10	Warrington	16

The Dewsbury Celtic game was played at Batley. The Pilkington Recreation game was played at St Helens.

Second Round

Featherstone R	23	New Hunslet	7
Huddersfield	13	Salford	3
Hull	8	Widnes	20
Oldham	11	St Helens	26
Wakefield T	6	Leeds	28
Warrington	29	Swinton	4
Wigan	10	Bradford N	22
Workington T	8	Castleford	8

Second Round Replay

Castleford	8	Workington T	8

Second Round, Second Replay

Castleford	20	Workington T	13
at Central Park, Wigan			

Third Round

Featherstone R	25	Castleford	15
Leeds	16	Bradford N	8
St Helens	31	Huddersfield	5
Warrington	6	Widnes	0

Semi-finals

Leeds	14	Featherstone R	9
At Odsal Stadium, Bradford			
Attendance: 12,824		*Receipts: £11,321*	
St Helens	12	Warrington	8
At Central Park, Wigan			
Attendance: 16,167		*Receipts: £13,959*	

Final

Saturday, 13 May at Wembley Stadium, London

Leeds	T	G	P	St Helens	T	G	P
Leeds	3	4	14	**St Helens**	2	3	12
W.Oulton		G		G.Pimblett		3G	
D.R.Smith	T			L.Jones			
N.Hague				D.Noonan			
L.P.Dyl				P.Glynn			
J.B.Atkinson	T			R.Mathias			
J.S.Homes		D		W.L.Francis	T		
J.Sanderson				K.Gwilliam			
M.Harrison				D.Chisnall			
D.Ward		2D		G.Liptrot	T		
S.Pitchford				M.James			
C.Eccles				G.Nicholls			
P.Cookson	T			E.Cunningham			
M.Crane				H.Pinner			

Substitutes:
K.Dick (for Sanderson)
R.Dickinson (for Harrison)

Lance Todd Trophy: G.Nicholls

Referee: W.H.Thompson (Huddersfield)
Half-time: 5-12
Attendance: 95,872   *Receipts: £330,575*

Cup presented by the Earl of Derby.

ball for David Smith to collect and sprint over for an unconverted try.

On 70 minutes a John Holmes fooled the St Helens defence when he quickly turned the ball back inside to Cookson who dived over for a try to put the sides level at 12-12. Oulton missed the conversion by inches.

Once again the rampant Leeds forwards drove the ball downfield and with less than ten minutes remaining, the ball was passed back to Holmes who dropped a brilliant left-foot goal to finally give his side the lead. Two minutes from time, David Ward dropped his second goal to put Leeds 14-12 ahead. The drama continued to the last second when Saints' Noonan just failed to hold a pass with the try line at his mercy.

Jubilant Chemics skipper Reg Bowden raises the Cup high following the presentation by Lord Daresbury in 1979.

THE first-ever sponsored Final, the State Express Challenge Cup, was one of the worst for many years. The first half was a scoreless, dour struggle dominated by relentlessly hard tackling and the occasional foray into the enemy's '25'. The respective defences were so tight that and evenly-matched that even the smallest crack to appear was swiftly and efficiently closed. Wakefield were at times the far more confident side, their intelligent and often bold manoeuvres regularly troubling, but never really threatening, the rigid and well-organised Widnes barriers.

Behind Wakefield's offensive was David Topliss who tirelessly roamed the field, constantly searching for a way through the Chemics' blanket defence. His awesome display of creative running and the endless attempts to coax the best from his teammates earned him the consolation prize of Lance Todd Trophy for Man of the Match.

For the Chemics, Laughton and Adams had good first halves but their subtle skills were all too brief for a huge crowd waiting patiently to be entertained.

The second half opened in pretty much the same way as the first — endless forward battles and very little variation of play by either side. Unlike the first half, however, gaps started to open more readily and the crowd's patience was at last rewarded.

After 49 minute, the stalemate was broken when Mick Burke kicked a long-range penalty awarded when Trinity's Bill Ashurst fouled Eric Hughes.

Twenty minutes into the half, Chemics' winger Stuart Wright exploded into action and took everyone by complete surprise. One account describes the action: 'Receiving possession from Eckersley, in his own half, and realising that the Wakefield forces were in some disarray, Wright surged irrepressibly forward. His burst took him in seconds midway into enemy territory. His run was followed by a nicely-judged kick to the corner, which in turn was followed by another thrilling sprint. Neither Diamond nor Sheard could catch him.'

From a seemingly impossible angle out on the touchline, Burke converted the try with ease and Widnes were 7-0 up. Four minutes later Keith Elwell edged the Chemics another point in front with a drop-goal.

162

Rugby League Cup Results

First Round

Barrow	10	York	7
Dewsbury	13	Blackpool B	6
Huddersfield	11	Whitehaven	9
Hull	17	Leeds	6
Hull KR	23	New Hunslet	15
Huyton	2	Keighley	14
Leigh	23	Leigh Miners Welfare	10
Oldham	23	Ace Amateurs	5
Rochdale H	15	Batley	0
St Helens	34	Doncaster	9
Salford	6	Bramley	6
Swinton	2	Bradford N	8
Wakefield	10	Featherstone R	7
Warrington	9	Castleford	15
Widnes	12	Workington T	5
Wigan	9	Halifax	6

Leigh Miners Welfare gave up ground advantage. The Oldham game was played at Salford.

First Round Replay

Bramley	2	Salford	2

First Round, Second Replay

Bramley	7	Salford	5

At Station Road, Swinton

Second Round

Barrow	25	Leigh	2
Bradford N	14	Hull KR	7
Castleford	31	Dewsbury	15
Huddersfield	31	Bramley	12
Keighley	12	Hull	33
Oldham	7	Wakefield T	19
Rochdale H	10	St Helens	11
Widnes	21	Wigan	5

Third Round

Bradford N	8	Hull	8
Castleford	6	St Helens	10
Huddersfield	0	Widnes	14
Wakefield T	8	Barrow	5

Third Round Replay

Hull	4	Bradford N	8

Semi-finals

Wakefield T	9	St Helens	7

At Headingley, Leeds
Attendance: 12,393   *Receipts: £14,195*

Widnes	14	Bradford N	11

At Station Road, Swinton
Attendance: 14,324   *Receipts: £16,363*

Final

Saturday, 5 May at Wembley Stadium, London

Widnes	T	G	P	Wakefield T	T	G	P
	2	4	12		1	0	3
D.Eckersley	D			L.Sheard			
S.Wright	T			A.Fletcher	T		
M.Aspey				K.Smith			
D.George				S.Diamond			
M.Burke		2G		B.J.Juliff			
E.Hughes	T			D.Topliss			
R.Bowden				M.Lampkowski			
J.Mills				J.Burke			
K.Elwell	D			A.Mccurrie			
G.Shaw				T.Skerrett			
M.Adams				W.F.Ashurst			
A.Dearden				Keith Rayne			
C.D.Laughton				G.Idle			

Substitutes:
M.O'Neill (for Dearden)
D.Hull (for George)

Lance Todd Trophy: D.Topliss

Referee: J.E.Jackson (Pudsey)   *Half-time: 0-0*
Attendance: 94,218   *Receipts: £383,157*

Cup presented by Lord Daresbury.

Trinity regrouped and rallied well, and when a promising move seemed to have run out of both ideas and energy, second-row forward Keith Rayne chipped the ball over the Widnes defence and Andy Fletcher nipped round Burke to touch down. Widnes complained that the winger had knocked the ball forward in the act of scoring but the referee would have none of it and the try stood. Keith Smith failed with the conversion attempt.

With ten minutes to play, Eckersley added a further point with a drop-goal, then Hughes bamboozled the Wakefield defence when he shaped to drop a goal but instead embarked on a 20-yard curving sprint that gave the Chemics their final try and a 12-3 victory.

AFTER 83 years of avoiding each other, neighbours and fierce rivals Hull and Hull Kingston Rovers finally met in the Challenge Cup Final.

With their fiercely partisan groups of supporters behind them, both sets of players knew the game was as much about the championship of the city of Hull as a major Final at Wembley.

From the kick-off, both sides seemed over-cautious, almost petrified of making a mistake. Then Kingston Rovers settled down and after eight minutes scored the first try of the match. From a tap restart, Rovers moved the ball quickly across the line and found Brian Lockwood who shaped to throw the ball long to Casey but fooled the Hull defence with a perfectly delayed short pass to Steve Hubbard who slipped through the gap to score. Hubbard failed with the conversion attempt but kicked the penalty awarded when Hull full-back Woods had fouled him as he touched down.

Hull's bad-tempered start began to worsen and in the 13th minute their hooker, Ron Wileman, caught Roger Millward far too high and late and left the little stand-off lying semi-conscious with his jawbone broken. Referee Lindop showed remarkable tolerance when he allowed Wileman to stay on the field for what the majority of the crowd thought would be an instant sending-off. After treatment, Millward courageously played on. The incident did little to distract the Hull players from their chosen tactics

Despite suffering from a broken jaw, Rovers captain Roger Millward holds the Cup high and manages a wry smile for the jubilant Robins followers in 1980.

Rugby League Cup Results

First Round

Ace Amateurs	5	Widnes	22
Barrow	31	Batley	11
Blackpool B	7	Bradford N	26
Dewsbury	2	Oldham	24
Featherstone R	13	Halifax	17
Huddersfield	11	Whitehaven	4
Hull	33	Millom	10
Huyton	0	Salford	25
Keighley	5	Castleford	21
Leigh	5	Leeds	12
Rochdale H	11	Doncaster	3
St Helens	16	Workington T	0
Swinton	2	Warrington	25
Wakefield T	24	Hunslet	17
Wigan	13	Hull KR	18
York	17	Bramley	16

The Ace Amateurs game was played at Craven Park, Hull.

Second Round

Barrow	4	Halifax	10
Huddersfield	3	Widnes	48
Hull	18	York	8
Hull KR	28	Castleford	3
Oldham	5	Wakefield T	10
Rochdale H	5	Salford	20
St Helens	10	Bradford N	11
Warrington	8	Leeds	2

Third Round

Bradford N	0	Hull	3
Halifax	7	Wakefield T	3
Hull KR	23	Warrington	11
Salford	8	Widnes	9

Semi-finals

Hull	10	Widnes	5

At Station Road, Swinton
Attendance: 18,347   *Receipts: £29,415*

Hull KR	20	Halifax	7

At Headingley, Leeds
Attendance: 17,910   *Receipts: £32,038*

Final

Saturday, 3 May at Wembley Stadium, London

	T	G	P		T	G	P
Hull KR	**1**	**4**	**10**	**Hull**	**1**	**1**	**5**
D.Hall				P.Woods			
S.Hubbard	T	3G		G.Bray			
M.Smith				G.Walters			
S.Hartley				T.Wilby	T		
C.A.Sullivan				P.Prendiville			
R.Millward		D		J.Newlove			
A.Agar				C.Pickerill			
R.Holdstock				K.Tindall			
D.Watkinson				R.Wileman			
B.Lockwood				R.Stone			
P.Rose				C.Birdsall			
P.Lowe				G.Lloyd		G	
L.Casey				S.Norton			
Substitutes:							
P.Hogan (for Hubbard)				B.Hancock (for Newlove)			
J.Millington (for Rose)				V.Farrar (for Stone)			

Lance Todd Trophy: B.Lockwood

Referee: G.F.Lindop (Wakefield)   *Half-time: 8-3*
Attendance: 95,000   *Receipts: £448,202*

Cup presented by Her Majesty Queen Elizabeth the Queen Mother.

and within minutes Hubbard kicked a penalty-goal awarded when Stone had punched Holdstock.

In the 28th minute Hull finally cut loose and a clever piece of play by Newlove and Pickerill created the room for Tim Wilby to sprint over the line for a good try. A nervous Sammy Lloyd placed and then replaced the ball several times before missing the conversion. Right on the stroke of half-time, Millward dropped a superb goal to give the Rovers an 8-3 lead.

The second half saw the players just as jittery as the first and their anxiety at the final pass led to referee Lindop disallowing five tries. In the 51st minute Sammy Lloyd finally kicked a goal, a well-struck effort from 35 yards out, and the Airlie Birds were within striking distance at just three points adrift.

Nine minutes from time, Lloyd obstructed Millward and Hubbard stepped forward to kick his third goal of the afternoon and seal the victory for the Robins. Minutes after the kick, Hubbard twisted his ankle and had to be carried from the field.

Man of the Match went to Brian Lockwood whose almost faultless display led one newspaper to comment: 'Lockwood embodied all that was best about Rovers. *He is a formidable combination of class and determination. He has a side-step that many a centre would envy and a footballing brain far in advance of a lot of stand-off halves.*'

Widnes celebrate their 1981 victory at the side of the Wembley pitch. Kneeling third from the right is Brian Lockwood, who had tasted victory the previous year as a Hull KR player.

FAVOURITES Widnes took the trophy with a remarkably easy victory over Hull KR in an entertaining game. Widnes were supremely confident throughout and played with a composure that highlighted their vast experience and total professionalism. Hull Kingston Rovers were the exact opposite, making far too many elementary mistakes and conceding penalties to such a degree that at times they effectively played themselves out of the game.

Kingston Rovers won the majority of first-half possession from the set-piece scrums but squandered control with a horrendous display of handling errors. When the ball did run loose, it was almost always a Widnes player who was first to snap it up. Apart from the scrums the Widnes pack dominated the forward play with Lockwood and his superb handling skills outstanding in his role of ball distributor.

Widnes revealed their eagerness in the third minute when Rovers's winger Peter Muscroft was caught offside. The Chemics took a quick tap penalty, Elwell passed to Mick Burke who had linked perfectly from full-back. Then a deliberate kick ahead allowed him to pass three defenders,

before re-gathering the ball to dive over near the corner. He failed to convert his try but the psychological importance of the first points had gone to Widnes.

Three minutes later, Steve Hubbard kicked a penalty but Burke retaliated with a goal in the 22nd minute, awarded when Rovers' Watkinson fouled Lockwood. In the 26th minute, Brian Lockwood cracked open the Rovers defence with a perfect pass to Burke. The full-back coaxed the defence towards him, then threw a pass to centre Mick George who tore through a huge gap to score. Burke converted and Widnes were 10-2 in front.

On the half-hour Steve Hubbard pulled two points back with a penalty but four minutes later the Chemics captain casually dropped a delightful goal to keep his side's seven-point lead. Two minutes into the second half, 20-year-old scrum-half Andy Gregory collected a Mick Adams pass and darted through the Rovers' defence for a fine individual try. Burke converted and then three minutes later added a penalty to give Widnes an 18-4 lead.

Rovers rallied and although their play was becoming

Rugby League Cup Results

First Round

Batley	7	Keighley	15
Blackpool B	2	Oldham	11
Bramley	5	Warrington	18
Castleford	42	Huyton	7
Dewsbury	15	Hunslet	10
Fulham	5	Wakefield T	9
Halifax	3	Wigan	2
Huddersfield	8	St Helens	10
Hull	14	Leeds	5
Hull KR	18	Barrow	13
Leigh	20	Whitehaven	6
Pilkington Recreation	7	York	18
Salford	17	Bradford N	13
Swinton	8	Featherstone R	10
Widnes	50	Doncaster	0
Workington T	17	Rochdale H	8

The Pilkington Recreation game was played on the St Helens ground.

Second Round

Dewsbury	10	Warrington	18
Featherstone R	10	Keighley	7
Hull KR	23	York	7
Oldham	18	Workington T	7
St Helens	5	Hull	3
Salford	12	Leigh	3
Wakefield T	18	Halifax	8
Widnes	7	Castleford	5

Third Round

Featherstone R	5	Widnes	21
Hull KR	19	Salford	8
Oldham	5	St Helens	6
Warrington	13	Wakefield T	9

Semi-finals

Hull KR	22	St Helens	5

At Headingley, Leeds
Attendance: 17,073   *Receipts: £30,615*

Widnes	17	Warrington	9

At Central Park, Wigan
Attendance: 12,624   *Receipts: £20,673*

Final

Saturday, 2 May at Wembley Stadium, London

	T	G	P		T	G	P
Widnes	3	5	18	**Hull KR**	1	3	9
M.Burke	T	4G		D.Hall			
S.Wright				S.Hubbard		3G	
M.George	T			M.Smith			
E.Cunningham				P.Hogan			
K.Bentley				P.Muscroft			
E.Hughes				S.Hartley			
A.Gregory	T			P.Harkin			
M.O'Neill				R.Holdstock			
K.Elwell				D.Watkinson			
B.Lockwood				S.Crooks			
L.Gorley				P.Lowe			
E.Prescott				C.Burton	T		
M.Adams		D		L.Casey			

Substitutes:

J.Myler (for Cunningham)   P.Proctor (for Crooks)
G.Shaw (for O'Neill)   J.Millington (for Holdstock)

Lance Todd Trophy: M.Burke

Referee: D.C.Kershaw (Easingwold)

Half-time: 11-4
Attendance: 92,496   *Receipts: £591,117*

increasingly desperate, they scored a fine try. A clever short ball from Len Casey, easily their best player on the day, gave second-row forward Chris Burton just enough time to crash over for a try. Steve Hubbard continued his Wembley goal-kicking feats with the conversion to put Rovers nine points behind Widnes but with little hope of catching them.

The victory put Widnes level with Wigan on six Wembley wins and a personal milestone for Brian Lockwood, a winner with three different clubs.

Mick Burke was awarded the Lance Todd Trophy for his fine all-round performance.

1982 Hull 18 Widnes 9

(after a replay)

'I THINK Widnes were lucky the final hooter went when it did,' was how Hull coach Arthur Bunting summed up the first draw at Wembley since 1954.

Widnes stormed into a 6-0 lead when Keith Elwell dropped a fourth-minute goal and then Eddie Cunningham powered his way over for a try which Mick Burke converted. Hull gradually clawed their way back into the game and three penalty-goals from Sammy Lloyd brought the game all-square again at half-time.

The Chemics took the lead again in the 51st minute, when Wembley Man of the Match Cunningham scored his second try, which substitute Andy Gregory converted. Ten minutes later, winger Stuart Wright intercepted a wild pass from Hull's Steve Evans and raced clear to score a brilliant individual try. Hull reeled a little but then slowly took control of the game. Airlie Bird loose forward, Steve 'Knocker' Norton burst through a gap in the Widnes defence and sprinted over the line for a well-deserved try. Sam Lloyd converted and Hull were just three points behind. Four minutes later they were back level when New Zealander Dane O'Hara collected a short ball from Lee Crooks and hurled himself over the line.

With the scores deadlocked at 14-14 the absorbing contest moved to a replay at Elland Road, the home of Leeds United.

Just as at Wembley, Widnes took the lead when full-back Mick Burke kicked a penalty in the 18th minute. They kept the lead for around a quarter of an hour, but then a quick tap penalty saw Norton race through the surprised Widnes pack before passing to Topliss who fed the supporting Gary Kemble the perfect pass to allow the full-back to outstrip the cover for a well-worked try. Crooks converted and Hull took the lead for the first time in 113 minutes of play.

Five minutes later Hull captain David Topliss fooled the Widnes defence with his sheer pace and sprinted over the line for an unconverted try. Widnes fought their way back with a penalty from Burke and then a superb sweeping movement ended in O'Loughlin sending Wright in at the corner. Burke was desperately unlucky when his towering conversion attempt hit a post.

In the 62nd minute, the Hull forwards launched a powerful assault down the centre of the field. Loose forward Norton drew the defence sideways, then turned the point of attack with a clever pass to Topliss, who once again dashed over for a try which Crooks converted to give the Airlie Birds a 13-7 lead. Widnes threatened a late victory when a Burke goal brought them to within four points, but seven minutes from time teenager Lee Crooks burst through the heart of the Chemics' defence to score under the posts. The second-row forward converted his own try and Hull were the Cup holders for the first time in 68 years.

Hull pose with the Challenge Cup at the Boulevard in 1982, for the first time for 68 years.

Rugby League Cup Results

Preliminary Round

Hull KR	22	Featherstone R	18

First Round

Batley	23	Huyton	15
Bradford N	14	Dewsbury	12
Bramley	4	Wakefield T	16
Cardiff C	8	Widnes	19
Carlisle	2	Castleford	17
Doncaster	6	Rochdale H	7
Fulham	14	Hunslet	4
Halifax	17	Huddersfield	12
Hull	29	Salford	15
Keighley	6	Barrow	12
Leigh	28	Warrington	17
St Helens	12	Wigan	20
Swinton	5	Oldham	15
Whitehaven	7	Hull KR	17
Workington T	32	Blackpool B	8
York	6	Leeds	34

Second Round

Barrow	1	Leeds	9
Batley	6	Castleford	31
Bradford N	17	Workington T	8
Fulham	5	Hull	11
Halifax	28	Rochdale H	7
Hull KR	17	Leigh	18
Wakefield T	18	Oldham	12
Wigan	7	Widnes	9

Third Round

Bradford N	8	Widnes	8
Hull	16	Halifax	10
Leigh	3	Castleford	8
Wakefield T	2	Leeds	20

Third Round Replay

Widnes	10	Bradford N	7

Semi-finals

Hull	15	Castleford	Il

At Headingley, Leeds
Attendance: 21,207   *Receipts: £41,867*

Widnes	11	Leeds	8

At Station Road, Swinton
Attendance: 13,075   *Receipts: £25,796*

Final

Saturday, 1 May at Wembley Stadium, London

	T	G	P		T	G	P
Hull	2	4	14	**Widnes**	3	3	14
G.E.Kemble				M.Burke		G	
D.B.O'Hara	T			S.Wright	T		
T.Day				K.O'Loughlin			
S.Evans				E.Cunningham	2T		
P.Prendiville				J.Basnett			
D.Topliss				E.Hughes			
K.Harkin				A.Gregory		G	
T.Skerrett				M.O'Neill			
R.Wileman				K.Elwell		D	
R.Stone				B.Lockwood			
M.Crane				L.Gorley			
G.Lloyd		4G		E.Prescott			
S.Norton	T			M.Adams			

Substitutes:
L.Crooks (for Crane)   A.Myler (for Burke)
    S.O'Neill (for Lockwood)

Lance Todd Trophy: E.Cunningham
Referee: G.F.Lindop (Wakefield) Half-time: 6-6
Attendance: 92,147   *Receipts: £684,500*

Final Replay

Wednesday, 19 May at Elland Road, Leeds

	T	G	P		T	G	P
Hull	4	3	18	**Widnes**	1	3	9
G.E.Kemble	T			M.Burke		3G	
C.A.Sullivan				S.Wright	T		
J.Leulaui				K.O'Loughlin			
S.Evans				E.Cunningham			
P.Prendiville				J.Basnett			
D.Topliss	2T			E.Hughes			
A.Dean				A.Gregory			
K.Tindall				M.O'Neill			
A.Duke				K.Elwell			
R.Stone				B.Lockwood			
T.Skerrett				L.Gorley			
L.Crooks	T	3G		E.Prescott			
S.Norton				M.Adams			

Substitutes:
M. Crane (for Norton)
Lance Todd Trophy: E.Cunningham
Man of the Match: D.Topliss
Referee: G.F.Lindop (Wakefield) Half-time: 8-2
Attendance: 41,171   *Receipts: £180,525*

Cup presented by Mr N.MacFarlane MP.

IN ONE of the most incident-packed Wembley Finals for years, Featherstone Rovers produced a display of such authority that they achieved the seemingly impossible and beat firm favourites Hull.

Before the game Hull had 99 per cent of the Rugby League world tipping them not just to win, but to do so by a wide margin. Outside the little mining village of Featherstone – and, if they had dared to say it, even in the village itself – Rovers were given no chance.

However, the heady mix of the Challenge Cup and Wembley Stadium is renowned for causing players to freeze, and there is no way of predicting which team will fare the worst when the numbness strikes. In 1983 it was the players of Hull who were stricken by the strange sickness, and between them they produced a pathetic display of Rugby League at its very worst. They lacked commitment and co-ordination and showed little interest in attempting to string together even basic moves.

The clever and confident play which they had used so well throughout the season simply evaporated in the Wembley arena and they became a tense and error-prone team.

In complete contrast to Hull, Featherstone were a strong, self-assured side that had planned and prepared for their victory with military-like precision. They knew from the onset that they had to prevent the Airlie Birds from spreading the ball out wide to their talented backs and to do this they had to concentrate on their defensive work, especially their tackling.

Rovers struck first blood in the seventh minute when their second-row forward David Hobbs surged through James Leuluai's attempted tackle and plunged over the line near the corner. Quinn failed with the conversion attempt but added a penalty-goal before half-time. In an eventful first half Hull lost Kevin Harkin following a collision with Rovers' Terry Hudson, and Featherstone had John Gilbert carried off with concussion when Paul Rose tackled him far too high. Rose's crude tackle earned him ten minutes in the sin bin, the first-ever player to receive such treatment at Wembley.

Hull shuffled their backs around and finally showed their capabilities in a brief spell at the start of the second half. First referee Whitfield awarded Hull a penalty-try when he adjudged Rovers' Hobbs had unfairly stopped Lee Crooks attempt to gather a kick-through on the line. Crooks added the two points to level the scores. Ten minutes later, Hull swept into a 12-5 lead when Leuluai crossed for a try and

Featherstone Rovers' Steve Quinn prepares to kick his first of four goals that were to help rank outsiders Rovers capture the Cup in 1983, for only the third time in their history.

Crooks kicked two goals. The Rovers stuck to their game plan and a try from Hobbs and two goals from Quinn saw the sides level again.

With only three minutes remaining, Steve Quinn landed a 20-yard shot at goal and Featherstone were worthy 14-12 winners.

Rugby League Cup Results

Preliminary Round

Wigan	14	Cardiff C	4

First Round

Barrow	18	Whitehaven	6
Blackpool B	11	Hull	19
Bradford N	23	York	5
Dewsbury	7	Huyton	13
Featherstone R	21	Batley	5
Huddersfield	5	Halifax	13
Hunslet	12	Hull KR	11
Oldham	5	Workington T	8
Rochdale H	4	Fulham	24
St Helens	52	Carlisle	0
Salford	12	Leigh	5
Swinton	21	Doncaster	13
Wakefield T	27	Keighley	5
Warrington	41	Bramley	3
Widnes	6	Leeds	12
Wigan	7	Castleford	17

The Featherstone Rovers game was played at Wakefield.

Second Round

Barrow	9	Castleford	14
Fulham	4	Bradford N	11
Hull	32	Wakefield T	15
Hunslet	17	Halifax	8
Leeds	13	St Helens	23
Salford	11	Featherstone R	17
Warrington	34	Huyton	2
Workington T	14	Swinton	9

Third Round

Hunslet	8	Castleford	13
St Helens	10	Featherstone R	11
Warrington	4	Hull	10
Workington T	0	Bradford N	17

Semi-finals

Featherstone R	11	Bradford N	6

At Headingley, Leeds
Attendance: 10,784   *Receipts: £22,579*

Hull	14	Castleford	7

At Elland Road, Leeds
Attendance: 26,031   *Receipts: £65,498*

Final

Saturday, 7 May at Wembley, Stadium, London

	T	G	P		T	G	P
Featherstone R	2	4	14	**Hull**	2	3	12
N.Barker				C.E.Kemble			
J.Marsden				D.B.O'Hara			
S.Quinn		4G		S.Evans			
J.Gilbert				J.Leuluai	T		
K.Kellett				P.Prendiville			
A.Banks				D.Topliss			
T.Hudson				K.Harkin			
M.Gibbins				T.Skerrett			
R.Handscombe				J.H.Bridges			
S.Hankins				R.Stone			
D.Hobbs	2T			P.Rose			
T.Slatter				L.Crooks	T	3G	
P.Smith				S.Norton			

Substitutes:

P. Lyman (for Gilbert)	T.Day (for Harkin)
G.Siddall (for Slatter)	M.Crane (for Day)

Lance Todd Trophy: D.Hobbs

Referee: R.Whitfield (Widnes)   *Half-time: 5-0*
Attendance: 84,475   *Receipts: £655,510*

Cup presented by Lord Gormley of Ashton in Makerfield, OBE.

Widnes centre Joe Lydon side-steps Wigan's Denis Ramsdale as he embarks on another blistering run in the 1984 Final. In support is Chemics' full-back Mick Burke.

WIGAN'S coach Alex Murphy tasted defeat at Wembley for the first time in six visits and in a remarkable outburst after the game laid the blame on the overseas pair of Cannon and Tamati. For most spectators, the public denouncement of the Australian and New Zealander seemed severe when the whole side had played badly. Indeed, Wigan, appearing at Wembley for the first time in 14 years, were a shadow of the side that had played so well in the rounds leading to the Final. Watched by an estimated following of 30,000 of their fans, the Riversiders turned in an inept and scrappy display that was punctuated with some of the worst basic errors seen at this grand old stadium.

Widnes, meanwhile, were solid and very efficient but, apart for the dazzling tries they scored, far from spectacular.

Wigan opened the scoring in the 14th minute with a penalty-goal from Colin Whitfield but then failed to worry the well-drilled Chemics defence. The only bright spots in the Wigan attack were when Shaun Edwards, who at 17 years, 6 months and 19 days was the youngest-ever player to appear at Wembley, linked up from his full-back position.

In the 26th minute the O'Neill brothers, Steve and Mike, linked well and opened the way for wingman John Basnett to race for the line and pass to Keiron O'Loughlin who juggled with the ball before finally touching down for the Chemics'

Rugby League Cup Results

Preliminary Round

Fulham	14	Swinton	4
Carlisle	12	Widnes	20

First Round

Barrow	12	Workington T	14
Salford	16	Leeds	24
Hunslet	21	Keighley	10
Bradford N	20	Featherstone R	4
Whitehaven	10	Fulham	17
Widnes	54	Dewsbury	10
Blackpool B	10	Hull KR	27
Doncaster	11	Batley	8
Halifax	7	Wakefield T	19
Rochdale H	8	York	17
Kent Invicta	20	Castleford	42
Warrington	34	Huddersfield	16
St Helens	16	Leigh	10
Cardiff C	6	Hull	34
Bramley	10	Wigan	10
Oldham	28	Huyton	10

First Round Replay

Wigan	34	Bramley	4

Second Round

Workington T	3	Leeds	12
Hunslet	7	Bradford N	17
Fulham	10	Widnes	12
Hull KR	40	Doncaster	7
Wakefield T	12	York	20
Castleford	23	Warrington	16
St Helens	24	Hull	14
Wigan	30	Oldham	6

Third Round

Leeds	13	Bradford N	13
Widnes	21	Hull KR	10
York	14	Castleford	12
St Helens	7	Wigan	16

Third Round Replay

Bradford N	10	Leeds	12

Semi-finals

Leeds	4	Widnes	15

At Swinton
Attendance: 14,046   *Receipts: £37,183*

York	8	Wigan	14

At Elland Road, Leeds
Attendance: 17,156   *Receipts: £52,888*

Final

Saturday, 5 May at Wembley Stadium, London

	T	G	P		T	G	P
Widnes	3	4	19	**Wigan**	1	1	6
M.Burke		3G		S.Edwards			
S.Wright				D.Ramsdale			
E.Hughes				D.Stephenson			
J.Lydon	2T			C.Whitfield		G	
J.Basnett				H.Gill			
K.O'Loughlin	T			M.Cannon			
A.Gregory				G.Stephens			
S.O'Neill		D		K.Hemsley	T		
K.Elwell				H.Tamati			
K.Tamati				B.Case			
L.Gorley				G.West			
M.O'Neill				M.Scott			
M.Adams				J.Pendlebury			
D.Hulme				W.Elvin			
F.Whitfield				B.Juliff			

Substitutes:

Hulme (for Hughes)	Elvin (for Whitfield)
Whitfield (for M.O'Neill)	Juliff (for Case)

Lance Todd Trophy: Joe Lydon
Referee: B.Thompson (Huddersfield)
Half-time: 12-2
Attendance: 80,116   *Receipts: £686,171*

first try. Full-back Burke added the two points. On the half-hour, a badly-judged kick by Wigan's Cannon saw the ball deflected to Les Gorley, who flicked it to Kevin Tamati. The New Zealand prop looked around and fired a quick pass out to Joe Lydon. The Widnes centre gathered the ball perfectly and in an amazing piece of acceleration, outstripped the entire Wigan defence to score a tremendous try which the ever-reliable Burke converted.

Steve O'Neill kicked a drop-goal at the start of the second half to put Widnes into a 14-2 lead, and in the 71st minute a rare Wigan excursion into Chemics' territory broke down when Gary Stephens dropped the ball inside the Widnes '25'.

First to respond was Joe Lydon, who collected the ball, nipped between two Wigan defenders and once again began to accelerate towards the Riversiders' try line. Well into his stride he rounded full-back Edwards with contemptuous ease, then sped past the cover defence to touch down for one of the finest-ever Wembley tries. Burke missed the conversion but landed a penalty-goal minutes later.

With six minutes to the final whistle, Kerry Hemsley, who had been flown from Australia for the Final, barged his way over for a consolation try that was far too late to do anything for his battered Wigan side.

1985 Hull 24 Wigan 28

THE 50th Challenge Cup Final held at Wembley provided one of the finest-ever games and records galore for an audience of millions worldwide.

A record total of ten overseas players, six in Hull colours, contributed to a record ten-try, 52-point thriller which gave winners Wigan a record-equalling seventh victory at Wembley. Poor Hull scored the same number of tries as Wigan, and scored more points than any other beaten side – but after six attempts they still could not win at Wembley.

The Airlie Birds opened the deluge of points in the second minute when Lee Crooks landed a penalty-goal. Nine minutes later ex-Aberavon Rugby Union wing Kevin James made full use of a gap carved out by Sterling and Kemble and touched down for Hull's first try. Crooks failed with the conversion.

The rampant Hull side had pinned Wigan inside their own '25' for much of the first quarter of an hour but still had only six points to show for their endeavours. On 17 minutes Wigan broke free of the Hull defence and Kenny elected to pass to Potter on the fifth tackle. The loose forward passed to Ferguson who jinked round O'Hara to score a fine try. Henderson Gill converted and Wigan were back on level terms. Ten minutes later the inspirational Kenny collected the ball from Mike Ford around the half-way line and swept past Kemble with a superb run to touch down in the corner. Stephenson converted.

Lee Crooks pulled two points back for Hull with a 33rd-minute penalty-goal but six minutes later Stephenson handed the ball to Gill for a thrilling 75-yard sprint down the touchline for the Riversiders' third try.

Three minutes into the second half, full-back Shaun Edwards exploded on to a Kenny pass to score at the side of the uprights. Gill converted to give Wigan a 22-8 lead.

Hull were reeling but managed to fight back with style. Australian Sterling tore through the Wigan defence to set up Steve Evans with a try in the 45th minute, but once again the

Wigan's Shaun Edwards jinks his way past the Hull defence in the 1985 Final.

Cherry and Whites scored a classic try when Ferguson picked up a loose ball and sprinted past Kemble to score.

Once again Hull fought back. Steve Norton and Paul Rose contrived a walk-over try for Leuluai, then ten minutes later

Rugby League Cup Results

Preliminary Round

Barrow	12	Halifax	26
Doncaster	6	Wakefield T	25
Leeds	68	Bridgend	6
Salford	14	Featherstone R	6

First Round

Bradford N	50	Southend I	18
Bramley	16	Blackpool B	15
Fulham	4	Halifax	17
Hull	52	Carlisle	6
Keighley	5	Runcorn H	12
Leeds	4	Widnes	14
Leigh	14	Huddersfield B	6
Mansfield M	10	Hunslet	34
Oldham	8	Castleford	14
Rochdale H	11	York	5
St. Helens	3	Hull K.R	8
Salford	31	Swinton	6
Sheffield E	19	Warrington	54
Whitehaven	8	Wakefield T	10
Wigan	46	Batley	8
Workington	28	Dewsbury	6

Second Round

Bradford N	13	Wakefield T	2
Bramley	24	Salford	10
Castleford	64	Workington T	4
Halifax	6	Hull	22
Leigh	27	Hunslet	28
Rochdale H	4	Hull KR	38
Warrington	14	Wigan	24
Widnes	36	Runcorn H	11

Third Round

Bradford N	6	Wigan	7
Castleford	58	Bramley	18
Hull	6	Widnes	6
Hunslet	7	Hull KR	27

Third Round Replay

Widnes	12	Hull	19

Semi-finals

Hull KR	11	Wigan	18

At Elland Road, Leeds
Attendance: 19,275   *Receipts: £70,192*

Hull	10	Castleford	10

At Headingley
Attendance: 20,982   *Receipts: £64,163*

Semi-final Replay

Hull	22	Castleford	16

At Headingley
Attendance: 20,968   *Receipts: £65,005*

Final

Saturday, 4 May at Wembley Stadium, London

	T	G	P		T	G	P
Hull	5	2	24	**Wigan**	5	4	28
G.Kemble				S.Edwards	T		
K.James	T			J.Ferguson	2T		
S.Evans	T			D.Stephenson		G	
J.Leuluai	2T			S.Donlan			
D.O'Hara				H.Gill	T	3G	
F.Ah Kuoi				B.Kenny	T		
P.Sterling				M.Ford			
L.Crooks		2G		N.Courtney			
S.Patrick				N.Kiss			
N.Puckering				B.Case			
J.Muggleton				G.West			
P.Rose				B.Dunn			
S.Norton				I.Potter			
G.Schofield				N.Du Toit			
G.Divorty	T			D.Campbell			
Substitutes:							
Schofield (for O'Hara)				Campbell (for Case)			
Divorty (for Puckering)							

Lance Todd Trophy: B.Kenny
Referee: R.Campbell (Widnes)   *Half-time: 8-16*
Attendance: 97,801   *Receipts: £760,322*

Sterling passed to Divorty and the big second-rower powered over the line for a try. Eight points behind with only six minutes remaining, Hull had the Riversiders visibly wilting. Two minutes from time, James Leuluai burst clear from half-way and scored Hull's third try of a breathless 12-minute spell. Gary Schofield attempted the conversion but once again he failed and Wigan held out for those final four minutes to leave Hull pondering those five missed conversion attempts.

The victorious Castleford side, with John Joyner lifting the trophy, after their 15-14 Wembley victory over Hull Kingston Rovers.

THE pre-match preparations of Castleford and Hull Kingston Rovers could hardly have contrasted more. Castleford, and especially their coach Malcolm Reilly, were oozing confidence, even naming their Wembley side in midweek. Rovers, on the other hand, had big problems. They had lost their second-row forwards Burton and Hogan with broken arms and had struggled all week to get George Fairbairn fit. Then on the very eve of the Final, influential Australian Gavin Miller pulled a hamstring. It was a huge blow to the plans of Rovers' coach Roger Millward, but he decided to keep the injury secret and gamble on playing the severely restricted Miller. The risk failed badly and the normally vigorous Miller was reduced to almost walking pace, his usual driving runs being replaced with a series of passes.

Castleford opened the scoring in the 20th minute when their Great Britain centre Tony Marchant swept 60 yards up the field for a classic centre's try. Martin Ketteridge converted the try to put Cas 6-0 in the lead. Seven minutes later, Rovers Kiwi centre Gary Prohm kicked a penalty-goal.

On 32 minutes Castleford scrum-half Bob Beardmore calmly stopped play and kicked a superb drop-goal to give his side an extra one-point cushion. A minute before half-time, Castleford second-row man Keith England blundered badly when he passed to Hull KR's Andy Kelly, who

transferred to Gary Prohm. He raced 50 yards to score a gift try.

Within minutes of the second half getting under way, Castleford stretched their lead when Bob Beardmore prodded the ball towards the Rovers line and the usually alert Prohm was far too slow to control the danger as the Castleford scrum-half nipped in to score.

Throughout the game Jamie Sandy, the tiny Australian wingman, had posed tremendous problems for the Rovers defence, his flying runs up the flank creating havoc for the Robins. In the 62nd minute Sandy cut loose again and in a superb run left three Hull defenders in his wake as he swept over for a glorious and well-deserved try.

At 15-6 it seemed there was little doubt that the Cup was on its way to Castleford. But on 67 minutes Gary Prohm redeemed himself for his earlier error and twisted, turned, then forced his way over for a try.

With a minute to go, Rovers substitute John Lydiat scored in the corner and put the Robins within a point of Castleford and the Cup. Australian stand-off John Dorahy stepped forward to take the conversion attempt from a very difficult but still kickable angle. After having seemed to have taken far too long to prepare for the kick, he struck the ball hard and straight, only to see it drift left of the posts, to leave Castleford with the victory they richly deserved.

Rugby League Cup Results

Preliminary Round

Carlisle	20	Mansfield M	14
Hull	38	Dudley Hill	10
Hunslet	20	Kells	8
Swinton	88	Leeds	30

First Round

Blackpool B	30	Runcorn H	10
Bradford N	10	Wakefield T	8
Bramley	8	Batley	6
Dewsbury	19	St Helens	22
Doncaster	18	Salford	12
Featherstone R	14	Widnes	18
Fulham	14	Barrow	26
Halifax	4	Leeds	24
Huddersfield	4	Rochdale H	10
Hull KR	22	Hull	6
Hunslet	6	Castleford	60
Keighley	2	Leigh	24
Oldham	56	Carlisle	10
Warrington	62	Sheffield E	11
Workington T	12	Wigan	56
York	18	Whitehaven	6

The Bradford Northern and Dewsbury Games were played at Headingley. The Fulham game was played at Wigan. The Oldham game was played at Oldham Athletic AFC. The Workington Town game was played at Workington AFC.

Second Round

Barrow	6	Castleford	30
Bradford N	20	Bramley	20
Leeds	28	Doncaster	10
Leigh	31	Blackpool B	10
Oldham	13	Warrington	6
Widnes	36	Rochdale H	20
Wigan	24	St Helens	14
York	6	Hull KR	34

Doncaster gave up ground advantage.

Second Round Replay

Bramley	2	Bradford N	36

Third Round

Hull KR	25	Leigh	10
Oldham	6	Bradford N	1
Widnes	10	Leeds	10
Wigan	2	Castleford	10

Third Round Replay

Leeds	5	Widnes	0

Semi-finals

Castleford	18	Oldham	7

At Central Park, Wigan
Attendance: 12,430   *Receipts: £38,296*

Hull KR	24	Leeds	24

At Elland Road, Leeds
Attendance: 23,866   *Receipts: £83,757*

Semi-final Replay

Hull KR	17	Leeds	0

At Elland Road, Leeds
Attendance: 32,485   *Receipts: £113,345*

Final

Saturday, 3 May at Wembley Stadium, London

	T	G	P		T	G	P
Castleford	3	2	15	**Hull KR**	3	1	14
G.R.Lord				G.A.Fairbairn			
D.Plange				G.Clark			
A.Marchant	T			M.Smith			
G.Hyde				G.J.Prohm	2T		
J.A.Sandy	T			D.Laws			
J.Joyner				J.K.Dorahy		G	
R.Beardmore	T	D		M.P.Harkin			
K.Ward				P.Johnson			
K.Beardmore				D.Watkinson			
B.Johnson				A.Ema			
K.England				A.Kelly			
M.Ketteridge		G		D.Harrison			
I.French				C.J.Miller			
Substitutes:							
D.Rookley (for Lord)				G.Smith (for Kelly)			
S.Horton (for K.Beardmore)				J.Lydiat (for Harrison)	T		

Lance Todd Trophy: R Beardmore

Referee: R.Whitfield (Widnes)   *Half-time: 7-6*
Attendance: 82,134   *Receipts: £806,676*

Cup presented by HRH Princess Alexandra.

1987 Halifax 19 St Helens 18

IT WAS 31 years since Halifax had visited Wembley and in a re-run of their last appearance they exacted revenge on the team that beat them 13-2 in 1956.

Halifax player-coach Chris Anderson made a huge gamble when he included himself in the team, knowing he was still suffering from a bad rib injury. The gamble paid off but Australian Anderson had a very quiet game and was certainly at fault when a missed tackle allowed Saints centre Elia to put Loughlin in for a try in the 53rd minute.

Nevertheless, Anderson's shrewd pre-match planning worked wonderfully well in the first half when Halifax swept to a 12-2 lead. Forwards Scott and Dixon launched themselves at the Saints' defence with a series of damaging charges. The tactics paid dividends in the 11th minute when Mick Scott broke through a sequence of attempted tackles and passed to Wilf George, who burst over the line for a try which St Helens hotly disputed. The Saints defenders argued that they had first been obstructed, then they had successfully pushed George into touch in goal. Referee Holdsworth dismissed their appeals and the try stood.

Paul Loughlin kicked a 20th-minute penalty-goal but 11 minutes later Halifax's forwards struck again when their Irish hooker Seamus McCallion evaded a clutch of defenders to crash over for a try which Colin Whitfield converted.

A minute into the second half, Mark Elia beat Halifax full-back Graham Eadie with his incredible pace and scored a try which Loughlin converted. Ten minutes later, Halifax replied in fine style when Eadie burst on to an inch-perfect pass and scored a try which Whitfield converted to give Halifax an 18-8 lead. Two minutes after that, Elia released Loughlin with a clever pass and the centre sped on for a brilliant try.

John Pendlebury dropped a shrewd goal for Halifax, then with 11 minutes remaining, Paul Round crossed for a converted try to put St Helens within a point of victory and the match into probably the most sensational final ten minutes of all time.

Eight minutes from the whistle, a clever move put Mark Elia over the line for a certain try, but just as he sailed through the air to touch down, John Pendlebury made a desperate lunge at the ball and the force of his blow made it fall harmlessly out of Elia's grasp. St Helens launched a series of attacks at the rapidly-tiring Halifax team and finally Andy Platt pierced the defence to pass to Elia, who crossed for a try. Pandemonium ensued when referee Holdsworth adjudged the pass to be forward and disallowed the 'try'.

Halifax held on and Saints and their coach Alex Murphy were left to rue their apparent disregard of a one-point drop-goal which would have taken the game to a replay.

Turning point of the 1987 Final as Halifax's John Pendlebury's desperate lunge displaces the ball from the grasp of Mark Elia and saves a certain try for St Helens.

Rugby League Cup Results

Preliminary Round

Castleford	74	Blackbrook	6
Elland	6	Heworth	10
Hunslet	13	York	0
Kells	4	Fulham	4
St Helens	18	Swinton	16
Workington T	0	Wigan	68

The Elland game was played at Halifax. The Kells game was played at Whitehaven. The Workington T game was played at Wigan.

Preliminary Round Replay

Fulham	22	Kells	14

First Round

Barrow	54	Batley	2
Blackpool B	10	Wakefield T	15
Bramley	2	Hull	10
Castleford	16	Widnes	24
Dewsbury	12	St Helens	48
Featherstone R	12	Hunslet	26
Fulham	10	Halifax	38
Huddersfield B	10	Whitehaven	32
Hull KR	29	Doncaster	14
Mansfield M	14	Heworth	7
Oldham	10	Wigan	8
Rochdale H	4	Carlisle	4
Runcorn H	6	Leigh	25
Salford	0	Leeds	4
Sheffield E	6	Keighley	8
Warrington	17	Bradford N	21

First Round Replay

Carlisle	30	Rochdale H	22

Second Round

Bradford N	6	Widnes	6
Halifax	29	Hunslet	10
Hull KR	42	Keighley	4
Leeds	26	Barrow	7
Leigh	18	Carlisle	6
Mansfield M	7	Hull	38
Oldham	14	St Helens	24
Wakefield T	2	Whitehaven	25

Second Round Replay

Widnes	29	Bradford N	12

Third Round

Halifax	35	Hull KR	7
Hull	8	Leigh	12
Leeds	7	Widnes	14
St Helens	41	Whitehaven	12

Semi-finals

St Helens	14	Leigh	8

At Wigan
Attendance: 13,105   *Receipts: £48,627*

Halifax	12	Widnes	8

At Leeds
Attendance: 16,064   *Receipts: £61,260*

Final

Saturday, 2 May at Wembley Stadium, London

	T	G	P		T	G	P
Halifax	**3**	**4**	**19**	**St Helens**	**3**	**3**	**18**
G.Eadie	T			P.Veivers			
S.Wilson				B.Ledger			
C.Whitfield		3G		P.Loughlin	T	3G	
G.Rix				M.Elia	T		
W.George	T			K.McCormack			
C.Anderson				B.Clark			
G.Stephens				N.Holding			
G.Beevers				T.Burke			
S.McCallion	T			G.Liptrot			
K.Neller				J.Fieldhouse			
P.Dixon				A.Platt			
M.Scott				R.Haggerty			
J.Pendlebury		D		C.Arkwright			
B.Juliff				P.Round	T		
N.James				P.Forber			
Substitutes:							
Juliff (for Anderson)				Round (for Haggerty)			
James for Beevers (70 mm.)							

Lance Todd Trophy: G.Eadie

Referee: John Holdsworth (Kippax)   *Half-time: 12-2*
Attendance: 91,267   *Receipts: £1,009,206*

DESPITE fielding a record five Australians in their side, Cup holders Halifax could do little to halt a Wigan side at their merciless best.

The first 20 minutes of the game were a poor advertisement for Rugby League as both sides struggled to settle down and play with any hint of cohesion. Halifax were desperately unlucky to lose inspirational loose-forward Les Holliday in the 20th minute when the club record signing left the field with knee problems.

However, his substitution seemed to encourage a change of strategy for Wigan, for they almost at once began to finally gel together and attack as one unit. Wigan's half-back pairing of Edwards and Gregory hit perfect form, completely monopolising the midfield and devising and performing a series of attacks that destroyed Halifax in an electrifying 11-minute spell before the half-time break.

Wigan's first points came after 27 minutes when a brilliant burst of speed put Shaun Edwards in the clear, only to be tackled a yard short of the line. Intelligent thinking from Kevin Iro saw the New Zealander collect the ball at acting half-back and break through the Halifax defence to score. Five minutes later Gregory fed the ball to Dean Bell and the Kiwi centre transferred perfectly to Henderson Gill over swept over the line in the corner.

Two minutes later Wigan were 12-0 in front when Kevin Iro capitalised on the huge gap his brother, Tony, had punched in the Halifax defence from a powerful run deep inside his own half. Almost on half-time, fast and clever handling between Edwards, Gill and Bell carved open a breach for Joe Lydon to sprint through for Wigan's fourth try.

Five minutes into the second half the diminutive but tremendously strong Andy Gregory flipped an adventurous pass to Tony Iro and the Kiwi simply strolled over the line for a try. Moments later Joe Lydon collected the ball from Halifax's restart and embarked upon one of his celebrated defence-splitting runs. The full-back sprinted 60 yards through the heart of the Halifax team before passing the ball

Captains collide. Wigan skipper Shaun Edwards looks inside as he is confronted by Halifax's Australian captain Graham Eadie during the 1988 Final.

Rugby League Cup Results

Preliminary Round

Bramley	6	Sheffield E	14
Carlisle	8	Whitehaven	8
Heworth	11	West Hull	4
Kells	0	Leeds	28
Leigh Miners	4	Hunslet	23
Warrington	48	Huddersfield	10

The Heworth game was played at York. The Kells game was played at Whitehaven. The Leigh Miners game was played at Leigh.

Preliminary Round Replay

Whitehaven	8	Carlisle	22

First Round

Dewsbury	10	Widnes	38
Doncaster	18	Batley	10
Featherstone R	32	York	21
Fulham	4	Mansfield M	16
Heworth	4	Halifax	60
Hull KR	14	Carlisle	6
Hunslet	10	Hull	27
Keighley	30	Workington T	4
Leeds	22	Castleford	14
Leigh	12	St Helens	22
Rochdale H	6	Barrow	4
Runcorn H	6	Springfield B	8
Salford	16	Swinton	6
Wakefield T	10	Sheffield E	14
Warrington	17	Oldham	6
Wigan	2	Bradford N	0

The Heworth game was played at York.

Second Round

Doncaster	16	Mansfield M	8
Halifax	30	Rochdale H	6
Hull	26	Sheffield E	6
Hull KR	35	Featherstone R	26
Keighley	2	Widnes	16
Salford	12	Springfield B	10
Warrington	20	St Helens	24
Wigan	30	Leeds	14

Third Round

Hull	27	Doncaster	12
Hull KR	4	Halifax	26
Salford	22	St Helens	6
Wigan	10	Widnes	26

Semi-finals

Salford	4	Wigan	34

At Burnden Park, Bolton
Attendance: 20,784   *Receipts: £95,876*

Halifax	0	Hull	0

At Leeds
Attendance: 20,534   *Receipts: £82,026*

Semi-final Replay

Halifax	4	Hull	3

At Elland Road, Leeds
Attendance: 25,117   *Receipts: £113,679*

Final

Saturday, 30 April at Wembley Stadium, London

	T	G	P		T	G	P
Halifax	2	2	12	**Wigan**	7	2	32
G.Eadie				J.Lydon	T	G	
M.Meredith				T.Iro	T		
T.Anderson	T			K.Iro	2T		
I.Wilkinson				D.Bell	T		
C.Whitfield		2G		H.Gill	T		
B.Grogan				S.Edwards			
S.Robinson				A.Gregory		G	
N.James	T			B.Case			
S.McCallion				N.Kiss			
K.Neller				A.Iford			
L.Holliday				A.Goodway			
P.Dixon				I.Potter			
J.Pendlebury				E.Hanley	T		
D.Fairbank				G.Byrne			
M.Scott				S.Wane			

Substitutes:
Scott (for Holliday)   Byrne (for Edwards)
Fairbank (for Robinson)   Wane (for Potter)

Lance Todd Trophy: A.Gregory

Referee: F.Lindop (Wakefield)   Half-time: 0-16
Attendance: 94,273   Receipts: £1,102,247

inside to Ellery Hanley, who outstripped what little remained of the defence and scored directly beneath the posts. Andy Gregory converted the try, Wigan's first goal of the afternoon, to put the Riversiders into a 26-0 lead.

Sensing total humiliation, Halifax rallied bravely and Australian wingman Tony Anderson scored a fine try which Whitfield converted. Wigan hit back ten minutes later when Dean Bell scored a try which Lydon converted.

Thirteen minutes from time Halifax added a little more respectability to the result when they scored the final points of the game when Neil James crossed the line for a try which Colin Whitfield converted.

Wigan's Andy Gregory collected the Lance Todd Trophy for one of the finest midfield displays ever seen at Wembley.

Wigan, in unfamiliar blue and white, after hammering St Helens 27-0 at Wembley.

WIGAN became the ninth club to retain the Challenge Cup in successive seasons with a superb display that excelled even their superb performance in the previous seasons defeat of Halifax. The Riversiders scored five superb tries and played quality football throughout the impressive victory over the Saints, but the majority of the discussion following the game was how badly St Helens had played.

Saints were absolutely atrocious. They fumbled and spilled the ball at an alarming rate and were never able to make any form of impression on the game. The chilling statistics of 27 handling errors by St Helens was a stark image of just how poor the team with such tremendous talent had played. Coach Alex Murphy denounced his team without mercy after the game saying: *"Several players saved their worst performance of the season for the most important day."*

Murphy was quite right, but many people questioned his own role in Saints' defeat, pointing to the fact that he left young Gary Connolly on the field when it was painfully obvious that the 17-year-old amateur was far from comfortable in his full-back role.

Wigan opened the scoring in the third minute when Connolly failed to control a Lydon downfield kick and within seconds Kevin Iro latched on to a clever pass from Hanley and crashed through some slipshod defence to score his first try of the afternoon. Joe Lydon added a penalty-goal

a quarter of an hour later to give Wigan a six-point lead.

In the 26th minute the unique skills of Ellery Hanley provided a second try when the Wigan captain, and the Lance Todd Trophy winner embarked on a powerful 45-yard run which beat four St Helens defenders and created one of the all-time classic Wembley tries. Lydon converted, and just after the interval Andy Gregory dropped a goal to put the Riversiders into a 13-0 lead.

Minutes later Kevin Iro elected not to pass to his unmarked brother Tony, and instead powered his way through a cluster of players for his second try. In the 65th minute Shaun Edwards broke free with ease and his superb run and simple pass gave a try under the posts for his half-back partner Andy Gregory. Joe Lydon kicked the conversion, his third goal of the game.

With around four minutes remaining, another scintillating Wigan attack saw Joe Lydon pass to Steve Hampson who dived over for a try in the corner. The touchdown was just reward for the full-back who had missed out on three previous Wembley Finals with a broken leg and two broken arms respectively.

It was to be the final score of the afternoon. Wigan had triumphantly laid to rest the ghosts of the 1961 and 1966 Wembley Finals when their traditional rivals had won on both occasions.

Rugby League Cup Results

Preliminary Round

Barrow Island	11	Thatto Heath	18
Leeds	32	Hunslet	6
Milford	0	Swinton	36
Wakefield T	18	Bramley	10
West Hull	2	Doncaster	48
York	35	Workington T	8

First Round

Barrow	38	Huddersfield	16
Carlisle	58	Mansfield M	I
Chorley B	8	Thatto Heath	4
Dewsbury	9	Oldham	40
Doncaster	6	Wigan	38
Fulham	10	Bradford N	28
Hull	4	Castleford	7
Rochdale H	24	Hull KR	28
Runcorn H	10	Keighley	28
Salford	14	Widnes	18
Sheffield E	23	Leigh	17
Swinton	5	St Helens	16
Wakefield T	34	Batley	4
Warrington	25	Halifax	8
Whitehaven	0	Featherstone R	32
York	9	Leeds	28

Second Round

Bradford N	4	Wigan	17
Castleford	18	Widnes	32
Hull KR	28	Chorley B	4
Leeds	24	Carlisle	4
St Helens	28	Barrow	6
Sheffield E	20	Oldham	32
Wakefield T	4	Featherstone R	10
Warrington	56	Keighley	7

Third Round

Hull KR	4	Warrington	30
Leeds	4	Widnes	24
Oldham	4	Wigan	12
St Helens	32	Featherstone R	3

Semi-finals

St Helens	16	Widnes	14

At Wigan
Attendance: 17,119   *Receipts: £70,411*

Wigan	13	Warrington	6

At Maine Road, Manchester
Attendance: 26,529   *Receipts: £144,056*

Final

Saturday, 29 April at Wembley Stadium, London

	T	G	P		T	G	P
Wigan	5	4	27	**St Helens**	0	0	0
S.Hampson	T			G.Connolly			
T.Iro				M.O'Connor			
K.Iro	2T			P.Veivers			
D.Bell				P.Louglilin			
J.Lydon		3G		L.Quirk			
S.Edwards				S.Cooper			
A.Gregory	T		D	N.Holding			
I.Lucas				T.Burke			
N.Kiss				P.Groves			
A.Shelford				P.Forber			
A.Platt				B.Dwyer			
I.Potter				R.Haggerty			
E.Hanley	T			P.Vautin			
D.Betts				D.Bloor			
A.Goodway				S.Evans			

Substitutes:

Goodway (for Potter)   Evans (for Dwyer)

Betts (for Kiss)   Bloor (for Loughlin)

Lance Todd Trophy: E.Hanley

Referee: R.Tennant (Castleford)   *Half-time: 12-0*
Attendance: 78,000   *Receipts: £1,121,293*

1990 Wigan 36 Warrington 14

In 1990, Wigan celebrated their record-breaking third successive Challenge Cup Final victory in the Wembley dressing room that was destined to be their second home.

WIGAN'S emphatic victory over Warrington created records galore. They became the first team to win the Cup for a third successive time and the most successful side in the competition's history with their 11th victory, 20th Final, 16th Wembley appearance and tenth Wembley win. Andy Gregory became the first player to win the Lance Todd Trophy twice at Wembley and his winners' medal was a record fifth.

Wigan's victory was also an immensely brave one. Shaun Edwards, already playing with a broken arm, suffered a horrendous double fracture of an eye socket and a depressed cheekbone in the tenth minute, but refused to leave the field until a few minutes from the final whistle.

During the week leading up to the Final, the Riversiders had serious doubts as to the fitness of such key players as Ellery Hanley, Joe Lydon, Kevin Iro and Andy Platt. The worries about Wigan's pre-match fitness gave Warrington great hope and several neutral observers tipped the Wire to halt the Cherry and Whites' relentless Cup victories. However, on the day they were little match for the might of

Wigan and despite giving a better performance than St Helens and Halifax, they were just as outclassed. One newspaper reporting: '*Warrington had little more to offer than honest physical endeavour, and the quiet that descended upon Wembley when Wigan led 14-2 was faintly embarrassing.*'

Wigan opened the scoring in the 11th minute when Joe Lydon kicked a penalty-goal, then went eight points in front 11 minutes later when Denis Betts scored a converted try following a bad mistake by the Warrington defence. Paul Bishop landed a penalty-goal to give Wire a glimmer of hope, but minutes later another badly-placed kick let Mark Preston in for the second Wigan try, which Lydon converted. The Wigan full-back kicked his fourth goal three minutes before half-time but, moments later, Wire captain Mike Gregory surprised both the crowd and the Riversiders' defence when he crashed over the line directly under the posts. Paul Bishop, whose clever run and pass had created the time and space for Gregory's try, converted and at 16-8 all was not totally lost for Warrington.

Eight minutes into the second half, Tony Iro scored his

Rugby League Cup Results

Preliminary Round

Fulham	23	Doncaster	16
Leeds	8	Bradford N	24
Millom	0	Bison	4
Oldham	30	Huddersfield	8
St. Helens	39	Castleford	12
Thatto Heath	2	Batley	45

First Round

Barrow	12	Sheffield E	22
Bramley	14	Helens	22
Chorley	6	Keighley	12
Fulham	14	Ryedale-York	14
Hull	46	Halifax	0
Hull KR	4	Wigan	6
Nottingham C	2	Dewsbury	32
Oldham	30	Workington T	8
Rochdale H	38	Carlisle	6
Runcorn H	12	Bradford N	22
Salford	56	Bison	6
Swinton	10	Wakefield T	10
Trafford B	14	Hunslet	7
Warrington	20	Featherstone R	12
Whitehaven	23	Leigh	22
Widnes	26	Batley	10

First Round Replays

Ryedale-York	12	Fulham	16
Wakefield T	32	Swinton	4

Second Round

Fulham	2	Bradford N	20
Hull	12	St Helens	24
Salford	7	Oldham	18
Wakefield T	27	Sheffield E	12
Warrington	20	Trafford B	11
Whitehaven	46	Keighley	10
Widnes	22	Rochdale H	16
Wigan	30	Dewsbury	6

Third Round

Bradford N	10	Warrington	12
St Helens	44	Whitehaven	10
Wakefield T	14	Wigan	26
Widnes	4	Oldham	16

Semi-finals

Wigan	20	St Helens	14

At Manchester United FC
Attendance: 26,489   *Receipts: £177,161*

Warrington	10	Oldham	6

At Wigan
Attendance: 15,631   *Receipts: £30,500*

Final

Saturday, 28 April at Wembley Stadium, London

	T	G	P		T	G	P
Wigan	6	6	36	**Warrington**	2	3	14
S.Hampson				D.Lyon	T		
J.Lydon		6G		D.Drummond			
K.Iro	2T			G.Mercer			
D.Bell				P.Darbyshire		G	
M.Preston	2T			M.Forster			
S.Edwards				M.Crompton			
A.Gregory				P.Bishop		2G	
A.Shelford				T.Burke			
M.Dermott				D.Mann			
A.Platt				N.Harmon			
D.Betts	T			B.Jackson			
A.Goodway				G.Sanderson			
E.Hanley	T			M.Gregory	T		
B.Goulding				B.McGinty			
I.Gildart				M.Thomas			

Substitutes:

Goulding (for Dermott)   Thomas (for Jackson)
Gildart (for Preston)   McGinty (for Bishop)

Lance Todd Trophy: A.Gregory

Referee: J.Holdsworth (Kippax)   *Half-time: 16-8*
Attendance: 77,729   *Receipts: £1,360,000*

first try when he cut through some feeble Warrington defending. Minutes later the Cherry and Whites pulled further away when a sweeping long-range attack saw Preston score his second try of the game. Ellery Hanley surged through some poor defence for a try which Lydon converted, and then Warrington's Gregory broke free from a scrum and, after a strong run, passed to Lydon who raced 40 yards to score a try which Darbyshire converted. It was some consolation but Wigan had the last say when Iro scored his second try following another tremendous run.

1991 Wigan 13 St Helens 8

Saints forwards Kevin Ward and John Harrison tangle with Wigan captain Ellery Hanley in 1991.

WIGAN continued their assault of the Challenge Cup record books with their fourth successive victory. It was the Riversiders' 12th win in 21 Finals, their 11th win in 17 Wembley appearances, their 20th successive Challenge Cup victory and the crowd paid record receipts of just over £1.5 million. Ellery Hanley became the first captain to collect the Challenge Cup on three successive occasions, and Andy Gregory played in his seventh unbeaten Wembley Final. Even defeated St Helens got in on the act – their 6ft 7ins forward John Harrison was the tallest-ever player at Wembley.

It could have all gone terribly wrong for Wigan, however. Playing ten games in 33 days had taken its toll on the players and the squad was plagued with a host of injuries. Before the game the Wigan doctor administered painkilling injections to Shaun Edwards, Andy Gregory, Martin Dermott, Andy Platt and Kevin Iro. He also gave influential captain Ellery Hanley an injection to help a badly-torn thigh muscle and then put the loose forward through a late fitness test on the

Wembley pitch. The drastic action prompted Australian coach John Monie to comment that his side was *'held together with needles and sticking plaster'.*

The plan worked, however, and although the Final was hardly ever a classic, and despite a jaded look about them, Wigan held off the challenge of their rivals St Helens to crown a memorable season with what was by now their traditional Wembley victory.

Wigan opened in a style that did little to suggest that they were either overworked or injured. They tore into the Saints' defence with Denis Betts leading the charge. St Helens did little to help their cause with a series of inept blunders and almost constant basic handling errors. They soon found that against the most formidable outfit in the game, mistakes of any kind would be instantly punished.

New Zealander Frano Botica opened the scoring with a penalty in the fifth minute. Two minutes later David Myers cut inside perfectly to score a clever, unconverted try. A

Rugby League Cup Results

Preliminary Round

Carlisle	8	Workington T	9
Hensingham	7	Dewsbury	24
Leigh East	12	Bradford N	24
Salford	44	Cutsyke	4
Sheffield E	19	Hull	6
Warrington	22	Huddersfield	4

The Hensingham game was played at Workington. The Leigh East game was played at Leigh.

First Round

Barrow	13	Hunslet	8
Bradford N	50	Leigh	4
Bramley	6	Oldham	38
Castleford	4	Wigan	28
Doncaster	4	Widnes	30
Halifax	46	Fulham	6
Keighley	36	Runcorn H	4
Leeds	40	Dewsbury	20
Nottingham C	10	Whitehaven	26
Rochdale H	14	Chorley	10
Ryedale-York	1	Warrington	8
Salford	36	Batley	14
Sheffield E	19	Featherstone R	12
Swinton	8	St Helens	18
Wakefield T	18	Trafford B	7
Workington T	18	Hull KR	12

The Bradford N game was played at Bradford City FC. The Swinton game was played at Manchester City FC.

Second Round

Barrow	4	Widnes	25
Bradford N	5	Leeds	0
Halifax	46	Whitehaven	12
Keighley	10	Warrington	42
Rochdale H	4	Wigan	72
St Helens	16	Wakefield T	2
Sheffield E	16	Salford	19
Workington T	15	Oldham	20

Third Round

Halifax	16	St Helens	24
Oldham	40	Salford	3
Warrington	14	Widnes	26
Wigan	32	Bradford N	2

Semi-finals

Wigan	30	Oldham	16
At Burnden Park, Bolton			
Attendance: 19,057		*Receipts: £116,937*	
St Helens	19	Widnes	2
At Wigan			
Attendance: 16,109		*Receipts: £81,342*	

Final

Saturday, 27 April at Wembley Stadium, London

	T	G	P		T	G	P
Wigan	2	3	13	**St Helens**	1	2	8
S.Hampson				P.Veivers			
D.Myers	T			A.Hunte	T		
K.Iro				T.Ropati			
D.Bell				P.Loughlin			
F.Botica	T	2G		L.Quirk			
S.Edwards				J.Griffiths			
A.Gregory		D		P.Bishop		2G	
I.Lucas				J.Neill			
M.Dermott				B.Dwyer			
A.Platt				K.Ward			
D.Betts				J.Harrison			
P.Clarke				G.Mann			
E.Hanley				S.Cooper			
B.Goulding				G.Connolly			
A.Goodway				P.Groves			
Substitutes:							
Goodway (for Clarke)				Connolly (for Veivers)			
Goulding (for Dermott)				Groves (for Neill)			

Lance Todd Trophy: D.Betts

Referee: J.Smith (Halifax)   *Half-time: 12-0*
Attendance 75,532   *Receipts: £1,610,447*

---

marvellous break by Betts cut open the Saints defence and Botica showed his class with a strong sprint for Wigan's second try. The Kiwi converted his own touchdown with a towering kick way out on the touchline.

Seven minutes into the second half, Andy Gregory extended Wigan's lead to 13 points with a clever drop-goal. The score inspired St Helens to a revival and led by their forever active scrum-half, Paul Bishop, they tore into the tiring Wigan team. Alan Hunte scored a try, which Bishop converted, in the 61st minute to put his side just seven points adrift. Bishop added a penalty-goal nine minutes from time but it was as far as St Helens could go, their atrocious handling constantly hampering their progress.

1992 Wigan 28 Castleford 12

DESPITE being the bookies' favourite to lose, Castleford went to great lengths to point out that they had never been defeated at Wembley and were confident of continuing the tradition that began in 1935.

From the kick-off, however, they looked nervous and hardly the confident side they had professed to be. And in the fifth minute the nerves told. Martin Offiah launched a harmless enough kick towards the Castleford line and full-back Graham Steadman seemed to have everything under control. What followed could be attributed to nerves or the sight of Offiah, arguably the fastest player in the game, bearing down on him. Steadman made a mess of the simple pick up, fumbling to such an extent that the Wigan wingman was able to kick the ball away from Steadman and score a simple try. Frano Botica kicked the goal.

In the 20th minute Wigan hooker Martin Dermott broke free of the Castleford defence and surged up the field. He transferred to the supporting Edwards who sprinted in for a fine try, which Botica converted. Three minutes before half-time Lydon dropped a one-point goal and then just before the break Offiah's sensational pace once again had the crowd on its feet. The forever adventurous Edwards kicked the ball deep into the Castleford half and, despite having a host of players in front of him, Offiah won the race to touch the ball down for a brilliant try. Botica once again converted the try with a precision kick.

Castleford started the second half a different team and some determined approach work by Nikau and Sampson created a fine opening for Richie Blackmore to score a try. Martin Ketteridge landed the extra two points. The six points worked wonders for Castleford and, led from the front by New Zealand international forward Tawera Nikau, they began to play with more flair and far less caution.

Around seven minutes later Offiah, whose performance earned him the Lance Todd Trophy, pounced on a loose ball and sprinted 45 yards for a breathtaking touchdown. The wingman's joy of being the first man to score a hat-trick at Wembley was short-lived, however, referee Whitfield disallowing the 'try' on the recommendation of his touch judge who had spotted a knock on when Offiah picked up the ball.

The Wigan followers hadn't long to wait for the next score however, for on the hour Steve Hampson scored a fine converted try to restore the Riversiders' 19-point gap. Cas stuck to their game plan and ten minutes after the Wigan try, full-back, Graham Steadman fooled the Wigan defence with a cheeky back pass to put Keith England in for a superb diving try. Martin Ketteridge kicked the conversion and at 25-12, Castleford regained a glimmer of hope before goals from Botica and Lydon sealed Wigan's fifth successive Wembley victory.

Wigan were given a harder fight than they had expected before lifting the Challenge Cup yet again with a 28-12 win over Castleford.

Rugby League Cup Results

Preliminary Round

Bramley	12	Leeds	36
Chorley B	13	Salford	64
Kells (Cumbria)	17	Hull Dockers	14
Nottingham C	0	Batley	36
Wakefield T	32	Huddersfield	18
Workington T	11	Carlisle	4

The Kells game was played at Whitehaven.

First Round

Barrow	7	Keighley C	7
Batley	20	Featherstone R	36
Dewsbury	14	Leigh	2
Doncaster	14	Swinton	4
Halifax	12	Hull KR	8
Highfield	12	London C	12
Kells (Cumbria)	14	Hunslet	32
Leeds	45	Ryedale-York	6
Oldham	3	Warrington	8
Rochdale H	28	Hull	32
Salford	6	Wigan	22
Scarborough P	4	Bradford N	52
Trafford B	0	Castleford	50
Whitehaven	4	Sheffield E	56
Widnes	2	St Helens	10
Workington T	13	Wakefield T	8

First Round Replays

Keighley C	14	Barrow	14
London C	24	Highfield	10

First Round Second Replay

Barrow	16	Keighley C	0

At Widnes

Second Round

Barrow	13	Bradford N	30
Dewsbury	10	Featherstone R	23
Halifax	66	Doncaster	8
Hunslet	12	Castleford	28
Leeds	12	St Helens	32
Sheffield E	6	Hull	11
Wigan	14	Warrington	0
Workington T	9	London C	2

Third Round

Castleford	19	Featherstone R	12
Halifax	4	Bradford N	12
St Helens	6	Wigan	13
Workington T	8	Hull	24

Semi-finals

Castleford	8	Hull	4

At Leeds
Attendance: 14,636   Receipts: £91,225

Wigan	71	Bradford N	10

At Burnden Park, Bolton
Attendance: 18,027   Receipts: £131,124

Final

Saturday, 2 May at Wembley Stadium, London

	T	G	P		T	G	P
Wigan	4	7	28	**Castleford**	2	2	12
J.Lydon		2D		G.Steadman			
F.Botica		5G		J.Wray			
D.Bell				St J.Ellis			
G.Miles				R.Blackmore	T		
M.Offiah	2T			D.Nelson			
S.Edwards	T			G.Anderson			
A.Gregory				M.Ford			
K.Skerrett				L.Crooks			
M.Dermott				G.Southernwood			
A.Platt				K.England	T		
D.Betts				G.Bradley			
B.McGinty				M.Ketteridge		2G	
P.Clarke				T.Nikau			
S.Hampson	T			T.Smith			
N.Cowie				D.Sampson			

Substitutes:

Hampson (for McGinty)   Sampson (for Crooks)

Cowie (for McGinty)   Smith (for Anderson)

Lance Todd Trophy: M.Offiah

Referee: R.Whitfield (Widnes)   Half-time: 19-0
Attendance: 77,286   Receipts: £1,877,564

189

1993 Wigan 20 Widnes 14

RANK outsiders Widnes gave Cup kings Wigan the hardest test of their record-breaking six consecutive Challenge Cup victories in a game that promised much but turned bitter in the heat of a second half littered with ill-tempered indiscretions and marching orders for Richie Eyres, the Widnes second-row forward.

Widnes settled into the game well and from the kick-off made a mockery of the pre-match pundits' predictions. The industrious Chemics, led and organised so well by scrum-half Bobby Goulding, were soon causing the well-drilled Wigan defence plenty of problems.

In the seventh minute the hard work paid off when Bobby Goulding, the former Riversiders' half-back, succeeded in opening a gap in the Wigan defence for Eyres to sail in, crash through a series of challenges and score a brilliant try. Jonathan Davies converted the try from way out on the touchline.

Stunned Wigan responded instantly and within minutes were on level terms, Kelvin Skerrett, the Riversiders' huge prop forward, using his immense strength to brush aside two very ineffectual tackles to score a try which Frano Botica converted. Undaunted, the Chemics stuck to their task and 37-year-old Kurt Sorenson belied his age when he burst through the Wigan defence and surged to the line, breaking through the attempted tackles of Botica and Hampson on the way. Once again Davies converted and Widnes had re-established their six-point lead.

As before, the joy was to be short-lived. Welsh wingman, John Devereux caught a Wigan kick and attempted to run straight through the on-coming Martin Offiah. In the collision that ensued the ball spilled loose and the ever-alert Offiah was the first to react, collecting the ball and then passing it to Dean Bell who ran unopposed for a simple touchdown. Botica converted, his kick beating the Wigan record of 176 goals in a season, set by Fred Griffiths in 1959.

On the stroke of half-time the precision kicking of Frano Botica extended the Riversiders' lead with a penalty-goal.

Wigan's Denis Betts comes face to face with Chemics captain Paul Hulme in the 1993 Final. In support are Kiwis Dean Bell and Frano Botica.

Rugby League Cup Results

Preliminary Round

Batley	20	Blackpool B	10
Widnes	62	Swinton	14
Wigan	40	Hull	2

First Round

Bradford N	28	Workington T	18
Chorley B	6	Batley	20
Dewsbury	4	Wigan	20
Featherstone R	22	St Helens	24
Halifax	66	Carlisle	16
Huddersfield	66	Nottingham C	1
Hull KR	30	Bramley	0
Hunslet	27	Ryedale-York	22
Keighley C	86	Highfield	0
Leeds	54	Barrow	18
Oldham	34	London C	6
Rochdale H	34	Doncaster	13
Salford	12	Wakefield T	20
Sheffield E	32	Leigh	5
Warrington	6	Castleford	21
Whitehaven	8	Widnes	20

Second Round

Castleford	34	Hunslet	16
Halifax	50	Batley	20
Hull KR	30	Keighley C	28
Leeds	68	Rochdale H	6
Oldham	20	Huddersfield	17
Sheffield E	6	Widnes	52
Wakefield T	18	Bradford N	20
Wigan	23	St Helens	3

Third Round

Halifax	18	Wigan	19
Hull KR	4	Widnes	4
Leeds	12	Castleford	8
Oldham	4	Bradford N	42

Third Round Replay

Widnes	16	Hull KR	11

Semi-finals

Widnes	39	Leeds	4

At Wigan
Attendance: 13,823   *Receipts: £83,914*

Wigan	15	Bradford N	6

At Elland Road
Attendance: 20,085   *Receipts: £150,167*

Final

Saturday, 1 May at Wembley Stadium, London

	T	G	P		T	G	P
Wigan	3	4	20	**Widnes**	2	3	14
S.Hampson				S.Spruce			
J.Robinson				J.Devereux			
J.Lydon				A.Currier			
A.Farrar				D.Wright			
M.Offiah				D.Myers			
F.Botica		4G		J.Davies		3G	
S.Edwards				B.Goulding			
K.Skerrett	T			K.Sorensen	T		
M.Dermott				P.Hulme			
A.Platt				H.Howard			
D.Betts				R.Eyres	T		
P.Clarke				E.Faimalo			
D.Bell	T			D.Hulme			
S.Panapa	T			J.O'Neill			
A.Farrell				S.McCurrie			

Substitutes:

Panapa (for Lydon)   O'Neill (for Faimalo)
Farrell (for Skerrett)   McCurrie (for Currier)

Lance Todd Trophy: D.Bell

Referee: R.Smith (Castleford)   *Half-time: 14-12*
Attendance: 77,684   *Receipts: £1,981,591*

Wigan flowed forward at the start of the second half and within two minutes Sam Panapa had latched on to Lance Todd Trophy winner Dean Bell's pass to score near the posts. Botica converted to give Wigan a 20-14 lead.

Widnes's frustration at twice losing the lead erupted in the 65th minute when Richie Eyres felled Martin Offiah with an elbow to the head. Referee Smith, after consultation with his touch judges, decided the punishment should fit the crime and promptly sent Eyres off.

In the final minutes of the game, Bobby Goulding's high and late tackle on Jason Robinson was the catalyst for a brief but ugly brawl that marred an otherwise absorbing contest. As one journalist commented: *'Rugby League is a game in which errors often carry a penalty. Widnes made far more than they could afford.'*

1994 Wigan 26 Leeds 16

Wigan 26, Leeds 16 – and a familiar sight at Wembley as the Challenge Cup goes back to Central Park once more after these celebrations.

WIGAN arrived at Wembley for the seventh successive season with more problems off the field than on it. Rumours about the continued job prospects of their Australian coach, John Dorahy, had been circulating for some weeks and on the eve of the Final, the gossip was that Ellery Hanley, their ex-loose forward, ironically playing for Leeds, was tipped for the job. Wigan chairman Jack Robinson suggested the rumour was *'scandalous'* but many pundits thought the constant back-stage talk would have an effect on the team. For the Wigan players, however, it was business as usual and the most pressing business was the retention of the Challenge Cup, as Martin Offiah had commented at the previous season's Final, *"The fear of losing is now perhaps a stronger spur than the adulation of winning."*

Leeds were also unmoved by the speculation surrounding their captain Ellery Hanley's supposedly imminent departure, concentrating more on the loose forward's fitness. The Loiners started the game well and played with a cool and confident air, sticking rigidly to a game plan prepared by their master tactician Doug Laughton. For around 12 minutes they more than matched the Cup holders and had genuine cause for optimism.

However, the whole complexion of the game changed in

just 12 seconds of pure magic from Martin Offiah, who gathered the ball and accelerated past the attempted tackles of two Leeds defenders. The Wigan wingman continued his run, by now a lightning sprint for the Leeds line, past Cummings, Schofield and former teammate, full-back Tait. His pace and sheer determination carried him almost the length of the field for a glorious try which BBC television commentator Ray French described as the best he had ever seen in 41 years of watching Wembley Finals.

Leeds were visibly distraught, a newspaper match report commenting: *'The physical and mental damage inflicted on Leeds in that brief time span was incalculable.'*

A try from Andrew Farrell and two conversions gave Wigan a 12-0 half-time lead and it looked almost certain that Leeds would crumble in the second period, opening the floodgates for another points bonanza from the Cup holders. However, the Leeds players came from the dressing-room with other ideas on their minds and one was certainly not instant submission.

From the onset they regained the composure they had lost following the Offiah try and clawed their way back into the game with a penalty from Holroyd and a fine try from powerful wingman Fallon. The comeback continued when

Rugby League Cup Results

Third Round

Batley	58	Dewsbury C	2
Barrow	34	East Leeds	10
Bramley	46	Redhill	20
Carlisle	42	Askham	8
Dewsbury	64	Hensingham	6
Doncaster	36	Wigan St Pats	4
Highfield	16	Saddleworth	13
Huddersfield	42	Woolston	6
Hunslet	58	Barrow Island	2
Keighley C	68	Oulton	0
London C	40	Shaw Cross	14
Rochdale H	32	Millom	0
Ryedale-York	52	Leigh MW	2
Swinton	30	Irlam Hornets	0
Whitehaven	44	West Hull	4
Workington T	24	Beverley	10

Fourth Round

Barrow	30	Bradford N	58
Batley	8	Keighley C	29
Bramley	11	Widnes	20
Carlisle	12	Workington T	13
Castleford	36	Salford	4
Doncaster	18	Dewsbury	6
Halifax	18	Warrington	22
Highfield	4	Whitehaven	15
Huddersfield	16	St Helens	23
Hull KR	16	Ryedale-York	6
Hunslet	20	Oldham	30
London C	14	Featherstone R	28
Rochdale H	18	Leeds	40
Sheffield E	42	Leigh	10
Swinton	10	Hull	18
Wigan	24	Wakefield T	16

Fifth Round

Doncaster	20	Oldham	0
Hull	21	Wigan	22
Hull KR	8	Featherstone R	30
Keighley C	14	Castleford	52
Leeds	38	Warrington	4
Whitehaven	4	St Helens	46
Widnes	22	Sheffield E	6
Workington T	0	Bradford N	32

Sixth Round

Castleford	30	Widnes	6
Leeds	33	Bradford N	10
St Helens	40	Doncaster	9
Wigan	32	Featherstone R	14

Semi-final

Castleford	6	Wigan	20

At Leeds
Attendance: 17,049   *Receipts: £115,842*

St Helens	8	Leeds	20

At Wigan
Attendance: 20,771   *Receipts: £135,722*

Final

Saturday, 30 April at Wembley Stadium, London

	T	G	P		T	G	P
Wigan	4	5	26	**Leeds**	3	2	16
G.Connolly				A.Tait			
V.Tuigamala				J.Fallon	T		
D.Bell				K.Iro			
Mather				C.Innes			
M.Offiah	2T			F.Cummings	T		
F.Botica		5G		G.Holroyd		2G	
S.Edwards				G.Schofield	T		
K.Skerrett				N.Harmon			
M.Dermott				J.Lowes			
A.Platt				H.Howard			
D.Betts				G.Mercer			
A.Farrell	T			R.Eyres			
P.Clarke				E.Hanley			
Substitutes:							
Cassidy (for Farrell)				O'Neill (for Harmon)			
Panapa (for Platt)	T			Vassilakopoulos (for Hanley)			

Lance Todd Trophy: M.Offiah

Referee: D.Campbell   *Half-time: 12-0*
Attendance: 78,348   *Receipts: £2,032,839*

Jim Fallon created a touchdown for Gary Schofield, and at 12-10 the tension mounted. Wigan's cold-blooded professionalism once again won the day, though, and tries from Lance Todd Trophy winner Offiah and Sam Panapa sealed the Riversiders' seventh victory.

Leeds did have the last say in the game when teenager Francis Cummings scored a converted touchdown to become the youngest-ever Wembley try scorer.

1995 Wigan 30 Leeds 10

Wigan celebrate yet again after beating Leeds 30-10 in the 1995 Final.

LEEDS and Wigan created history when they became the first two clubs to meet at Wembley in successive seasons. The celebrations were, however, all Wigan's as they collected the Cup for the eighth successive time with a breathtaking display of open, running rugby.

The Riversiders were far above Leeds in every aspect of the game. On attack they had mastered the new ten-metre rule to such an extent that their forwards were running at speed when the leisurely Loiners defence finally arrived to attempt to stop them. The powerful props, Skerrett and Cowie, caused the Leeds defence constant problems and when fully supported by the rest of the rampant Riversiders pack, the Loiners were in deep trouble. Intensifying the damage was hooker, Martin Hall, whose unpredictable and probing runs from acting half-back proved to be a constant source of chaos in an already disorderly Leeds defence.

It was Leeds who began the scoring as early as the second minute when Graham Holroyd kicked a penalty-goal, but Jason Robinson opened the Riversiders' account when he sprinted close to the touchline for fully 40 metres before diving over the line for a classic try. Such was the young wingman's confidence that he cheekily blew a kiss to the crowd before touching the ball down. Eight minutes later, loose forward Phil Clarke passed to Henry Paul who twisted and turned the Loiners inside out before crossing for a try. Botica converted, as he had with the previous try.

Leeds rallied a little before the break but the superb Wigan defence never faltered and all the Loiners' efforts were rewarded with was a penalty-goal kicked by Holroyd.

The second half soon turned into the all-familiar Wembley romp as the incomparable Wigan players exposed every single Leeds weakness, then punished them with a brilliant display of total football. It was shoddy and lethargic defending at a play-the-ball that allowed Jason Robinson to sprint clear of three men for a superb long-range try four minutes after the break. Botica converted to give Wigan an 18-2 lead.

Ten minutes later, Hall's towering performance around the base of the ruck was finally rewarded when the hooker once again took full advantage of relaxed Leeds marking at a play-the-ball and scampered over the line for a try. Throughout the game, the strong runs of Wigan's centre · Va'aiga Tuigamala had caused Leeds problems, as many as three players being enlisted to haul the Western Samoan to the ground.

In the 64th minute the powerhouse once again crashed through a tackle and pounded towards the Loiners' last line of defence, only to sell an astute dummy before sprinting over the line for the Riversiders' final try. Frano Botica kicked his fifth goal, beating Neil Fox's 32-year-old record of 39 goals in three Finals, to give Wigan an splendid 30-10 victory.

Rugby League Cup Results

Third Round

Barrow	56	East Leeds	0
Batley	32	Shaw Cross	4
Bramley	42	Woolston	2
Carlisle	34	Dudley Hill	4
Dewsbury	72	Kells	12
Highfield	4	Beverley	27
Huddersfield	44	Wigan St Judes	10
Hull KR	58	Thornhill	6
Hunslet	64	Wigan St Patricks	4
Keighley C	68	Chorley	0
Leigh	40	Heworth	28
London B	30	Ellenborough	10
Rochdale H	48	Lock Lane	16
Ryedale-York	50	Barrow Island	20
Swinton	30	Millom	10
Whitehaven	64	Moorends	12

Fourth Round

Beverley	20	Batley	30
Carlisle	2	Widnes	40
Doncaster	12	Sheffield E	22
Featherstone R	50	Barrow	22
Huddersfield	36	Halifax	30
Hunslet	32	Salford	32
Keighley C	24	Dewsbury	12
Leeds	31	Bradford N	14
London B	20	Hull KR	26
Oldham	70	Bramley	10
Ryedale-York	18	Rochdale H	12
Swinton	22	Leigh	34
Warrington	17	Castleford	2
Whitehaven	24	Wakefield T	12
Wigan	16	St Helens	16
Workington T	30	Hull	6

The Beverley game was played at Hull.

Fourth Round Replays

St Helens	24	Wigan	40
Salford	52	Hunslet	10

Fifth Round

Batley	4	Wigan	70
Hull KR	14	Whitehaven	18
Keighley C	0	Huddersfield	30
Leeds	44	Ryedale-York	14
Salford	10	Featherstone R	30
Sheffield E	7	Widnes	19
Warrington	6	Oldham	17
Workington T	94	Leigh	4

Quarter-finals

Leeds	50	Workington T	16
Oldham	23	Huddersfield	12
Whitehaven	14	Featherstone R	42
Widnes	12	Wigan	26

Semi-finals

Wigan	48	Oldham	20

At Huddersfield
Attendance: 12,749   *Receipts: £115,705*

Leeds	39	Featherstone R	22

At Elland Road, Leeds
Attendance: 21,485   *Receipts: £175,245*

Final

Saturday, 29 April at Wembley Stadium, London

	T	G	P		T	G	P
Wigan	5	5	30	**Leeds**	1	3	10
H.Paul	T			A.Tait			
J.Robinson	2T			J.Fallon			
V.Tuigamala	T			K.Iro			
G.Connolly				C.Innes			
M.Offiah				F.Cummings			
F.Botica		5G		G.Schofield			
S.Edwards				G.Holroyd		3G	
K.Skerrett				H.Howard			
M.Hall	T			J.Lowes	T		
N.Cowie				E.Faimalo			
D.Betts				G.Mercer			
M.Cassidy				R.Eyres			
P.Clarke				E.Hanley			
P.Atcheson				G.Mann			
A.Farrell				N.Harmon			
Substitutes:							
Farrell (for Cassidy)				Mann (for Howard)			
Atcheson (for Skerrett)				Harmon (for Faimalo)			

Lance Todd Trophy: J.Robinson

Referee: R.Smith (Castleford)   *Half-time: 12-4*
Attendance: 78,550   *Receipts: £2,040,000*

Jubilant St Helens skipper Bobby Goulding holds the Challenge Cup aloft after the breathtaking spectacle of the 1996 Final.

THE first Final of the Super League era produced an epic 13-try thriller of sheer excitement and emotion, the like of which had never before been seen at Wembley. The incessant points scoring action started in the fourth minute when a high kick from Goulding saw Scott Gibbs break free from Loughlin and direct a high pass to Steve Prescott who raced over for a try. Fifteen minutes later Prescott hacked on a clever grubber kick by Bobby Goulding and dropped over the line for a try.

A clever piece of play from Paul, Dwyer and Loughlin put Jonathan Scales in the clear and the Bulls' wingman scores a fine try in the corner which Paul Cook converted with a towering kick. On the half-hour Cook squared the scores with a penalty-goal, but two minutes later Saints Danny Arnold wrong-footed the Bulls defence with a brilliant side step to score a try and put St Helens back in the lead. Seven minutes to the break, a strong run from Nathan Graham and Matt Calland set up a try directly under the posts for Robbie Paul. Cook converted and the Bulls hit the front for the first time.

Thirteen minutes into the second half, the Bulls surged into a 26-12 lead, thanks to tries from Dwyer and Paul, both of which are converted by Cook.

However, within four minutes, Bobby Goulding began a chain of events that changed the course of the game in a seven-minute spell. The Saints scrum-half hoisted a high kick towards the Bradford line which Nathan Graham, the Bulls' full-back, naively allowed to bounce straight into the arms of Keiran Cunningham who scored a try which Goulding converted. Three minutes later Goulding tried his luck with another perfect kick at the Bulls' line and once again Graham failed to collect and Saints' Booth scored a try which Goulding again converted.

Sensing the shattered nerves of Graham, Goulding once again launched a high spinning ball in the direction of the Bulls' line and for the third time in seven minutes Saints scored when Pickavance pounced to ground the ball. Goulding converted and St Helens were in front by four points.

Within minutes the supremely confident Saints lengthened their lead when they blasted a hole in the Bulls' defence and Danny Arnold scored his second try of the

Rugby League Cup Results

Third Round

Barrow B	14	Doncaster D	0
Bramley	22	Heworth	18
Carlisle	36	West Bowling	6
Chorley C	12	Thatto Heath	27
Highfield	20	West Hull	35
Hull KR	44	Eastmoor	12
Hunslet H	30	Skirlaugh	18
Leigh C	58	Egremont	6
Swinton	52	Thornhill	4
York	30	Lock Lane	10

Fourth Round

Bradford B	60	Batley	18
Carlisle	18	Wakefield T	34
Castleford	16	St Helens	58
Dewsbury	12	London B	10
Huddersfield	14	Sheffield E	35
Hull	52	Hunslet H	18
Hull KR	0	Leigh C	24
Keighley C	12	Barrow B	9
Oldham B	4	Warrington	26
Rochdale H	54	Thatto Heath	8
Salford R	35	Featherstone R	12
Swinton	22	Leeds	27
West Hull	10	York	6
Whitehaven	6	Halifax	18
Wigan	74	Bramley	12
Workington T	10	Widnes	17

Fifth Round

Dewsbury	16	Widnes	36
Halifax	24	Sheffield E	20
Hull	42	Keighley C	10
Leigh C	12	Bradford B	44
Rochdale H	20	St Helens	58
Salford R	26	Wigan	16
Warrington	10	Leeds	30
West Hull	8	Wakefield T	40

Quarter-finals

Bradford B	30	Wakefield T	18
Halifax	24	Leeds	35
Hull	0	Widnes	20
Salford R	26	St Helens	46

Semi-finals

St Helens	25	Widnes	14
At Wigan			
Attendance: 13,424		*Receipts: £89,760*	
Bradford B	28	Leeds	6
At Huddersfield			
Attendance: 17,139		*Receipts: £106,597*	

Final

Saturday, 27 April at Wembley Stadium, London

	T	G	P		T	G	P
Bradford B	5	6	32	**St Helens**	8	4	40
Graham				Prescott	2T		
Cook		6G		Arnold	2T		
Calland				Gibbs			
Loughlin				Newlove			
Scales	T			Sullivan			
Bradley				Hammond			
Paul	3T			Goulding		4G	
McDermott				Perelini	T		
Dwyer	T			Cunningham	T		
Hamer				Leatham			
Donougher				Joynt			
Nickle				Booth	T		
Knox				Northley			
Substitutes							
Fairbank (for Hamer)				Martyn (for Northey)			
Medley (for Nickle)				Pickavance (for Martyn)	T		
Donohoe (for Knox)				Matautia (for Leatham)			
Hassan (for Graham)				Hunte (for Perelini)			

Lance Todd Trophy: R.Paul

Referee: S.Cummings *Half-time: 14-12*
Attendance: 75,994 *Receipts: £1,893,000*

game. Bradford refused to lie down, however, and their gifted scrum-half Robbie Paul surged through a gap on half-way, then duped Prescott with a subtle change of pace to score the first-ever hat trick of tries at Wembley. Cook goaled and Bradford were back to within two points of the Saints.

There was to be no fairy tale ending for Bradford, however, a defence-splitting diagonal run by Bobby Goulding setting up Apollo Perelini for the 13th try of the game, which Goulding converted.

1997 Bradford Bulls 22 St Helens 32

The 1997 Final, and Saints celebrate their second successive Challenge Cup Final victory over Bradford Bulls. Although not captain on the day, Chris Joynt, who had taken over as skipper while Bobby Goulding was serving suspension, collected the trophy.

ALTHOUGH not the points scoring orgy of the 1996 game, Bradford and St Helens produced a sparkling contest with flashes of pure brilliance. The Bulls were pre-match favourites, their team-building over the winter had produced a powerful outfit that was dominating the Super League season. Saints had their stars and match winners, too, but were missing Alan Hunte, their immensely talented centre, who had failed to shake off a torn hamstring.

Bradford began the game with a ferocious onslaught towards the St Helens line and only some solid, and at times scrambling defensive work kept the Bulls from scoring. Having survived the attack, the Saints countered and, in the tenth minute a chip kick over the Bulls' try line by Bobby Goulding gave the supporting Tommy Martin the chance to score a brilliantly-worked try. Within minutes Bradford were streaming forward again and Steve McNamara finally managed to pierce the Saints' defence, before slipping a short pass to Sonny Nickle who dashed 40 metres before passing to Peacock who, contemptuously brushed aside Prescott's attempted tackle to sweep over the line for a try.

The Bulls' forwards gradually began to dominate the game and they were soon breaking tackles and creating huge gaps in the Saints' defence. In the 20th minute an over-optimistic pass from Saints' loose forward Karl Hammond was plucked from the air by Paul Loughlin, who raced over for a try. McNamara converted and the Bulls were six points in the lead, seemingly in command, and coasting for victory.

However, just as the previous year, the boot of Bobby Goulding came back to haunt Bradford. The ever-alert Goulding kicked the ball diagonally behind the Bulls' defence and sent it bouncing over the try line where it was once again met by Tommy Martin for a try. Goulding gratefully accepted the extra two points on offer and St Helens were back on level terms.

Seconds before the half-time break, Hammond launched himself at the line and, with four Bradford defenders clinging to him, somehow managed to ground the ball for a try of real strength and character. Goulding converted and Bradford left the field wondering how they were six points adrift in a game that they had almost sewn up.

Rugby League Cup Results

Third Round

Barrow B	16	Siddal	8
Batley B	48	Prescot P	12
Carlisle Border R	34	BRK	8
Dewsbury R	44	West Hull	18
Doncaster D	15	Oulton R	14
Featherstone R	48	Moldgreen	14
Huddersfield G	82	East Leeds	0
Hull S	42	Lock Lane	0
Hull KR	44	Mayfield	4
Hunslet H	54	Woolston R	6
Keighley C	62	Redhill	4
Lancashire L	24	Hull D	4
Leigh C	68	Wigan St Patricks	10
Rochdale H	30	Walney C	6
Swinton L	46	Bramley	0
Wakefield T	52	Ovenden	0
Whitehaven W	12	Skirlaugh	6
Widnes V	56	Clayton	2
Workington T	86	Thatto Heath	0
York	14	Dudley Hill	21

Fourth Round

Batley B	4	Paris St Germain	38
Carlisle Border R	62	Dudley Hill	2
Castleford T	18	Salford R	36
Dewsbury R	26	Doncaster D	15
Featherstone R	14	Widnes V	12
Huddersfield G	16	Hull S	16
Hull KR	16	Halifax Blue Sox	20
Hunslet H	10	Bradford B	62
Lancashire L	5	London B	48
Leigh C	18	Sheffield E	62
Oldham B	48	Rochdale H	6
St Helens	26	Wigan W	12
Wakefield T	9	Swinton L	4
Warrington W	66	Barrow B	6
Whitehaven W	8	Leeds R	48
Workington T	14	Keighley C	24

Fifth Round

Carlisle Border R	20	Featherstone R	32
Halifax Blue Sox	8	Keighley C	21
Leeds R	48	Dewsbury R	22
London B	12	Bradford B	34
Salford R	8	Paris St Germain	4
St Helens	54	Hull S	8
Wakefield T	14	Oldham B	22
Warrington W	31	Sheffield E	18

Quarter-finals

Keighley C	0	St Helens	24
Leeds R	32	Featherstone R	12
Oldham B	12	Bradford B	38
Warrington W	10	Salford R	29

Semi-finals

St Helens	50	Salford R	20

At Wigan
Attendance: 12,580   *Receipts: £101,957*

Bradford B	24	Leeds R	10

At Huddersfield
Attendance: 18,193   *Receipts: £206,555*

Final

Saturday, 2 May at Wembley Stadium, London

Bradford Bulls	T 4	G 3	P 22	St Helens	T 5	G 6	P 32
Spruce				Prescott			
Ekoku				Arnold			
Peacock	T			Haigh			
Loughlin	T			Newlove			
Cook				Sullivan	T		
Bradley				Martin	2T		
Paul				Goulding		6G	
McDermott				Perelini			
Lowes	T			Cunningham			
Reihana				O'Neill			
Nickle				Joynt	T		
Dwyer				McVey			
McNamara		3G		Hammond	T		
Substitutes:							
Tomlinson			T	Pickavance			
Medley				Matautia			
Knox				Northey			
Calland				Morley			

Lance Todd Trophy: T.Martin

Referee: S.Cummings   *Half-time: 10-16*
Attendance: 78,022   *Receipts: £2,033,426*

Six minutes into the second half, Bradford's misfortune continued when their influential half-back Robbie Paul left the field injured. The half-back returned 12 minutes later but by then St Helens were 18 points in front thanks to tries from Joynt and Sullivan and two goals from the efficient Goulding.

Bradford mounted a mini revival in the 63rd minute when a kick and chase by James Lowes enabled Australian Glen Tomlinson to score a try which McNamara converted. A Goulding penalty edged Saints to 32 points before Lowes and McNamara added six points to the Bulls' total to make a ten-point difference, a margin which was a little less one-sided.

Sheffield Eagles players pose proudly with the Challenge Cup after they astonished everyone by turning the form book upside down to beat hot favourites Wigan.

SHEFFIELD Eagles, cruelly dismissed as no-hopers by just about everyone connected with the game, created the biggest upset ever in the 101-year history of the Challenge Cup by beating 14-1 odds-on favourites in a tremendously exciting Final.

The Eagles, who were only formed in 1994, refused to listen to the pre-match hype that had branded them instant losers and came to Wembley with an astute game plan and immense self-belief.

Coach John Kear concentrated on every single detail of the day with his players and instilled a bond so great that they beat the unbeatable.

It soon became apparent in the pre-match build-up that the Eagles were intently focused on the game and within five minutes of the kick-off they proved it. On their second set of tackles, Sheffield swept down the field and set up the perfect position for scrum-half Mark Aston. The eventual Lance Todd Trophy winner exploited Wigan's diminutive Jason Robinson with a towering kick across the field which Nick Pinkney plucked from the air to score a try. Aston failed with the difficult conversion.

Wigan counted with a series of attacks which were marred by poor handling. Meanwhile, Sheffield's superb scrambling defence held firm and just around the time everyone expected the Warriors to take a grip on the game, the Eagles swooped again. Pinkney was held near the Wigan line on the sixth tackle and, incredibly, when Moore played

the ball to restart the game no Wigan player was there to take it up.

Aston dived on the loose ball to regain the valuable possession in a perfect position. The ball was swept across the field and Matt Crowther dived over for a try which Aston converted. Sheffield were 10-0 to the good.

Wigan were still far from convincing on attack, relying on a penalty goal from Andrew Farrell for their first points of the game. With minutes to go to the interval, Mark Aston remembered the old adage about never coming away from an attack without scoring and promptly dropped a goal.

Eleven minutes into the second half, Sheffield did the seemingly impossible and stretched their lead a further four points when Turner drove through four Wigan defenders to score from close range. Aston added a further two with the conversion and, at last, people began to believe the Eagles could do it.

Despite displaying some glaring symptoms of shell-shock, the Warriors clawed their way back into the game and began to put together something approaching their usual game. After 56 minutes play, McCormick, Betts and Henry Paul combined perfectly to send Mark Bell crashing over the line for the best try of the game. It was the final score. Wigan did their utmost but it was far too late, as most newspapers covering the game inevitably commented, the Eagles had finally landed.

Rugby League Cup Results

Third Round

Barrow Border R	52	Farnworth	8
Batley B	44	Oulton R	2
Bramley	10	Ellenbrough R	16
Dewsbury R	40	Thornhill	2
Doncaster D	18	Featherstone L	23
Eastmoor D	14	Egremont R	20
Featherstone R	56	Woolston R	0
Hull KR	34	Queens	16
Hunslet H	44	Skirlaugh B	12
Keighley C	66	Saddleworth R	16
Lancashire L	46	West Hull	0
Leigh C	44	Hunslet W	4
Moldgreen	10	Ovenden	20
Rochdale H	44	Leigh Miners R	4
Swinton L	74	Folly Lane	6
Wakefield T	44	BRK	6
Whitehaven W	48	Lock Lane	7
Widnes V	48	Oldham	8
Workington T	12	Haydock	8
York	37	Norland	5

Fourth Round

Barrow Border R	22	Widnes V	36
Batley B	20	London B	44
Egremont R	18	Workington T	0
Ellenbrough R	14	Hunslet H	12
Featherstone L	20	Hull KR	56
Featherstone R	24	St Helens	56
Halifax Blue Sox	28	Huddersfield G	8
Keighley C	0	Wigan W	76
Lancashire L	28	Dewsbury R	28
Leeds R	12	Castleford T	15
Leigh C	11	Sheffield E	66
Ovenden	0	Salford R	74
Rochdale H	10	Bradford B	48
Swinton L	39	York	21
Wakefield T	6	Warrington W	42
Whitehaven W	12	Hull S	26

Fourth Round Replay

Dewsbury R	31	Lancashire L	14

Fifth Round

Castleford T	26	Bradford B	21
Dewsbury R	0	Wigan W	56
Hull S	78	Ellenbrough R	0
Hull KR	46	Swinton L	24
London B	21	Halifax Blue Sox	18
Sheffield E	84	Egremont R	6
St Helens	35	Warrington W	22
Widnes V	6	Salford R	48

Quarter-finals

Castleford T	22	Sheffield E	32
London B	46	Hull KR	18
Salford R	41	Hull S	10
Wigan W	22	St Helens	10

Semi-finals

Sheffield E	22	Salford R	18
At Headingley			
Attendance: 6,961			
London B	8	Wigan W	38
At Huddersfield			
Attendance: 11,058			

Final

Saturday, 2 May at Wembley Stadium, London

	T	G	P		T	G	P
Wigan Warriors	1	2	8	**Sheffield Eagles**	3	3	17
Radlinski				Sovatabua			
Robinson				Pinkney	T		
Moore				Taewa			
Connolly				Senior			
Bell	T			Crowther	T		
Paul				Watson			
Smith				Aston		2G	1D
Holgate				Broadbent			
McCormack				Lawless			
Mestrov				Laughton			
Haughton				Carr			
Betts				Shaw			
Farrell		2G		Doyle			
Substitutes:							
Cowie				Wood			
Gilmour				Stott			
O'Conner				Turner	T		
Cassidy				Jackson			

Lance Todd Trophy: M.Aston

Referee: S.Cummings (Widnes)   *Half-time: 11-3*
Attendance: 60,669

The Lance Todd Trophy

Lance Todd, the famous New Zealander, pictured in his 1907-08 All Blacks tour jersey.

Dean Bell, the 1993 winner, is presented with the Lance Todd Trophy by Ken Allen, general sales manager of ESAB.

THE Lance Todd Trophy is awarded for the Man of the Match at Wembley and is one of the most coveted individual honours in the game.

Lance Todd made his name in Britain in 1907-08 as a member of the New Zealand All Blacks squad that played a gruelling 35-match tour of the Northern Union strongholds. Todd was a great success on the tour, appearing in 22 games, including all three Test matches against the Northern Union, his play attracting the interest of many of the bigger English clubs. Wigan finally captured Todd, signing him immediately after the third and final Test which had been taken to Cheltenham in an effort to spread the gospel of the 13-a-side code of rugby football.

Twenty thousand Wigan fans witnessed his debut at Central Park, where, despite Todd scoring a try, his new club lost 9-3 to Oldham. The diminutive New Zealander stayed with Wigan until his transfer to Dewsbury, for the then vast amount of £400, in January 1914. Todd made a try-scoring debut for the Yorkshire side but his career with them was cut short by the outbreak of World War One.

Todd later made his name as manager of Salford and a commentator for BBC Radio. In November 1942 he was killed when his car crashed in the blackout whilst returning from a game at Oldham.

So great was his popularity within the game that Australian Harry Sunderland, Warrington director Bob Anderson and journalist John Bapty decided a lasting reminder of his contribution to the game should be found. They hit upon the idea of a Man of the Match award for the game's showcase event and the award was first presented to Wakefield's Billy Stott following the 1946 Wembley Final.

Today the trophy's recipient is decided by a vote of members of the Rugby League Writers' Association present at the Final. Some of the greatest names in the game have been awarded the trophy. In 1948, Bradford Northern's Frank Whitcombe became the first holder from the losing side, and in 1953 Huddersfield's Peter Ramsden became the youngest when he received the award on his 19th birthday. Hull's Tommy Harris is still the only hooker to be awarded the trophy, and Ray Ashby and Brian Gabbitas are still the only two players to share the trophy, following their performances in the memorable Hunslet v Wigan Final in 1965. Two Wakefield Trinity players have experienced the despair of winning the trophy in defeat, Don Fox in 1968 and David Topliss in 1979.

David Topliss descends the famous Wembley steps a totally dejected winner of the Lance Todd Trophy.

1946	Billy Stott	Wakefield T	(v Wigan)	Centre
1947	Willie Davies	Bradford N	(v Leeds)	Stand Off
1948	Frank Whitcombe	Bradford N	(v Wigan)	Prop
1949	Ernest Ward	Bradford N	(v Halifax)	Centre
1950	Gerry Helme	Warrington	(v Widnes)	Scrum-half
1951	Cec Mountford	Wigan	(v Barrow)	Stand off
1952	Billy Ivison	Workington T	(v Featherstone R)	Loose forward
1953	Peter Ramsden	Huddersfield	(v St. Helens)	Stand off
1954	Gerry Helme	Warringfon	(v Halifax)	Scrum-half
1955	Jack Grundy	Barrow	(v Workington T)	Second row
1956	Alan Prescott	St Helens	(v Halifax)	Prop
1957	Jeff Stevenson	Leeds	(v Barrow)	Scrum-half
1958	Rees Thomas	Wigan	(v Workington T)	Scrum-half
1959	Brian McTigue	Wigan	(v Hull)	Second row
1960	Tommy Harris	Hull	(v Wakefield T)	Hooker
1961	Dick Huddart	St Helens	(v Wigan)	Second row
1962	Neil Fox	Wakefield T	(v Huddersfield)	Centre
1963	Harold Poynton	Wakefield T	(v Wigan)	Stand off
1964	Frank Collier	Widnes	(v Hull KR)	Prop
1965	Ray Ashby	Wigan		Full-back
	Brian Gabbitas	Hunslet		Stand off
1966	Len Killeen	St Helens	(v Wigan)	Winger
1967	Carl Dooler	Featherstone R	(v Barrow)	Scrum-half
1968	Don Fox	Wakefield T	(v Leeds)	Prop
1969	Malcolm Reilly	Castleford	(v Salford)	Loose forward
1970	Bill Kirkbride	Castleford	(v Wigan)	Second row
1971	Alex Murphy	Leigh	(v Leeds)	Scrum-half
1972	Kel Coslett	St Helens	(v Leeds)	Loose forward
1973	Steve Nash	Featherstone R	(v Bradford N)	Scrum-half
1974	Derek Whitehead	Warrington	(v Featherstone R)	Full-back
1975	Ray Dutton	Widnes	(v Warrington)	Full-back
1976	Geoff Pimblett	St Helens	(v Widnes)	Full-back
1977	Steve Pitchford	Leeds	(v Widnes)	Prop
1978	George Nicholls	St Helens	(v Leeds)	Second row
1979	David Topliss	Wakefield T	(v Widnes)	Stand off
1980	Brian Lockwood	Hull KR	(v Hull)	Prop
1981	Mick Burke	Widnes	(v Hull KR)	Full-back
1982	Eddie Cunningham	Widnes	(v Hull)	Centre
1983	David Hobbs	Featherstone R	(v Hull)	Second row
1984	Joe Lydon	Widnes	(v Wigan)	Centre
1985	Brett Kenny	Wigan	(v Hull)	Stand off
1986	Bob Beardmore	Castleford	(v Hull KR)	Scrum-half
1987	Graham Eadie	Halifax	(v St Helens)	Full-back
1988	Andy Gregory	Wigan	(v Halifax)	Scrum-half
1989	Ellery Hanley	Wigan	(v St Helens)	Loose forward
1990	Andy Gregory	Wigan	(v Warrington)	Scrum- half
1991	Denis Betts	Wigan	(v St Helens)	Second row
1992	Martin Offiah	Wigan	(v Castleford)	Winger
1993	Dean Bell	Wigan	(v Widnes)	Loose forward
1994	Martin Offiah	Wigan	(v Leeds)	Winger
1995	Jason Robinson	Wigan	v Leeds)	Winger
1996	Robbie Paul	Bradford B	(v St Helens)	Scrum-half
1997	Tommy Martin	St Helens	(v Bradford)	Stand off
1998	Mark Aston	Sheffield E	(v Wigan)	Scrum-half

The Cup Comes Home

The victorious Hull side return home in somewhat sedate style in 1914.

FROM the very first Final of 1897, the return of the Challenge Cup has often been an occasion equally as important as the Final itself. In the formative years of the competition, success in winning what was to become the game's major trophy gave rise to tremendous celebrations, the like of which had never been witnessed in many towns and cities. When 'The Gallant Youths' of Batley brought the Cup home for the first time in 1897, one hundred fog warning signals were placed on the railway lines, heralding the team's entrance to the station. In 1912 the arrival of the team and trophy created such excitement in Dewsbury town centre that one member of the waiting crowd suffered a fatal heart attack.

In modern times the return of the Cup still holds a very special place in the hearts of the victorious club's supporters and thousands still take to the streets to welcome home their team, and, perhaps more significantly, the Challenge Cup.

A brass band leads Halifax through the town centre in 1931.

The victorious Bradford Northern side aboard a converted coach in 1947.

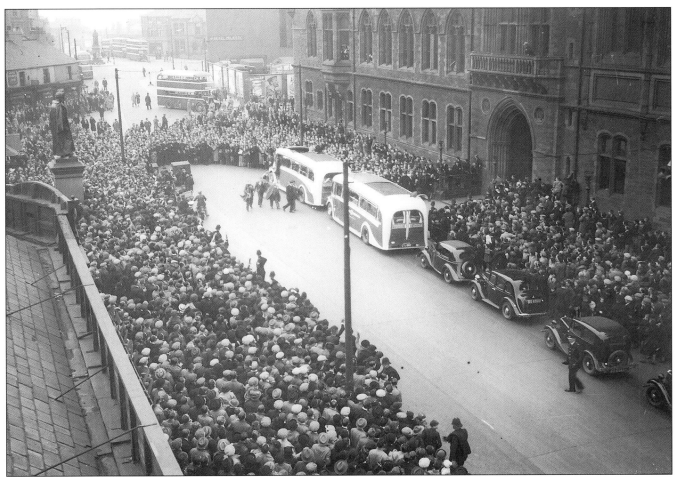

Crowds throng the centre of Barrow, desperate to catch a glimpse of their team's return from Wembley in 1955.

Challenge Cup Records

All Rounds

Team

Highest Score: 1914 Huddersfield 119 Swinton Park 2.

Individual

Most goals in a match: 22 by Jim Sullivan Wigan v Flimby and Fothergill, 1925.
Most Tries in a match: 11 by George West Hull KR v Brookland Rovers, 1905.
Most points in a match: 53 (11T, 10G) by George West Hull KR v Brookland Rovers, 1905.

Final Records

Most wins: Wigan 16
Most Finals: Wigan 26
Highest score: St Helens 40 v Bradford Bulls, 1996.
Widest margin: Huddersfield 37 v St Helens 3.
Biggest attendance: 102,569 Halifax v Warrington, 1954 replay at Odsal Stadium, Bradford.

Individual

Most tries: 3 by Bob Wilson, Broughton Rangers 1902; Stanley Moorhouse, Huddersfield 1913; Tom Holliday, Oldham 1927; Robbie Paul, Bradford Bulls 1996.
Most goals: 8 by Cyril Kellett Featherstone Rovers, 1973.
Most points: 20 by Neil Fox Wakefield Trinity, 1960.

Challenge Cup Roll of Honour

Year	Winners		Runners-up		Venue	Attendance	Receipts
1897	Batley	10	St Helens	3	Leeds	13,492	£624.17.7
1898	Batley	7	Bradford	0	Leeds	27,941	£1,586. 3.0
1899	Oldham	19	Hunslet	9	Manchester	15,763	£946.16.0
1900	Swinton	16	Salford	8	Manchester	17,864	£1,100.0.0
1901	Batley	6	Warrington	0	Leeds	29,569	£1,644.16.0
1902	Broughton R	25	Salford	0	Rochdale	15,006	£846.11.0
1903	Halifax	7	Salford	0	Leeds	32,507	£1,834.8.6
1904	Halifax	8	Warrington	3	Salford	17,041	£936.5.6
1905	Warrington	6	Hull KR	0	Leeds	19,638	£1,271.18.0
1906	Bradford	5	Salford	0	Leeds	15,834	£920.0.0
1907	Warrington	17	Oldham	3	Broughton	18,500	£1,010.0.0
1908	Hunslet	14	Hull	0	Huddersfield	18,000	£903.0.0
1909	Wakefield T	17	Hull	0	Leeds	23,587	£1,490.0.0
1910	Leeds	7	Hull	7	Huddersfield	19,413	£1,102.0.0
Replay	Leeds	26	Hull	12	Huddersfield	11,608	£657.0.0
1911	Broughton R	4	Wigan	0	Salford	8,000	£376.0.0
1912	Dewsbury	8	Oldham	5	Leeds	15,271	£853.0.0
1913	Huddersfield	9	Warrington	5	Leeds	22,754	£1,446.9.6
1914	Hull	6	Wakefield T	0	Halifax	19,000	£1,035.5.0
1915	Huddersfield	37	St Helens	3	Oldham	8,000	£472.0.0
1920	Huddersfield	21	Wigan	10	Leeds	14,000	£1,936.0.0
1921	Leigh	13	Halifax	0	Broughton	25,000	£2,700.0.0
1922	Rochdale H	10	Hull	9	Leeds	32,596	£2,964.0.0
1923	Leeds	28	Hull	3	Wakefield	29,335	£2,390.0.0
1924	Wigan	21	Oldham	4	Rochdale	41,831	£3,712.0.0
1925	Oldham	16	Hull KR	3	Leeds	28,335	£2,879.0.0
1926	Swinton	9	Oldham	3	Rochdale	27,800	£2,551.0.0
1927	Oldham	26	Swinton	7	Wigan	33,448	£3,170.0.0
1928	Swinton	5	Warrington	3	Wigan	33,909	£3,158.1.11
1929	Wigan	13	Dewsbury	2	Wembley	41,600	£5,614.0.0
1930	Widnes	10	St Helens	3	Wembley	36,549	£3,102.0.0
1931	Halifax	22	York	8	Wembley	40,368	£3,908.0.0
1932	Leeds	11	Swinton	8	Wigan	29,000	£2,479.0.0
1933	Huddersfield	21	Warrington	17	Wembley	41,874	£6,465.0.0
1934	Hunslet	11	Widnes	5	Wembley	41,280	£6,686.0.0
1935	Castleford	11	Huddersfield	8	Wembley	39,000	£5,533.0.0
1936	Leeds	18	Warrington	2	Wembley	51,250	£7,070.0.0
1937	Widnes	18	Keighley	5	Wembley	47,699	£6,704.0.0
1938	Salford	7	Barrow	4	Wembley	51,243	£7,174.0.0
1939	Halifax	20	Salford	3	Wembley	55.453	£7,681.0.0
1940	No competition						
1941	Leeds	19	Halifax	2	Bradford	28,500	£1,703.0.0
1942	Leeds	15	Halifax	10	Bradford	15,250	£1,276.0.0
1943	Dewsbury	16	Leeds	9	Dewsbury	10,470	£823.0.0
	Dewsbury	0	Leeds	6	Leeds	16,000	£1,521.0.0
	Dewsbury won on aggregate 16-15						
1944	Bradford	0	Wigan	3	Wigan	21,500	£1,640.0.0
	Bradford	8	Wigan	0	Bradford	30,000	£2,200.0.0
	Bradford won on aggregate 8-3						
1945	Huddersfield	7	Bradford N	4	Huddersfield	9,041	£1,184.3.7
	Huddersfield	6	Bradford N	5	Bradford	17,500	£2,050.0.0
	Huddersfield won on aggregate 13-9						

Year	Winners		Runners-up		Venue	Attendance	Receipts
1946	Wakefield T	13	Wigan	12	Wembley	54,730	£12,013.13.6
1947	Bradford N	8	Leeds	4	Wembley	77,605	£17,434.5.0
1948	Wigan	8	Bradford N	3	Wembley	91,465	£21,121.9.9
1949	Bradford N	12	Halifax	0	Wembley	*95,050	£21,930.5.0
1950	Warrington	19	Widnes	0	Wembley	94,249	£24,782.13.0
1951	Wigan	10	Barrow	0	Wembley	94,262	£24,797.19.0
1952	Workington T	18	Featherstone R	10	Wembley	72,093	£22,374.2.0
1953	Huddersfield	15	St Helens	10	Wembley	89,588	£30,865.12.3
1954	Warrington	4	Halifax	4	Wembley	81,841	£29,706.7.3
Replay	Warrington	8	Halifax	4	Bradford	102,569	£18,623.7.0
1955	Barrow	21	Workington T	12	Wembley	66,513	£27,453.16.0
1956	St Helens	13	Halifax	2	Wembley	79,341	£29,424.7.6
1957	Leeds	9	Barrow	7	Wembley	76,318	£32,671.14.3
1958	Wigan	13	Workington T	9	Wembley	66,109	£33,175.17.6
1959	Wigan	30	Hull	13	Wembley	79,811	£35,718.19.9
1960	Wakefield T	38	Hull	5	Wembley	79,773	£35,754.16.0
1961	St Helens	12	Wigan	6	Wembley	94,672	£38,479.11.9
1962	Wakefield T	12	Huddersfield	6	Wembley	81,263	£33,390.18.4
1963	Wakefield T	25	Wigan	10	Wembley	84,492	£44,521.17.0
1964	Widnes	13	Hull KR	5	Wembley	84,488	£44,840.19.0
1965	Wigan	20	Hunslet	16	Wembley	89,016	£48,080.4.0
1966	St Helens	21	Wigan	2	Wembley	*98,536	£50,409.0.0
1967	Featherstone R	17	Barrow	12	Wembley	76,290	£53,465.14.0
1968	Leeds	11	Wakefield T	10	Wembley	87,100	£56,171.16.6
1969	Castleford	11	Salford	6	Wembley	*97,939	£58,848.1.0
1970	Castleford	7	Wigan	2	Wembley	95,255	£89,262.2.0
1971	Leigh	24	Leeds	7	Wembley	85,514	£84,452.15
1972	St Helens	16	Leeds	13	Wembley	89,495	£86,414.30
1973	Featherstone R	33	Bradford N	14	Wembley	72,395	£125,826.40
1974	Warrington	24	Featherstone R	9	Wembley	77,400	£132,021.05
1975	Widnes	14	Warrington	7	Wembley	85,098	£140,684.45
1976	St Helens	20	Widnes	5	Wembley	89,982	£190,129.40
1977	Leeds	16	Widnes	7	Wembley	80,871	£241,488.00
1978	Leeds	14	St Helens	12	Wembley	*96,000	£330,575.00
1979	Widnes	12	Wakefield T	3	Wembley	94,218	£383,157.00
1980	Hull KR	10	Hull	5	Wembley	*95,000	£448,202.90
1981	Widnes	18	Hull KR	9	Wembley	92,496	£591,117.00
1982	Hull	14	Widnes	14	Wembley	92,147	£684,500.00
Replay	Hull	18	Widnes	9	Elland Rd	41,171	£180,525.00
1983	Featherstone R	14	Hull	12	Wembley	84,969	£655,510.00
1984	Widnes	19	Wigan	6	Wembley	80,116	£686,171.00
1985	Wigan	28	Hull	24	Wembley	*97,801	£760,322.00
1986	Castleford	15	Hull KR	14	Wembley	82,134	£806,676.00
1987	Halifax	19	St Helens	18	Wembley	91,267	£1,009,206.00
1988	Wigan	32	Halifax	12	Wembley	*94,273	£1,102,247.00
1989	Wigan	27	St Helens	0	Wembley	*78,000	£1,121,293.00
1990	Wigan	36	Warrington	14	Wembley	*77,729	£1,360,000.00
1991	Wigan	13	St Helens	8	Wembley	75,532	£1,610,447.00
1992	Wigan	28	Castleford	12	Wembley	77,286	£1,877,564.00
1993	Wigan	20	Widnes	14	Wembley	*77,684	£1,981,591.00
1994	Wigan	26	Leeds	16	Wembley	*78,348	£2,032,839.00
1995	Wigan	30	Leeds	10	Wembley	*78,550	£2,040,000.00
1996	St Helens	40	Bradford B	32	Wembley	75,994	£1,893,000.00
1997	St Helens	32	Bradford B	22	Wembley	78,022	£2,033,426.00
1998	Sheffield E	17	Wigan	8	Wembley	60,669	

* indicates a capacity attendance, the limit being fixed annually taking into account variable factors.

Bibliography

Huxley, J. *The Rugby League Challenge Cup*
Huxley, J. and Morris, G. *Wembley Magic*
Fletcher, R and Howes, D. *Rothmans RL Year Books.*
Record keepers club handbooks
Dalby, K. *The Headingley Story*

Newspapers
The Manchester Guardian
Yorkshire Post
Hull Daily Mail
Rugby Leaguer
Batley News
Dewsbury Reporter
Bradford Telegraph
Athletic News